THE FAMILY TREE
IRISH
GENEALOGY GUIDE

THE FAMILY TREE
IRISH
GENEALOGY GUIDE

How to Trace Your Ancestors in Ireland

CLAIRE SANTRY

FAMILY
TREE
BOOKS

CINCINNATI, OHIO
shopfamilytree.com

Contents

PART 1: LINKING YOUR FAMILY TREE TO IRELAND

CHAPTER 1
Learn more about your ancestry with this history of the Irish in America: traditions, famous Irish-Americans, and why you should celebrate your Irish heritage.

CHAPTER 2
Set yourself up for research success. This chapter will help you start your genealogy research, with expert first steps, genealogy best practices, and important research principles.

CHAPTER 3
Discover the ancestors who braved the New World with this chapter's guides to finding your ancestral townland and religion and tracing immigrant ancestors in US records like passenger lists, naturalization records, and the federal census.

PART 2: GETTING TO KNOW THE OLD COUNTRY

CHAPTER 4
Delve into your homeland's turbulent past with this quick guide to Irish history (and how it affects your research), from the High Kings of Ireland to the Great Famine to today.

CHAPTER 5
Journey to your ancestors' lands. This chapter discusses Irish administrative divisions, plus how to use geographical resources like maps, gazetteers, and atlases.

CHAPTER 6
Decode confusing names with this chapter's tips for understanding Irish given names, surnames, and naming conventions.

CHAPTER 7
Locate your ancestors in the official records of the old country. This chapter discusses Ireland's civil registration system, which of its vital records survive, and how to find them.

CHAPTER 8
Explore the faith lives of your ancestors with this chapter's guide to baptism, marriage, and burial records created by the Catholic Church, the Church of Ireland, and other religious institutions.

Introduction

My mother always insisted she was descended from the High Kings of Tara. It seemed an unlikely pedigree for someone raised in relative poverty in County Carlow, and she certainly had no evidence to support her claim. But there had been a fire, it seemed, and all the paper records were lost. Hmm. Myths, exaggerations, smoke and mirrors: the essential tools of the storyteller. And the fibber. It was easy enough for me to smile and move on from a childhood belief in our noble tradition.

But another myth—that a 1922 fire destroyed all Irish records—proved harder to ignore. The facts were indisputable: An explosion and fire at the Public Record Office in Dublin during the Civil War destroyed scores of Irish records. This seemed to me the first insurmountable brick wall to my research, and it kept me from digging too deeply into my ancestry for several decades.

It wasn't until the end of the 1990s that I realized that the fire, while a catastrophe, hadn't consumed every last scrap of Ireland's genealogical heritage. A stone mason, installing a headstone near the grave of my great-grandmother in Wicklow, mentioned that the death records for all of those residing in the cemetery were held in Dublin at the General Register Office. This revelation—that many historical documents had *not* been in the PROI when the fuse was lit—finally launched my family history research journey.

And that was all I needed to get started. I clocked up a good few miles visiting archives and libraries in the capital in the years that followed, but I didn't mind. I was, finally, becoming acquainted with my ancestors. I was to find no Gaelic lords, of course. Instead, my maternal line branched out to seafarers and carpenters in Wicklow, blacksmiths in

Wicklow and Wexford, and laborers in Tipperary, while my father's line stretched back in a long line of laborers, all firmly rooted in southwest Cork.

Unfortunately, the myth of the all-record-consuming fire still circulates. Thanks to the Internet and the best endeavors of the Irish genealogical community, fewer would-be Irish family historians are discouraged by the story, but it still makes the rounds. To some extent, it has been replaced by the more general, widely accepted notion that "Irish genealogy is difficult."

I'll accept that Irish genealogy can be challenging. It depends to a large extent on which period of history you're researching, where (geographically) your family lived, and what information you start with or can gather along the way. But it is undoubtedly a whole lot easier than it used to be. Irish-Americans no longer face only the choice between taking expensive research trips to Ireland or commissioning professionals. Millions of Irish family history records, especially those used by beginners, are now online—and nearly all of them are free.

This book will give you a thorough grounding in genealogical techniques and point you towards the records you need to search, both in the United States and in Ireland. It's full of tips, essential explanations about the collections, and strategic advice.

I hope it will inspire you to start out on your own journey to connect with your Irish ancestors and heritage.

Claire Santry
January 2017

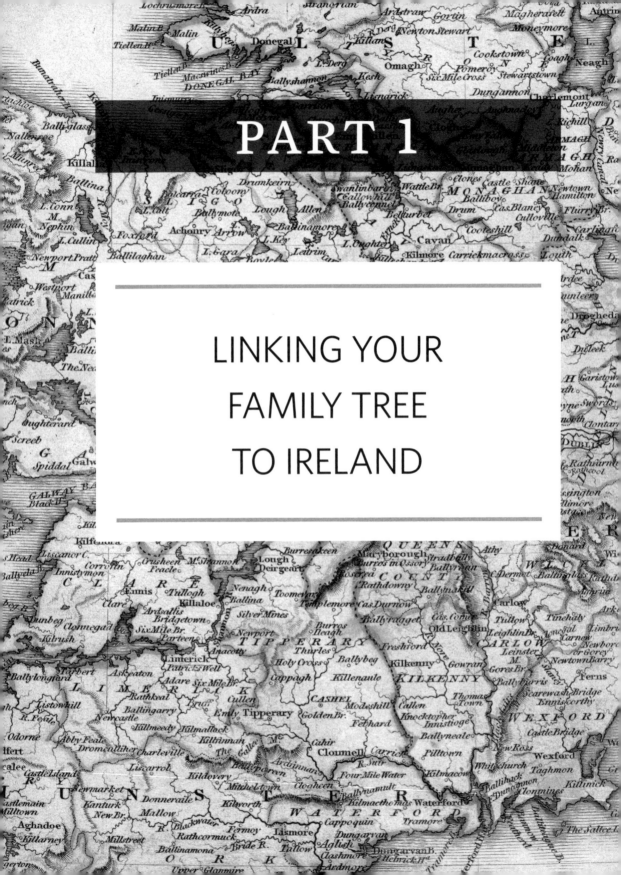

PART 1

LINKING YOUR FAMILY TREE TO IRELAND

Discovering Your Irish Heritage

Whether you were brought up immersed in Irish traditions or have only recently discovered your ancestors from the Emerald Isle, you're probably already familiar with some aspects of your Irish heritage. You'd have to be living under a rock to not have encountered St. Patrick's Day, Irish dancing, and "the little fella"—the leprechaun. You'll also know that being Irish has a certain cultural cachet, in part because of Irish-Americans' classic underdog backstory of overcoming the odds in the face of prejudice, abuse, and extreme poverty, and partly because of the community's reputation for being big-hearted and charming.

Beyond the stereotype and hype, however, you may have asked yourself about the people who connect you to this heritage. What motivated them to leave Ireland, an island that's only the size of South Carolina but has such important historical and cultural significance? How did your ancestors get to America, and what were their early experiences as immigrants? What about the family and friends they left behind?

This first chapter is an overview of the Irish-American immigrant experience, providing you with a basic understanding of the cultural, social, and political world in which your ancestors lived. Check it out as you embark on your own journey into your family's history.

IMMIGRATION TO THE UNITED STATES

Irish-American history dates back to the late sixteenth century with the transportation of petty criminals and, in the mid-1600s, prisoners captured during Oliver Cromwell's bloody conquest of Ireland. Many of these early immigrants were used as slave labor on Caribbean tobacco plantations, but significant numbers also journeyed there voluntarily; one of the largest Irish communities emerged in Barbados. The descendants of these first Irish-Americans were among the early settlers of the Carolinas.

This was the first surge of Irish immigration to North America. In numerical terms, it was tiny—barely a ripple—compared to the hundreds of thousands that would follow in three distinct waves: the largely Protestant and artisan Irish who arrived between 1720 and 1845; the starving citizens escaping almost certain death in Ireland's Great Famine in the late 1840s; and the poor, unskilled, and initially reviled Catholics desperate for opportunity who arrived from the mid-1850s to the start of World War I in 1914. We'll explore each of these periods in turn, as they each tell a different story of Ireland, the Irish, and the land that these immigrants would come to call home.

Emigration from Ireland, 1720–1845

After Cromwell's conquest of Ireland, the British authorities introduced a series of restrictive Penal Laws that limited the freedoms and opportunities for Irish Roman Catholics and, to a lesser extent, Protestant Dissenters (those who refused the authority of the Church of Ireland, such as Presbyterians). While they suffered discrimination in Ireland, the Presbyterians were generally more economically independent than their Catholic neighbors. Many were artisans, shopkeepers, and professionals, and they believed they would find tolerance and greater freedom in North America.

The trickle of these Scots-Irish Presbyterians crossing the ocean turned into a fairly steady stream in the early 1720s, and rose and fell in response to economic peaks and troughs over the next fifty years. By 1775, an estimated two hundred thousand had migrated. Philadelphia and Delaware were the most popular arrival ports for these new settlers, mainly because the linen trade routes along this coast were already well established.

While the ships traveling to Ireland arrived full of flaxseeds needed for Ireland's linen industry, they returned with emigrants keen to satisfy America's labor shortage and collect the high wages they had heard about. In return for free passage, some signed up for several years of unpaid work. And once freed of their contractual obligations, these settlers moved into the Appalachian regions, the Ohio Valley, New England, the Carolinas, and Georgia, many buying land and returning to their farming traditions. By 1790, the

United States' Irish immigrant population numbered 447,000, with two-thirds originating from Ulster (Ireland's northernmost province).

Irish Roman Catholic immigrant numbers during the 1700s were considerably smaller, especially in the first half of the eighteenth century when each of the thirteen colonies enacted laws that discriminated against them. In 1704, for example, Maryland created a tax of twenty shillings on Irish servants "to prevent the importing of too great a number of Irish Papists into this Province." A decade later, South Carolina forbade the immigration of people "commonly called native Irish, or persons of scandalous character or Roman Catholics," yet offered a land grant of three hundred to four hundred acres to Irish Protestants. Other colonies took similar action.

But Catholics had other reasons for not leaving Ireland. Firstly, Catholic immigration to North America was forbidden by law until after the Revolutionary War, and, secondly, they had no means to pay their passage even if they could avoid the authorities. Unlike their Presbyterian neighbors, Catholic prospective immigrants rarely had skills, and most owned nothing of value to sell to raise funds. Finally, Catholics had a third, purely emotional reason for their apparent inertia: their deep-rooted attachment to their Gaelic ancestral land. For most Catholic Irish families, emigration meant exile. Even so, small numbers found the means and chose to sever their connections with the old country, typically sailing from Dublin, Cork, Kinsale, or Waterford.

The pace of Irish immigration into America increased in the early nineteenth century as tales of adventure and prosperity started to filter down to the unskilled and illiterate in Ireland. They sailed to seek their fortunes, often finding employment as laborers on some of America's early, huge infrastructure projects such as the Erie Canal and the Philadelphia and Columbia Railroad. The majority of immigrants, however, continued to be of Scots-Irish and/or Protestant heritage. They were quickly assimilated, not least because English was their first language, and most (but certainly not all) had skills or some small savings on which to start building their new lives.

Famine Immigration, 1846–1855

In 1845, potato blight struck the harvest in Ireland, and the disease created a catastrophe because the potato was the main (if not only) food source for many Irish people. When the crop failed completely in each of the three following years, the poorest members of Irish society faced starvation, disease, and homelessness. An exodus from the island began with some 215,000 immigrating to North America. Ships from Northern Europe generally sailed only in spring and summer to avoid ice and bad weather, but ships continued to sail from Ireland in the harsh winter of 1846. Most headed southwest, to US ports.

Alarmed at the level of destitution and illness arriving with these vessels, the US Congress quickly passed two new legislative acts to make the voyage even more expensive. That following March, the minimum fare to New York rose to seven pounds, an amount way beyond the reach of most families facing starvation in Ireland. Even so, all tickets had been sold by the middle of April.

For those who could not afford such a fare, the only alternative was to take a ship to Canada. These voyages were cheaper, partly because they were crossing to a British colony, and partly because standards on board were low and the ships were crammed to bursting with human cargo. Typically chartered by landowners in Ireland who wanted to be rid of starving tenants who could not pay their rent, these often unseaworthy vessels set sail with inadequate provisions of drinking water, food, and sanitation, and became known as "coffin ships." The statistics for 1847 tell the tale: Some two hundred ships had crossed from ports in Ireland or Liverpool, England, to British Canada, and one-third of their passengers (more than sixty thousand individuals) died either on the journey or shortly after arrival, most of them from cholera or typhus. Many of those who survived were motivated to get beyond the clutches of the British. They traveled across Canada, settling for short periods to find work that would fund the next part of their journey until they crossed into the United States.

The stereotypical Catholic Irish was hotheaded, violent, drunk, ignorant, and of ape-like appearance, as depicted in this cartoon called "The Usual Irish Way of Doing Things," published in *Harper's Weekly* in 1870.

Whether arriving via the northern overland route or East Coast ports, some one million Irish are estimated to have arrived in the United States during the Famine years. This was the first big wave of poor refugees to arrive from Europe, and they were not met with the warmest reception. Most were Catholic and spoke only Irish, and they often had no skills and no financial resources. Met with extreme prejudice (mainly from the English settlers; see image **A**), they settled into the lowest rung of society. Waging a daily battle for survival, they lived in unsanitary, unsafe accommodations and eked out an existence from laboring and other unskilled manual work.

Post-Famine Irish in the United States

When the economy was strong, Irish immigrants to America were (relatively) welcome. But when boom times faded away, as they did in the mid-1850s, social unrest followed. In addition to struggling to find work because of the economic downturn, Irish immigrants faced the additional challenge of being perceived as "taking jobs from Americans." Being already low in the pecking order, the Irish suffered great discrimination. "No Irish

Mapping the Irish-Born in America, 1870

In 1870, the Irish-born population of the United States was 1,855,827, the single largest foreign-born group. The greatest number by far (just under 32 percent of them) lived in New York, where 528,806 settled. The second-largest population was in Pennsylvania (235,798), just ahead of Massachusetts (216,120). Making up the rest of top ten states for Irish-born inhabitants were Illinois (120,162), New Jersey (86,784), Ohio (82,674), Connecticut (70,630), Missouri (54,983), California (54,421), and Wisconsin (48,479).

Created from data held in the ninth (1870) census, this map showing the density of the Irish-born population was published in 1874.

Need Apply" became a familiar comment in job advertisements, and anti-immigration, nationalist groups like the Know-Nothing party flourished amidst the growing distrust of foreigners.

While some blacksmiths, stonemasons, bootmakers, and shopkeepers were among the flood of Catholic Irish who arrived during the Famine, the majority lacked the professional skills necessary for higher-paid labor. On ship passenger manifests, many men claimed to be laborers, and many women said they were domestic servants. In most cases, they had little or no previous experience in these roles; these positions were the limit of their aspirations.

They sought a job—or, more precisely, a wage—and they didn't really care too much about the details. Being unskilled, uneducated, and typically illiterate, many Irish immigrants accepted the most menial jobs that other immigrant groups did not want, working long hours for minimal pay. Their cheap labor was needed by America's expanding cities for the construction of canals, roads, bridges, railroads, and other infrastructure projects.

Attitudes toward the Irish began to change during the Civil War, when thousands of Irish wholeheartedly participated in the armed forces. Irish immigrants and their descendants made up a majority in at least forty Union regiments, and their actions gained the respect and acceptance of many of their fellow Americans. A couple of decades on, second- or even third-generation Irish-Americans had moved up the social and managerial ladder from their early laboring work. Some even entered the professional class.

This was not the case for the majority, of course. In the 1900 census, hundreds of thousands of Irish immigrants lived in poverty, mostly in urban slums. But economic circumstances improved for a significant proportion, and the Irish (as a group) were gaining footholds in the workplace, especially in the labor/trade union movement and the police and fire services. And with their numbers (especially in the large Irish populations in Boston, Chicago, and New York), they were able to elect Irish candidates as well as candidates sympathetic to the Irish people's plight.

At the start of the twentieth century, Irish-born immigrants made up 2.12 percent of the US population. More importantly, Irish-Americans—those Americans born to Irish parents—made up 6.53 percent. By 2013, the number of Americans claiming Irish heritage was more than 33 million, or nearly 11 percent of the total population, nearly five times the total population of Ireland (6.4 million).

FAMOUS IRISH-AMERICANS

Since the influx of Irish immigrants began in the eighteenth century, the Irish have fully integrated themselves into American society. They have produced thousands of American sports stars, film stars, writers, and captains of industry and commerce.

Their representation at the top of political ladders is pretty impressive, too, with at least ten US Presidents having proven Irish ancestry, including: Ronald Reagan (Ballyporeen, County Tipperary), George H.W. Bush (Counties Down and Cork), and Barack Obama (whose maternal line reaches back to a shoemaker who immigrated to the United States in 1850 from Moneygall, County Offaly). But perhaps the most famous Irish-American president was John F. Kennedy, who had a full set eight of Irish great-grandparents. Fittingly, even the White House was designed by an Irishman, James Hoban from County Kilkenny. Some more famous Americans with Irish ancestry are listed in the sidebar.

IRISH TRADITIONS AND CULTURAL INFLUENCE

Where would America be without its annual outing of green beer, corned beef and cabbage, and shamrock-shaped spectacles? St. Patrick's Day is undoubtedly the biggest single event in the Irish heritage calendar, even if it is celebrated slightly differently on the two sides of the Atlantic. In Ireland, you'll find no green beer or corned beef (the traditional cuisine is pork), but most cities and even some towns put on a parade of some size. Dublin's parade—the highlight of a four-day festival of arts, culture, and entertainment in venues across the capital—is huge, and continues a tradition that started in New York City, where the world's first St. Patrick's Day parade took place on March 17, 1762, thanks to Irish soldiers serving in the English army. In time, this parade became an annual event, and it's the highlight of Irish-American Heritage Month, a concept introduced in 1995 and proclaimed each year by the US president.

Unlike St. Patrick's Day, Halloween is a holiday that definitely has its origins in Irish culture. It harks back to the Celtic festival of *Samhain* (pronounced "Sow-ain"), the last day of the Celtic year and the day when boundaries between the "Otherworld" and the human world became less secure, and banshees, fairies, shapeshifters, and other spirits would play tricks on the unsuspecting. To ward off the evil of the night, celebrants lit bonfires, created lots of noise, and wore ugly masks to confuse the spirits.

Between these two major events, the Irish-American community throws many festivals to celebrate other aspects of their culture. Some are small gatherings, but several attract hundreds of thousands of visitors to watch and listen to world-class professional musicians (harpists, fiddlers, uilleann pipers), dancers, storytellers, and other performers. Attendees at these events also take part in sporting challenges, cooking classes, Irish-themed lectures, and (of course) genealogy consultations.

While at these celebrations, you might encounter popular Irish sports: Gaelic football, hurling, and camogie. Gaelic football is a mixture of soccer and rugby, two sports that are growing in popularity across the world. In hurling (for men) and camogie (for women), players use a curved oak stick (called a hurley) to pass and carry a baseball-sized ball

Famous Americans with Irish Ancestry

- Muhammad Ali, boxer and political activist
- Neil Armstrong, astronaut
- Joe Biden, US senator and vice president of the United States
- Bill Bryson, author
- James Cagney, actor and dancer
- Raymond Chandler, author
- George Clooney, actor and director
- Eddie Cochran, musician
- Davy Crockett, pioneer and folk hero
- Bing Crosby, musician and actor
- Tom Cruise, actor
- Walt Disney, animator and entrepreneur
- F. Scott Fitzgerald, author
- Michael Flatley, dancer and musician
- Henry Ford, entrepreneur and manufacturer
- Bill Haley, musician
- Mary Harris Jones (Mother Jones), educator and community organizer
- Gene Kelly, actor and dancer
- Grace Kelly, actress and princess of Monaco
- John F. Kennedy, thirty-fifth president of the United States
- Robert F. Kennedy, US senator
- Frank McCourt, author and educator
- John McEnroe, tennis player
- Maureen O'Hara, actress and singer
- Barack Obama, forty-fourth president of the United States
- Ronald Reagan, fortieth president of the United States
- Mickey Spillane, author
- George Washington, general and first president of the United States
- John Wayne, actor

(called a sliothar) across a field and into the opponent's goal, similar to hockey and soccer. All three activities (which share some elements with each other) are rough, fast-moving, contact sports. If you prefer your shins to be bruise-free, you might stick to the supporters' seats, but the game promises an exhilarating event whether you're playing or spectating.

These tough sports arrived in North America with Irish immigrants in the early and mid-1800s. They are managed today by the United States Gaelic Athletics Association (GAA). As you'd expect, most of the oldest established clubs are in the cities with the largest Irish-American populations, but the games have continued to spread further afield. There are now at least fifty GAA-affiliated clubs playing regularly across the United States.

A less energetic way to sample your Irish heritage is to reach for Irish food that your immigrant ancestor would have enjoyed. Traditional Irish cuisine is simple "peasant" food, with many recipes inevitably featuring the potato. Perhaps the best-known dish is Colcannon, a favorite for Halloween, which mixes mashed potatoes with chopped kale or savoy cabbage and spring onion. (Don't hold back with the butter!) Another dish, a hearty Irish stew of lamb, onion, and potato (with optional pearl barley and carrots), always goes down well on a chilly evening. For those seeking a buzz, drink up a Guinness or some Irish whiskey. You can pair those beverages with a loaf of soft-textured, yeast-free Irish soda bread that you can rustle up in no time; it requires minimum kneading and is easy enough for children to make. What a lovely way to introduce the next generation to their heritage!

KEYS TO SUCCESS

- Start digging deeper into your heritage by picking a topic you're naturally drawn to, be it music, cuisine, folklore, dance, literature, geography, or history, and give it an Irish flavor. For example, do you love cooking? Try some Irish recipes. Love folklore? Learn about Irish fairies (they're nothing like the do-gooder types of other cultures) or Irish marriage traditions. Interested in colonial heritage? Explore the history of the Scots-Irish.

- Locate your nearest Irish cultural center and attend one of its exhibitions, lectures, performances, or other social events.

- Attend one of the many annual Irish festivals held in the United States. They come in all sizes, and usually include music, dance, and the opportunity to try traditional Irish activities (such as hurling or spinning) and sample Irish foods and drinks.

2

Jump-Starting Your Irish Research

With all that you've probably heard about Irish genealogy being notoriously difficult, you may be nervous about setting off on an uncharted journey into your Irish family history. Even if you are up for the challenge, you may not be sure how or where to begin the research, or maybe you were disappointed with your progress in a previous research attempt and want to start again with a more strategic approach. As with most successful journeys, solid preparation is key to Irish genealogy research, so this chapter will guide you through the early stages and present the basic genealogical principles, concepts, and techniques that will help you unlock your ancestral past.

FIRST STEPS

Although your impulse may be to rush headlong into the nearest archive or online database with every known name and date of your immigrant ancestors, your first steps should be taken much closer to home. Before embarking on any journey, you need to know where you are and have some sense of where you are headed, so you'll need to assess what you already know about your ancestors, what information you hope to uncover, and what you can realistically expect to achieve through your research.

This preparatory stage of your family history project involves a five-step strategy to help you decide the direction and focus of your research.

① Record What You Already Know

The first principle of genealogical research is to start with yourself and work methodically backwards, linking each generation to the previous generation. It may seem counterintuitive to start with yourself rather than with the story of your immigrant ancestor, but you may save yourself months of research following the wrong family. You are also likely to miss out on several clues left behind in their paper trails. So start by documenting your own name, birth dates, and birthplace, and do the same for your parents and (if you can) your grandparents. Continue to sketch out a basic family tree, generation by generation, adding any details you have of any other ancestors.

② Seek Out Ancestral Memorabilia

Now for a treasure hunt! In as systematic a way as possible, start rummaging about in the attic, wardrobes, cupboards, under the bed ... anywhere family memorabilia might be boxed up or otherwise lurking. Be on the lookout for family Bibles, memorial/mass cards (image **A**), family documents, newspaper clippings, war medals, birth announcements, baptism certificates, diaries, invoices, wedding invitations, and official papers. Any of these items could hold vital genealogical information that will steer you on the right course for the next research stages.

Old letters can be particularly valuable finds, not only for the information revealed within the correspondence but also for providing return addresses and postmarks. Photographs of people, places, and events are also important; these snapshots of the past often have dates, names, and locations noted on the back.

Keep an eye out, too, for documents that suggest membership in any Irish social organizations or regular attendance at specific churches.

③ Build Your Family Tree

It's now time to get yourself organized. Using five-generation pedigree charts, family group charts, and biographical outlines, start to record the information you've gathered. You can download some forms to do so for free online **<www.familytreemagazine.com/info/basicforms>** and fill them in by hand. They are standard forms used by genealogists, and they will help you keep track of your ancestors.

Alternatively, you can record the details directly into genealogical software, either using an off-the-shelf family history program or one of the online family tree builders on sites such as Ancestry.com **<www.ancestry.com>**, Findmypast **<www.findmypast.com>**, MyHeritage

"We have loved her in life, let us not forget her in death, until we have conducted her by our prayers into the eternal abode of bliss."—*St. Ambrose.*

Eternal rest grant unto her, O Lord, and may the perpetual light of Thy glory shine on her.

Blessed be the Holy and Immaculate Conception.

In Loving Memory
—OF—
TERESA BANNON
30 West Street, Drogheda,

Who died on 8th March, 1884.

R. I. P.

Grant, we beseech Thee, O Lord, that the soul of Thy servant, TERESA, on whom Thou didst confer many graces whilst on earth, may for ever rejoice in celestial bliss through Our Lord Jesus Christ. Amen.

Immaculate and afflicted Heart of Mary, pray for us.

"We have loved us not forget him in life, let him in death."

Sweet Heart of Jesus, be Thou my love,—300 days, each time.

Sweet Heart of Mary, be my salvation,—300 days, each time.

IN THE MOST HOLY NAME OF JESUS,
PRAY FOR THE REPOSE OF THE SOUL OF
Willie Nolan,
Athenry, Co. Galway,

Who died at New York
On the 4th January, 1917,
AGED 32 YEARS.

R. I. P.

Immense Passion! O Profound Wounds! O Profusion of Blood! O Sweetness above Sweetness! O Most Bitter Death! Grant eternal rest. Amen.—400 days' Indulgence

Memorial cards usually provide some genealogical information and refer to the deceased's place of residence. As such, the survival of a memorial card suggests an important connection between the deceased's family and the person who retained the card.

<www.myheritage.com>, and FamilySearch.org <www.familysearch.org>. It's worth spending some time exploring the options and comparing features, tools, flexibility, and ease of use (and discussing them with other family historians) before committing yourself.

Whichever method you choose, the facts you'll be recording at this stage will mainly consist of names; dates and places of birth, marriage, and death; and occasional snippets of biographical detail about some individuals.

Recording these details in standard formats, whether on screen or on paper, will quickly show you the gaps in your knowledge so you can identify areas requiring further research.

④ Interview Relatives

One of the richest sources of family history is a living relative, so an essential part of your early research should be spent gently coaxing vital details and clues from family members' memories.

Approach these interviews with sensitivity and patience, because not everyone wants to talk about the past. Some may be reluctant to discuss "the old days" because of unhappy

Record Information Consistently

Right from the start of your research, you'll want to establish a consistent format for your note-taking. Memory is fallible; you may think you'll remember all the background to that hastily scribbled transcription of a date or place, but you might find it doesn't make quite as much sense when you reread it three weeks later.

- **Abbreviations:** If you hurriedly record a date next to the name of an ancestor, will you remember the relevance of that date when you revisit your note? If, for example, you write *Patrick Ryan b1853*, will you or any other researchers who subsequently use your research know if that date relates to Patrick's birth, baptism, or burial? It's fine to use abbreviations, as long as you are consistent.
- **Names:** Write names—including first, middle, last, and maiden names—as they are spoken. Some genealogists capitalize surnames to identify them as such.
- **Dates:** In Ireland, the date is usually recorded in a day/month/year sequence, rather than month/day/year as in North America. This can cause confusion, and leave researchers unsure, for example, whether Aunt Nellie was born on February 10 (2/10 in North America, but 10/2 in Ireland) or October 2 (10/2 in North America, but 2/10 in Ireland). To avoid confusion, don't use numbers for months; always spell out the name of the month or use its first three letters. It is also good practice to use four numerals for the year, e.g., 1783 or 1883, rather than just '83.

experiences and severed relationships, or perhaps a fear of exposing family secrets that a previous generation may have considered shameful. Some may also want to avoid speaking ill of the dead or confronting the sadness of remembering and discussing missed family members.

Start by interviewing your closest relatives—your parents and grandparents—if possible, then extend your net to aunts, great uncles, cousins, godparents, and even close friends of deceased blood relatives. While extended family members may insist they know nothing that could help your research, they may have inherited items from your immigrant ancestors (e.g., old photos or other papers that could shed light on your family's history). Encourage them to talk to you anyway, and see what they are prepared to share.

Whenever possible, conduct your interviews face to face. If this isn't practical, you have a number of alternatives: telephone, Skype **<www.skype.com>**, FaceTime **<support.apple.com/en-us/HT204380>**, or even e-mail or paper letter. Be sure your interviewees are comfortable with the chosen method, and obtain their advance agreement to the conversation being recorded. Again, you have several recording options to chose from: a traditional tape recorder, a digital recording device, a video camera, or a smartphone/tablet app.

Some people may not be willing to be filmed or recorded for posterity, in which case you may have to resort to pen-and-paper notes. However, you could suggest that the recording will be private between the two of you and will be erased after you have transcribed it.

For face-to-face interviews, bring your pedigree and family history charts and ask for help filling them out. See if your relative can provide descriptions of appearance, character, occupation, habits, or home for each person on the chart.

Whichever method you agree on, ensure you are completely familiar with the equipment and check that it is working properly before the interview begins.

However you conduct the interview, let your relative see copies of any old photos you may have gathered (send them in advance, if necessary). Photographs are extremely useful for prompting recollections about people, events, and locations. Formal wedding groups can help you establish relationships between some of the people whose names you've encountered in your research. Allow your relative to reminisce while studying these photos; this is where you are likely to hear the kind of stories you won't find in dusty archives or online record databases, and you may pick up some gems while you listen.

You will also want to ask your interviewees some specific questions, chosen according to their relationship with your ancestors. If they knew your immigrant ancestors, for example, you can focus on what they know of their journey to America. Ask direct questions: Where and when did they arrive? Did they travel with any family or friends? From where in Ireland did they travel? What was the name of their hometown or county? Who did they leave behind in Ireland? Did they meet other family in America, or did other family members subsequently join them?

If your interviewee didn't know your immigrant ancestors, concentrate on what they were told by other family members about the immigration story, what happened after their arrival, and any other tales of their lives or their children's lives. You can find more interview tips online at <**www.familytreemagazine.com/article/ oral-history-interview-question-lists**>.

Unless your relative is a family historian, he is unlikely to know all the dates, locations, and facts you're seeking. His information may also be confusing or not entirely accurate,

---

RESEARCH TIP

Treat Family Stories as Clues

Stories handed down through generations may be based on fact, but they may have changed (intentionally or not) along the way. Indeed, some may bear little resemblance to the historical reality. As a result, treat family stories as clues that inspire further research, rather than proven facts.

but you should record it faithfully in your transcriptions notes nonetheless. You'll often find some grain of truth in the stories, plus some ways of unravelling inconsistencies.

Aim to transcribe the entire interview while it is still fresh in your mind. If you intend to store the recording in a digital format, be sure to keep a paper copy of your transcript as a backup.

⑤ Identify Your Research Goals

A research plan needs clearly stated goals, and you'll want to prepare at least one goal for each branch of your family that you are curious to explore. This plan will help you focus on what you're hoping to achieve, develop realistic expectations, and provide a to-do list that's always ready to inspire you and keep you productive.

Creating a research plan involves five basic steps:

1. **Articulate a research question.** Identify the principal person you want to research, then be specific about what you want to accomplish. Ask yourself what it is that you want to learn about your ancestor. Is it how and when your immigrant ancestor arrived in North America? Is it to discover the name of your great-grandmother? Is it to confirm the family tale of your ancestor's daring exploits in the Revolutionary War? Include long- and short-term goals, but try to sum up the main objective in one question.

2. **List any known facts.** After evaluating the information you've gathered to this point, record what you know. Note the name of your principal research target and the names of those connected or associated to him or her. Add dates of births, marriages, and deaths, plus the places associated with these events if you have documentary evidence to confirm them. List also any possible surname variations.

3. **Formulate a working hypothesis.** Making educated guesses where necessary, write a summary of what you know about the life of your principal ancestor. If you are looking at a short time frame (e.g., your ancestor's life after arriving in North America), just concentrate on that period of his or her life.

RESEARCH TIP

Be Realistic
Don't be too ambitious in setting your research goals. For the majority of us with Irish ancestors, searching for our Irish roots leads us to poor, landless laborers. As such, their lives were not well-documented and, where records do survive, they are unlikely to date from much before 1810, at best.

Weigh Up the Evidence

When different sources give conflicting information, give more weight to the source created most closely to the time the event occurred. For example, if your sources for a birth date are an obituary and a baptism register entry, the latter is a primary source and thus more likely to be correct, as it was documented closer to the person's birth.

4. **Identify related records.** Make a list of the US sources you need to investigate to reach your goal (e.g., to confirm or disprove assumptions you have made). Become familiar with the US records most likely to prove/disprove your hypothesis, such as an immigrant ancestor's Civil War pension file or your great-great-grandparents' marriage certificate. At this stage, you should also find out not only where those types of records are available, but also if they still exist.

5. **Define research steps.** Decide the best order of databases to consult or repositories to visit to find the records you need. Use free research calendar forms <www.familytreemagazine.com/info/researchforms> to organize and keep track of materials you've searched so you don't duplicate your efforts.

As your research journey progresses, you should revise your plan to incorporate new discoveries. New information may direct you to different sources, and some discoveries may even require a complete change of focus and a fresh plan. Once you've decided where you want your research to go, you're ready to start seeking out the records.

KEY GENEALOGY PRINCIPLES

As research into your Irish family gets underway and you begin to gather records of your ancestors, note the details and sources of each discovery and follow tried-and-true genealogical research concepts and techniques. Approaching your research with these established methods will help you correctly evaluate the records you find and should steer you away from unnecessary dead ends and brick walls.

Understand Primary and Secondary Information

Genealogists use many different types of sources to find the information needed to build family trees, and they categorize them as primary and secondary sources. Each category is further classified as an original or derived source.

A **primary source** is a document or other item that was written or created close to the time or event it records by someone whom you can reasonably expect had their facts

Examples of Primary and Secondary Sources

Primary

- Civil registrations/certificates of birth, marriage, and death
- Church baptism, marriage, and burial registers
- Cemetery interment registers
- Headstones (death dates)
- Wills and deeds
- Naturalization records
- Passenger manifests and arrival lists
- Diaries and letters written at the time of the event

Secondary

- Newspaper birth, marriage, and death announcements, obituaries, and news stories
- Indexes to record collections
- Oral histories
- Biographies and genealogies
- Headstones (birth dates)
- Family Bibles

straight. Some examples of primary sources are vital records (e.g., birth, marriage, and death certificates), military service records, wills, deeds, and census returns.

Although generally considered highly accurate and trustworthy, primary sources can contain errors, especially when the information was recorded years after the event. Headstone inscriptions may fall into this category, for example, when the person instructing the letter cutter (having been present at the person's death) was confident of a death date, but may be relying on a secondary source or hearsay for the birth date. Similarly, some people providing information to officials may not have been entirely truthful; think of the patriotic but underage would-be soldier telling fibs to the recruiting sergeant, or the woman who knocks off a few years to be younger than her beau. Human frailties, desires, and ambitions have resulted in many untruths being faithfully recorded in documents down the centuries.

A **secondary source** is a document or other item that was not created at the time of the event described. Often these kinds of resources are interpretations of other primary or secondary sources, so they may have been influenced by bias or other emotions. Secondary sources include family genealogies, old letters, books, family lore, and biographical histories. Oral interviews that are not timely, firsthand witness accounts are also in this category.

While some of these memories may be perfectly accurate, secondary sources are often provided by someone who is recollecting events and, as such, they are more prone to errors than primary sources. As a family historian, you'll want to trace each piece of information from a secondary source back to a primary source. Failing that, you'll want to assess the accuracy of the secondary information against other secondary sources.

An **original source** for genealogical purposes is the very first record or photograph of an event. A baptism register entry is a notable example, as it would have been the first documentary recording of the event. As such, original sources are considered the most accurate.

Each subsequent copy of an original is a **derived source**, whether reproduced by hand, camera, photocopier, or scanner, onto paper or microfilm or as photographs or digital files. While some photographic derivatives—copies created by photocopiers, scanners,

B

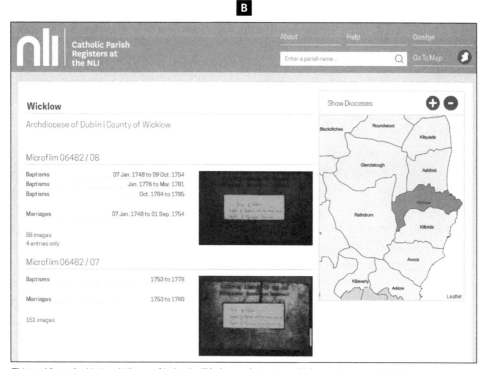

This tool from the National Library of Ireland will help you determine which records are available for your ancestor's town. For example, if your Roman Catholic family came from Wicklow Town, you may be able to trace them through registers back to 1747.

and cameras—are almost as good as originals, the main distinction between originals and derivatives is that errors are more likely to have crept into the latter. For example, a typed copy of a handwritten baptism register page would be a derivative source even if typed up on the same day, because it may contain unintentional errors.

Learn Which Records Are Available

It's a sad fact that Irish recordkeeping has a (well-earned) poor reputation. For several reasons—Penal Law restrictions, poverty, fire, flood, explosion—Ireland's documentary heritage suffers from huge gaps in both geographical and time coverage.

The result is a mixed bag of available records. For many, the paper trail will evaporate in the first half of the nineteenth century, but you can still discover more about your Irish origins by learning about the history, traditions, religious practices, and cultural settings of earlier undocumented ancestors. Some collections have survived intact (images **B** and **C**), but that doesn't mean the collection will be of value to every researcher. The civil registration records of births, marriages, and deaths, for example, are complete, but of no use to those looking for records that pre-date 1845/1864 when the system was introduced. Other records—the nineteenth-century census returns being the most obvious—are almost completely lost to researchers, while church records of all denominations except Quakers are hit-and-miss.

This situation is not unique to Ireland. When you're researching your immigrant ancestor's life in North America, you may encounter a similar barrier raised by geography and time. Don't bother looking for an official birth certificate for your Minnesota ancestor born in 1863, for example, because Minnesota didn't start issuing such documents until 1900. But relocate that ancestor to Massachusetts, and you can find vital records back to the 1600s.

Finding out the laws and record-keeping practices of the places where your ancestors lived will spare you the frustration of chasing records that don't exist.

RESEARCH TIP

Revisit Documents You've Filed

A document can contain much more information than we appreciate at first glance. You may discover a particular fact or correlation of facts on a second pass that you didn't originally see. For this reason, be sure to cast a refreshed pair of eyes over your records. As you learn more and more about your ancestors, you can look at these documents from a more-informed perspective and spot inconsistencies or other clues that would not have occurred to you at an earlier stage of your research.

Major Record Collections Used by Irish Genealogists			
Collection	Start date	End date	Notes
Deeds	1708	Current	Complete
All-Ireland census	1821		Only fragments survive
All-Ireland census	1831		Only fragments survive
All-Ireland census	1841		Only fragments survive
All-Ireland census	1851		Only fragments survive
All-Ireland census	1901		Complete
All-Ireland census	1911		Complete
Civil registration of births	1864	Current	Complete
Civil registration of marriages	1845	1863	Civil and non-Catholic weddings only. Complete
Civil registration of marriages	1864	Current	Civil and all church weddings. Complete
Civil registration of deaths	1864	Current	Complete
Church of Ireland registers	1619	Current	More than half of historical registers lost in the 1922 fire
Roman Catholic registers	1671	Current	Most registers date from the early 1800s
Presbyterian registers	1674	Current	Most registers date from the 1820s
Griffith's Valuation and Revision/Cancelled books	1848–1864	Current (Republic of Ireland); 1930s (Northern Ireland)	Complete
Tithe Applotment Books	1823	1837	Complete
Wills	1858	1922	Some earlier wills and indexes also available

This chart shows most of the major record collections consulted by Irish family historians. As you can see, most of the surviving sources begin in the first half of the nineteenth century.

Create Timelines

Creating individual biographical chronologies or timelines for each ancestor is a useful way to keep track of an individual's life, allowing you to view it in the context of the social and political events that may have impacted it. A timeline will also highlight the gaps in your research and help you identify the types of records you need to consult.

It's possible to create simple, personalized timelines in tabular format, then weave in historical and local events gathered from your own study of the period and place (image **D**). A number of digital tools can create chronologies for you. Most genealogical

D

TIMELINE: William Santry (1825-1902)	
1825	Baptized on 8 April, third child of Patrick Santry and Catherine Mahony of Gurranagoleen, a townland c. one mile from Clonakilty in Co. Cork. Rossletteri & Lisavaird parish. Sponsors Jeremiah Callanan & Mary McCarthy.
1829	Catholic Emancipator Act grants equal rights to Roman Catholics
1831	Census of Ireland. Returns for Clonakilty area destroyed in 1922
1837	Queen Victoria comes to the throne of the United Kingdom
1838	Poor law unions introduced to collect taxes and provide relief for the poor. Clonakilty area covered by Bandon PLU
1841	Census of Ireland. Paper returns for Clonakilty area destroyed 1922
1845-1849	The Great Hunger. Millions die of starvation and famine fever. Millions emigrate. West Cork is one of the worst affected areas.
1848	Griffiths Valuation carried out in County Cork.

A timeline shows what you've already learned about the life and times of your ancestor. It also reveals areas requiring further research.

software packages include a range of built-in customizable timeline features, but there are also standalone programs available such as Genelines by Progeny Genealogy <www.progenygenealogy.com/products/timeline-charts.aspx> and Tiki-Toki <www.tiki-toki.com>. You could also try a free online program such as HistoryLines <www.historylines.com>.

Whatever method you use to create your chronology, you should record every life event you've already established for your ancestor—their vital details of birth, marriage, and death. Add in the dates and places of the birth of each child (which may produce a clear migration path) and the dates and locations of all residences as recorded in census returns. Next, add in any relevant military records—enlistment and service details, notable battle engagements, injuries or health concerns, discharge and pension arrangements—and any other details such as immigration, naturalization, and educational or occupational successes.

When all the personal and historical events are in place, take a hard look for what might be missing from the timeline. Where are the gaps in your ancestor's life? Record where you have already searched for details and what information or clues these sources revealed, then note the collections where you need to look next.

Watch Your Style

Learn how to produce quality source citations. You can choose from a number of widely accepted styles, among them Modern Language Association (MLA) and the Chicago Manual of Style (CMS). FamilySearch.org has a good overview of various style guides and hints for further reading **<www.familysearch.org/wiki/en/Cite_Your_Sources_(Source_Footnotes)>**.

Record Your Sources

Recording where and when you found information is another discipline every family historian should make second nature. If you don't document your sources, you may find yourself unnecessarily duplicating some of your work down the line.

Whether formally written or not, source citations—the footnotes that set out the source of the information you are relying upon—add credibility to your genealogical research. Good citations provide sufficient information to enable you or another researcher to retrieve the document again, so you should include at least the name of the repository, the reference number of the source, and the date it was accessed.

Most genealogy software programs include either dedicated fields where you can cite your sources or a notes section where you can enter details of where your information originated. Different resources and websites also make citing sources easier than ever, as programs such as EasyBib **<www.easybib.com>** will generate citations in various styles.

For more in-depth study, you can also consult *Evidence Explained: Citing History Sources from Artifacts to Cyberspace* by Elizabeth Shown Mills (Genealogical Publishing Company, 2015) or view Mills' website **<www.evidenceexplained.com>**. The Board for Certification of Genealogists also has its own Genealogical Proof Standard (GPS) that it uses to evaluate the reliability of research; you can learn more about it on the Board's website **<www.bcgcertification.org/resources/standard.html>**.

Keep a Research Log

As your research progresses and the amount of data you gather accumulates, you will find it increasingly difficult to remember all the sources you have explored. A basic research log is a list of each source you have consulted and the information each revealed, saving you from forgetting where you left off in your research. A research log provides you with a handy list of what you have already searched, and this should prevent you from doing duplicate work by returning to the same source material unnecessarily. Recording the details of searches and what you discovered will also remind you of how you reached conclusions in

Starting Your Search for Immigrant Ancestors

After taking your first steps, you'll emerge with a clear direction for your research, and you'll be ready to start exploring records. There is no one-size-fits-all process for going about this because each family—and each individual within it—will present unique challenges. Below are the various stages of a typical research project. They can be easily adapted to suit the circumstances of your own family history.

You can learn more about tracing your Irish immigrant ancestor in chapter 3. If you are ready to jump across the pond, you can skip number 1.

Establish your ancestor's date of arrival.

The date is pivotal to your family history research, as you'll find earlier records in Ireland or Britain, while later records are in North America. Bear in mind that as the sea crossing got shorter during the nineteenth century, some Irish immigrants made the journey several times before settling in their new home.

Research place names, first names, and surnames.

If you know only Ireland as a place of origin for your immigrant ancestor, concentrate on North American records that provide the names of parents and siblings and at least a home county in Ireland. If your family was Roman Catholic, note the Latin versions of first names, and find out what nicknames or modifications those names may have had, especially in written form. Investigate surname variations, be flexible about their spellings, and accept that the prefixes of *O'-* and *Mc-/Mac-* were randomly omitted and added (see chapter 6).

Search websites and online databases.

Between global suppliers such as Ancestry.com, Findmypast, and FamilySearch.org, family history societies, and specialized volunteer-led websites, billions of North American records live in online databases. Take time to learn how to best use each search engine.

4

Investigate brick-and-mortar North American repositories.

It's not all online! Many important records have not been digitized, so you may find you need to contact the holding archive to order a photocopy or to make an appointment for a personal visit.

5

Familiarize yourself with the location in Ireland.

Once you have established a location in Ireland, learn about the relevant administrative boundaries that apply for different record sets, and of the records that survive for that area. *Tracing Your Irish Ancestors* by John Grenham (Genealogical Publishing Company, 2012) has a county-by-county breakdown.

6

Search Irish record collections.

Access records online, for free (National Archives of Ireland **<genealogy.nationalarchives. ie>**, National Library of Ireland **<registers.nli.ie>**, Irish Genealogy **<irishgenealogy.ie>**) and for-pay (Findmypast, RootsIreland **<rootsireland.ie>**).

7

Reach out to other Irish family historians.

You can now connect with generous and enthusiastic genealogists on social media sites such as Facebook **<www.facebook.com>** and Twitter **<www.twitter.com>**, websites of regional and local societies in Ireland, and online forums such as Boards.ie **<www.boards. ie/b/forum/1288>** and RootsChat **<www.rootschat.com/forum/ireland>**.

8

Reach out to repositories and experts.

Identify when, where, and how to access the records you need, and make contact with the appropriate repository to order copies if they are not online. Some repositories do not offer copy services, so you may need to consider hiring a local professional genealogist to access the records on your behalf.

your research. The log can be developed further as a list of websites, books, databases, and archive collections you intend to consult in the future, along with your reasons for wanting to search them. And if you're collaborating with other family members, research logs are a handy mechanism for keeping everyone up-to-date on the progress of the research.

Exactly what you include in your research log is up to you. At its most simple, the log should include the date, record/collection name, call number, book title and page number, name of repository or website URL, type of record (original document, transcription, microfilm, index, etc.), the result of the search (both positive and negative), and a source citation.

You can also include the research objective (what you are hoping to find out about your ancestor); the source type (primary or secondary, original or derivative); an evaluation of the status, clarity, or condition of the record; a transcription or summary of the information revealed; and an analysis of the result.

A research log created as a spreadsheet (see Microsoft Excel **<products.office.com/en-us/excel>** or Google Drive **<drive.google.com>**) will suit most researchers and have plenty of functions for organizing and analyzing data. Another option is to learn how to use a more general note-taking program such as Evernote **<www.evernote.com>**, which has quickly become a popular tool among genealogists for researchers on the move. For more on Evernote, see *How to Use Evernote for Genealogy* by Kerry Scott (Family Tree Books, 2015).

Think Laterally: Collateral and Cluster Research

While the main goal of your genealogical research may be to learn about your direct-line ancestors, casting a wider net to find your ancestors' siblings, neighbors, acquaintances, friends, and coworkers provides a broader and more accurate picture of your family as well as a deeper understanding of your Irish heritage. This practice of searching for complete families, not just a single lineage, is called whole-family genealogy. This shift in focus often opens up entirely new avenues to explore—ones that you might not have considered if you had followed only the direct family line.

Collateral research explores individuals whom you're not directly related to: your ancestors' siblings, aunts, uncles, and cousins. While researching additional historical individuals might take more time, it can also yield more benefits. Doing so can turn up vital information about preceding generations that you *are* directly related to, plus records that you wouldn't have had access to if you were searching only your direct-line ancestors. For example, perhaps only one member of your ancestor's generation knew the maiden name of his or her mother and had the good sense to record it in a letter or on a memorial card, or an older sibling may remember more about the family's immigration than a younger sibling. And as recordkeeping improved over time, your ancestor's younger sibling might have been asked for more specific detail about his or her background when enlisting into the military or applying for a passport or pension.

Cluster research broadens out further to look at the family in the context of a larger community. This kind of research extends to the neighbors, friends, and migrating companions of a core family group, exploring each member and examining the connections between them. The relationships within communities will be less linear than those of the core family group, being mixed up with aunts, cousins, friends, and in-laws. These groups' compositions tend to be more fluid, too, with relatives joining and leaving the community as time (or the group) moved on.

By broadening your research laterally, you will collect many more clues to investigate and may avoid some brick walls. If luck is really on your side, you might even find yourself sifting through a private archive of family records and memorabilia. Chapter 3 provides more details on using collateral and cluster research. Use the Cluster Research Worksheet at the end of this chapter when conducting your searches.

KEYS TO SUCCESS

Begin by writing down everything you already know about your family's history. Transpose the basic details of names and dates, if known, into a basic family tree chart so you can keep different generations together. This will help you establish the relationships between them.

Create your research plan and adopt a methodical approach before looking for records. If you don't know what your objectives are, you could waste a lot of time and money gathering information that doesn't answer your most important questions nor bring you nearer to your goals.

Learn the difference between primary and secondary sources, and treat the information you find in each accordingly. Prove your information from a secondary source with the more reliable information of a primary source. If you can't, treat the detail as an unverified clue.

Cite your sources, as this will allow you to trace your information back to documents and give credit and standardization to your research. And as the amount of information you collect grows, you'll need to remain consistent in how you record your discoveries.

CLUSTER RESEARCH WORKSHEET

Person of Interest

Name	
Birth	
Marriage	
Death	
Other details	

Person of Interest's Cluster

Name				
Relationship to person of interest, if known				
Birth				
Marriage(s)				
Death				
Other events/ details				

3

Identifying Your Immigrant Ancestor

Just like many other European immigrants who arrived in the United States looking for work, tolerance, and a life of new opportunity, the Irish didn't leave a perfect paper trail for their genealogically inclined descendants to follow. They were neither expected nor encouraged to include more than "from Ireland" on official forms requesting a birthplace, an unfortunate reality for Irish researchers. In this chapter, we'll identify strategies and US sources that will help you discover your ancestor's name, place of origin, and religion, the three most vital pieces of information in Irish immigrant research.

Before getting underway, you need to cast off any notions that your family's surname has always been spelled the way it is now. The spelling of surnames did not become standardized until the very late nineteenth and early twentieth centuries. And when you consider the high levels of illiteracy among Irish immigrants, you'll realize that the names in your family tree could have been recorded in many different ways. You'll learn a lot more about variant surnames (and first names) in chapter 6, and you should keep a list of all the likely options handy as you research.

Beyond the Ellis Island Myth

Despite all the evidence against it, the myth that the names of immigrants were changed by inspectors at Ellis Island persists. However, this suggestion has long since been disproven, as Ellis Island agents didn't even create passenger lists, much less botch the spelling in them. This reality is true for Irish immigrants as well, particularly as there was no need to "Anglicize" Irish names; Anglicization in Ireland occurred long before the mid-nineteenth century exodus from Ireland, as evidenced by the lack of Irish-language names on passenger manifest lists. As with lists of immigrants from other countries, these lists of travelers were drawn up before the ship sailed. They were created by Irish agents who would have understood local accents. If there was a mistake in the written spelling, it may have been the "fault" of the steamship agent.

Immigrants whose names changed soon after arrival in the United States likely made that decision to fit into their new surroundings. For this reason, a lot of Irish shed a symbol of their past by losing the O'- or Mc'- in their surnames. Others may have abbreviated or changed their names to sound less Irish, less Catholic, or more "American" in response to the prevailing anti-Irish sentiment in the nineteenth century.

DETERMINING RELIGION AND TOWNLAND

In addition to knowing your ancestor's correctly spelled name and surname, you'll also need to identify his or her religion as well as townland (an administrative division). With those additional pieces of information, you can identify more Irish records to research as well as distinguish your ancestor from other people with similar names.

Finding Your Ancestor's Religion

Almost all Irish immigrants to North America were members of the Roman Catholic, Church of Ireland, Presbyterian, Methodist, or Society of Friends (Quaker) faiths. Most researchers can make an educated guess about the beliefs of their own ancestors based on the faith of more-recent relatives, but you should be prepared for the unexpected. For example, mixed marriages occurred more frequently than we tend to realize (especially in urban areas), and this could also have permanently altered the religious direction of your family line. Freed from Ireland's strict religious regimes, some new immigrants may have cast off religious affiliation altogether.

Other factors can influence which religious faith your ancestors practiced—and thus, which faiths they were recorded as being a part of. When their numbers were fairly low in the early nineteenth century, many Catholics switched to the prominent local denomination to fit in. For example, if you find ancestors in the early nineteenth century who were members of the Congregational Church in New England, you should not assume they were members of this church in Ireland; they were much more likely to have been Catholics who converted upon arriving.

You may also find it helpful to learn about the history of the specific religion in that area, as it may be very different from its national or state history. For example, Presbyterian, Baptist, and Methodist denominations were split into several branches, and you'll need to know which one your ancestor belonged to when you search for records. The

Sources for Townland of Origin

The chart below sets out the US sources where you may find mention of your ancestor's townland of origin. They are arranged in descending order of probability of revealing at least a town name. While you should search through all these records for clues about your family and your immigrant ancestor, the table allows you to prioritize your research and set realistic expectations.

Sources	Examples	Tips
Relatives and family friends, especially older generations	Parents, aunts, uncles, cousins, grandparents; friends of these	Ask about family lore and any recollections of other family members. Seek out memorabilia and documentation.
Family memorabilia	Bibles, photographs, letters, memorial cards, leases, deeds	Record place names or other clues about location.
Cemetery	Headstone inscriptions	Check burial plot details for other members of the family who may not be recorded in the inscription.
Newspapers	Obituaries, birth and marriage announcements, reports of local civil involvement, society news, "Missing Friends" advertisements	See chapter 11 on printed sources for more.
Church records	Baptism, marriage, burial registers	Look for annotations in registers' margins noting parish of origin.
Naturalization records	Declarations of intention (first papers) and petitions for naturalization (second or final papers)	Citizenship papers may be in different towns and in any court. Papers filed since 1906 are most likely to note place of origin.
Military records	Civil War records, WWI draft registrations	Seek out Civil War widows pension records; the details are often fulsome. Army records sometimes give the birthplace of the recruit or his father.
Vital records	Birth, marriage, and death certificates	An official occasionally noted a place of origin.

website of the local diocese or other central office of the church or congregation may offer a brief overview, but seek out county histories and church directories at the local library for a more in-depth understanding, or contact a genealogical society or historical group.

If you're lucky enough to have inherited a family Bible or to have unearthed memorial cards in the memorabilia hunt suggested in chapter 2, you should be able to identify the correct religion and parish of origin. Otherwise, your first port of call should be the regular baptism, marriage, and burial registers of the most likely church in the locality where your ancestor settled. See the Vital Records section later in this chapter for more.

Identifying Your Ancestor's Townland

To track your ancestors back to the Emerald Isle, you will need to know where the family lived. Ireland may be small compared to the United States, but you still can't expect to find the strip of land your forebears once toiled on with nothing more than a name and maybe an approximate date of birth. You need to establish the precise location of that strip—or the name of the street where the family lived—before you can start looking in Irish records.

TRACKING IMMIGRANTS IN US SOURCES

Before you start your research in Ireland, you first need to exhaust all US sources, working generation by generation to your immigrant ancestor. In the course of this research, you might be tempted to stop after finding your family's religion and place of origin in Ireland, but I urge you to continue your research as far back as the records allow. During this research process, you will be gathering a wealth of information about your family, and any of it could prove extremely useful when you start your search in Ireland.

In-depth research in US sources means studying a number of different record types, and we'll spend the rest of this chapter looking at the most important of these and identifying the likely clues they contain. You can find and download a checklist of these records (and other important US resources) from *Family Tree Magazine* **<www.familytreemagazine.com/upload/images/PDF/recordschecklist.pdf>**.

Censuses

The first US census was taken in 1790, and a new census has been conducted every ten years since. Currently, researchers can access census records through 1940; future censuses will become available seventy-two years after their creation to protect respondents' privacy. Almost all of these records—except the 1890 census, which was destroyed by a fire in 1921—are available and indexed on websites such as Ancestry.com **<www.ancestry.com>** and FamilySearch.org **<www.familysearch.org>**. From 1850 onwards, the US census

Catch the Ship in Derry

Immigrants from the Ulster counties of Derry, Donegal, and Tyrone used the port of Londonderry as their preferred route to North America in the mid-nineteenth century. The passenger lists from two companies out of Londonderry are the subject of *Irish Passenger Lists, 1847–1871* by Brian Mitchell (Genealogical Publishing Company, 2008). This book includes the names and residences in Ireland of more than twenty-seven thousand passengers to North America, many disembarking in Philadelphia. The book can also be accessed on Ancestry.com.

requested information on all members of a household (earlier censuses required only details about the head of household) and, from 1880, the relationship of each individual to the head of the household. Many states also conducted their own censuses between the federal censuses, so be sure to check if your ancestor's home state conducted a survey during her lifetime.

Most researchers find it helpful to begin their search with the most recent federal census available and work backwards from recent family members to earlier generations. As you work through relevant census years, you may find personal information changes. Ages, in particular, seem to be very fluid, and first names may alter, too, switching from formal names to nicknames or abbreviated versions: Jeremiah to Jerry, Bridget to Delia, Margaret to Peggy, Bartholomew to Bart, etc. As always, spellings of surnames may change, and the prefixes *O* and *Mc* may be omitted or added over the years.

While the place-of-birth information on census returns rarely notes anything other than *Ireland* (or *Irish Free State* after 1922), some censuses asked useful questions about the number of years an immigrant had been in the United States or about the respondent's naturalization status. If the respondent had received citizenship, the census notes the year.

Naturalization Records

Not every immigrant chose to become a citizen. But those who wished to do so under-went a two-step system of naturalization that was introduced in the late eighteenth century. The process could be started and finished at any local, state, or federal court. In practice, individuals usually went to the county court nearest to their residence. An immigrant could take the first step—the "declaration of intent" to become a citizen—after living in the United States for at least two years. This was followed three years later by a "petition for naturalization" (known as "second" or "final" papers), which would result in a certificate of citizenship. (Note: The two steps did not have to take place in the same court.)

T650

Family name	Given name or names
Tierney	John

Address	
	Portland, Maine.

Certificate no. (or vol. and page)	Title and location of court U.S.District.
3 - 575.	Portland, Maine.

Country of birth or allegiance	When born (or age)
Clare, Ireland.	Aug. 1825.

Date and port of arrival in U. S.	Date of naturalization
New York. May 1, 1844.	Mar. 15, 1860.

Names and addresses of witnesses

W. B. Richards,   Portland, Maine.

Edward Flanigan,   Portland, Maine.

U. S. DEPARTMENT OF JUSTICE, Immigration and Naturalization Service. Form No. 1-IP. 16—17302

Not all early naturalization applications recorded birthplace simply as "Ireland." John Tierney, who immigrated in 1844, was a proud Clare man.

Naturalization papers often include at least a county of birth in Ireland, and some provide a town or even townland. Infuriatingly, most record "Ireland" only. However, the papers can contain information that points you towards additional records and research areas: a date of immigration, the name of the ship on which your ancestor traveled, a birth date or age, or the places of residence in America. You might even consider researching the person who sponsored your ancestor's naturalization application, as he or she may be a member of extended family, a colleague, or a fellow member of a religious congregation.

Your immigrant ancestor may not have completed the naturalization process. Many were granted "first papers" but did not subsequently apply for "final papers," and many others never chose to start the process. Married women and children under age twenty-one were granted citizenship through the husband or father, so you will not find separate records for them.

On September 26, 1906, the process of applying for naturalization was standardized and became a federal process. You can request naturalization records from after this date at the United States Citizenship and Immigration Services <www.uscis.gov/genealogy> for a fee. Online naturalization records are sprinkled across the major commercial databases; see Joe Beine's German Roots website <www.germanroots.com/naturalization.html> for state-by-state links, and you can access microfilmed records at local Family History

Centers (resource centers run by the Church of Jesus Christ of Latter-day Saints). You'll find more information about accessing citizenship records on the US National Archives and Records Administration (NARA) website **<www.archives.gov/research/naturalization/ naturalization.html>** (image **A**).

Some immigrants returned to Ireland after becoming citizens, and they often applied for passports to achieve this end. Until 1941, this wasn't technically necessary (except for certain short-lived periods during the Civil War and World War I). Passport applications dating from 1795 to 1925 are held by the NARA, which has a useful overview of these records at **<www.archives.gov/research/passport>**. Many of these are also online at Ancestry.com. The records hold useful genealogical information, including the birthplaces of the applicant and of his or her parents, dates of immigration and naturalization, occupations, and physical descriptions. Individual files may also include cover letters, affidavits from witnesses, and certificates.

Immigration Records

Irish immigrants arrived in the United States from any number of ports, as well as overland from Canada. The actual numbers cannot be adequately gauged, as standard recordkeeping was often nonexistent or inefficient and many records have not survived. Still, New York is recognized as the most popular port of arrival for Irish immigrants during the nineteenth century, followed (in no particular order) by Baltimore, Boston, New Orleans, and Philadelphia. Ships also arrived in some of the smaller ports along the East Coast, such as Savannah (Georgia), New Haven (Connecticut), and Rhode Island.

Until January 1, 1820, masters of ships were not legally obliged to present their ships' passenger lists to US officials, so US immigration records from this early period are scarce. However, two pre-1820 lists—"Arrivals at New Orleans 1813–1819" and "Arrivals at Philadelphia 1800–1819"—are available on microfilm at NARA **<www.archives.gov/research/ immigration/passenger-arrival.html>**. Additionally, NARA's collection holds many post-1820 lists for both small and major ports of arrival. Until 1882, these were known as customs passenger lists, then passenger-arrival lists. Like naturalization records, earlier passenger manifests don't usually state individual travelers' towns of origin. Later passenger records (after the 1890s or so) will usually include the town name.

All of NARA's passenger lists are available on microfilm at Family History Centers. They have also been digitized and indexed on Ancestry.com.

Vital Records

Every US state records the births, marriages, and deaths of its inhabitants, even if the starting point of such recordkeeping varies widely. The average start date for statewide

Destination: New York

New York is thought to have received the largest numbers of Irish immigrants. Ancestry.com has passenger lists for New York arrivals from 1820 to 1891. Those dating from 1851 are easier to search and have the most information, including the exact date of arrival, the name of the ship, and the names, ages, and occupations of those who sailed with the immigrant.

Unfortunately, these records provide only two clues relating to the origin of the immigrant: the port of departure of the ship and the passenger's nationality. It was not until the Immigration Act of 1893 that the passenger's former address in Ireland was recorded.

One of the largest individual collections of passenger records is "New York, Irish Immigrant Arrival Records, 1846–1851," which holds details of about six hundred thousand Irish immigrants who left the country during the Famine. Less than 5 percent of these record a place of residence. The collection is searchable for free on FamilySearch.org and on subscription at Ancestry.com and Findmypast.

Castle Garden's website **<www.castlegarden.org>** contains details of about 10 million people who passed through Castle Garden, America's first official immigration reception center. It opened in 1855, but the free transcribed records (which are not complete) date from 1830 to 1892.

The Ellis Island Passenger Search collection (available at on the foundation's website **<www. libertyellisfoundation.org>**) is an online database of fifty-one million passengers who were processed through America's official reception center from 1892 to 1957. It's free and contains digital images of ships' manifests and more. Passenger records by this time contained details of next of kin, places of birth, and places of last residence and age, as well as the names and addresses of where the traveler was headed (often a relative's or sponsor's home). Some even offered basic descriptions of the individual.

collection of these vital records is the early 1900s. Fortunately, some towns, cities, and counties introduced local government registration systems much earlier. In Massachusetts, for example, the records date to 1790. A state-by-state listing of vital records availability, both online and offline, is at VitalRec.com **<www.vitalrec.com>**, while the National Center for Health Statistics **<www.cdc.gov/nchs/w2w/index.htm>** maintains a database of the official state providers of certificates. The largest online collections of vital records are on subscription at Ancestry.com, Findmypast **<www.findmypast.com>**, and MyHeritage **<www.myheritage.com>**, and free of charge on FamilySearch.org.

While birth records don't usually provide any proof of immigration, they occasionally note birthplaces of the baby's parents. Similarly, marriage records historically required the bride and groom to provide the names and birthplaces of their parents. Bear in mind that the official completing the registration would probably have been unfamiliar with the correct spelling of Irish place names and may have recorded them phonetically. The

MICHAEL SANTRY			
FIRST NAME	MICHAEL	RELATIVE LEFT BEHIND	
LAST NAME	SANTRY	NAME OF RELATIVE LEFT BEHIND	
OCCUPATION	LABORER	ADDRESS OF RELATIVE LEFT BEHIND	
AGE	22	TICKET	
SEX	Male	PAID BY	Self
LITERACY	Unknown	IN THE US BEFORE	Unknown
SHIP	NANANTUM	IN THE US WHEN	
ARRIVED	2 Mar 1849	IN THE US WHERE	
COUNTRY	IRELAND	GOING TO SOMEONE IN THE US	Unknown
PORT OF DEPARTURE	LIVERPOOL	RELATIONSHIP TO THAT SOMEONE IN THE US	
PLACE OF LAST RESIDENCE		NAME OF RELATIVE IN THE US	
PROVINCE OF LAST RESIDENCE	UNKNOWN		
CITY OR VILLAGE OF DESTINATION	UNITED STATES	ADDRESS OF RELATIVE IN THE US	
PLAN	Unknown	CITY OF RELATIVE IN THE US	
PASSAGE	Unknown	COUNTRY OF BIRTH	IRELAND
MONEY		PLACE OF BIRTH	

The 1849 arrival of my great-great-grandfather's cousin Michael is noted in Castle Garden's records after he'd traveled from Cork to catch the *Nanantum* in Liverpool.

same problem may apply to death registrations; the forms usually asked the informant for the birthplace of the deceased.

In addition to being wary of spelling, you should also treat with caution any information on a death certificate unless the informant was a close relative who you can reasonably expect to have known the correct details. Joe Beine's DeathIndexes.com <www.deathindexes.com> is a handy gateway site to death, burial, and probate records and obituaries. See the Headstones section for additional resources.

Church records can reveal reliable information about your ancestors' backgrounds. Priests and other clergymen often developed close relationships with members of their congregation and would be in a strong position to know personal details about their parishioners. Roman Catholic priests, for example, were usually Irish themselves, and exchanging background details about a place of origin and its inhabitants would have been enjoyed as a bonding exercise between individuals, whether or not the priest was familiar with the old community. Priests were also regularly called upon to arrange marriages between two underage people, between two people of different religions, or between two cousins, again involving the release of familial details. Sometimes these details will have been annotated in the church register; otherwise, the dispensation papers are kept in diocese archives and you may need to be patient to gain access.

Always note the names of godparents, sponsors, and witnesses in church records. More often than not, they were members of the extended family or close friends from the same place in Ireland. If your own ancestors didn't leave a decent paper trail, you might find that the people who performed these duties at important life events have a more reliable set of records.

To find out where your ancestors worshipped, search Google by parish name and locality to find details of likely churches. Alternatively, try the USA Churches online directory <www.usachurches.org>. When you contact a church or diocese to enquire about access to their registers, bear in mind that church records are not public records. Any access or information provided from them will be at the discretion of the priest or clergyman. Be as clear as possible about what it is you are seeking, and ask for *all* the information, including annotations connected with the register entry. Annotations can be extremely revealing, as the priest may have requested proof of baptism from the home parish in Ireland before agreeing to a marriage.

Keeping the Savings Safe

In both New York and Philadelphia, Irish immigrants took advantage of specialist banks set up to help them manage their finances and send money home. The Emigrant Savings Bank was established in 1850 in New York, and its records include the place and year of birth of the account holder and often other details. The originals are held at New York Public Library <www.nypl.org>. The records are also on microfilm via the Family History Library <www.familysearch.org/catalog/search> and at Ancestry.com.

The Diocese of Philadelphia introduced a similar banking arrangement in May 1848. Set up for Catholics (rather than just for Irish), it became known as the Bishop's Bank. Age and county of birth (at least) were noted with details of deposits, and some records include physical descriptions or family connections. The ledgers are free at Villanova University's Digital Library <digital.library.villanova.edu/Item/vudl:202764>, and the originals are held by the Philadelphia Archdiocesan Historical Research Center.

The FAN Principle

If you've conducted research all the way back to your immigrant ancestor and still can find no evidence of religion or place of origin in Ireland, it's time to "go wide," using the collateral and cluster techniques mentioned in chapter 2. These methods develop the FAN principle, which champions researching an individual's friends, associates, and neighbors (hence, FAN). This is a perfect match for Irish genealogy because Irish people have always had a natural sense of "clan" and often settled in clusters with people they knew. Pay special attention to these FANs:

Friends

- witnesses to an ancestor's naturalization
- executors in probate records
- sponsors of children at baptism
- witnesses to marriages
- guardians of deceased family's children
- boarders living with your ancestor's family in census returns

Associates

- people arriving on the same immigrant ship
- witnesses to wills and deeds
- buyers named in estate sales
- colleagues and business partners

Neighbors

- people living next-door to your ancestor in census returns
- people with the same surname living in the same street in census returns
- people appearing in city directories at adjoining addresses to your ancestor's business

Newspapers

The mass digitization of newspapers has opened up new opportunities to find obituaries, reports of accidents, happy events, probate issues, court appearances, and much more besides. All of that could possibly include information about a place of origin. Learn more about the value of newspapers and where to access them in chapter 11.

Headstones

A townland, city, or county of origin was often noted on the tombstones of Irish immigrants. Since, in nearly all cases, close relatives commissioned inscriptions, the details on tombstones are generally more reliable than some other death records. Likewise, the death certificate may hold details of the undertaker and burial place, or you may have to seek out the most likely cemetery for people living in the area where your ancestor died.

If you can't visit a cemetery yourself, you may find a kind genealogist has already transcribed and photographed the headstone and uploaded details to Find A Grave <www.findagrave.com>, BillionGraves <www.billiongraves.com>, or Interment.net <www. interment.net>. Alternatively, you could approach a local genealogical society to find out if it has completed any transcriptions in the cemetery. You should also find out if there is an interment list for the cemetery; while this will probably not record a specific place of origin beyond "Ireland," an interment list may include the names of others buried in the plot but not memorialized on the stone.

Military Records

Army records can be valuable sources of information. The most likely to reveal genealogical information and help you narrow down to a place of origin are military service records, pension applications, and draft registration cards.

Civil War pensions will be your most valuable military records if your ancestor came to the United States before the 1860s. Military pensions were claimed by soldiers, their widows, and their children, and applications may hold birth and marriage dates and locations. Importantly, pensions often state the name of the county or precise townland in Ireland. For information about where these files are held, see NARA's Civil War resource list <www.archives.gov/research/military/civil-war/resources.html>.

While Ancestry.com holds many Civil War collections and indexes, one of the most revealing collections, the Civil War "Widow" Pension application files, is now being digitized and made accessible at Ancestry.com's sister site, Fold3 <www.fold3.com>. These files relate to Civil War veterans whose service ended between 1861 and 1910 (i.e., they include soldiers who may not have died during the conflict, but who died later of injuries or diseases sustained during the war). Case files include where and when a man served, details of his service, his life before the war, and his family, including information about his widow, children, and sometimes his parents. The level of detail is often remarkable.

WWI draft registrations are another useful source of information about military ancestors and their relatives. About twenty-four million draft cards for men born between 1872 and 1900 survive. They have been indexed and can be searched at Ancestry.com and Fold3. They include the date and location of birth of the soldier, plus his citizenship status and his father's birthplace. All too often, the place of birth is "Ireland," but a good proportion will tell you the county and some will tell you a town or townland of origin (image B).

B

In his WWI draft papers, Daniel J. Driscoll noted his place of birth as the small town of Drimoleague in County Cork.

WHAT IF YOU STILL CAN'T FIND THE TOWNLAND?

After painstakingly working through all this research on not just your direct ancestor but also his extended family and acquaintances, you have hopefully found a place of origin. You may have successfully narrowed down the location to a county or more focused area, but the name of the exact townland or street may still be proving elusive. What now?

Depending on the time you have available, the size of the area you have identified, and (to a large extent) the popularity of your ancestral surname, your next step might be to work through all the parish and other land records for that locality. It would be a big commitment and would involve a lot of work, but you'll be rewarded if you're able to discover the place your Irish ancestor once called home.

KEYS TO SUCCESS

Don't be rigid about the spelling of your family name. While the name would have been Anglicized before your immigrant's arrival in North America, the spelling would not have been standardized and an *O'-* or *Mc-* prefix may have been lost or found since.

Check all US ports for your immigrant ancestor's arrival if you are having trouble locating him in records. New York, Boston, and Philadelphia were the largest ports of arrival for Irish immigrants, but many Irish passengers sailed to other, smaller East Coast ports.

Complete a full sweep of research in US records before continuing your research in Ireland. All the information gathered at this stage helps you create a fuller picture of your family's history and will ensure you have a solid base of clues when you start delving into Irish records.

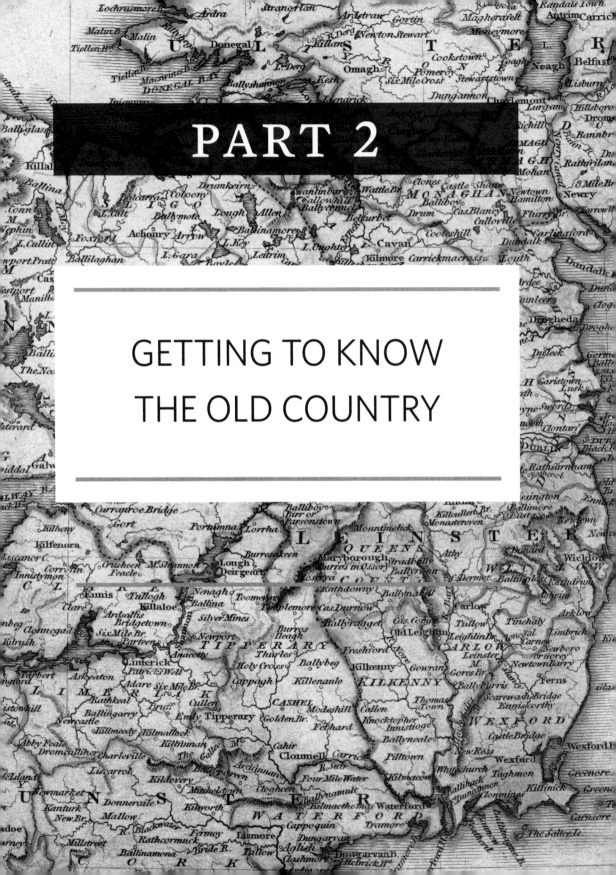

PART 2

GETTING TO KNOW
THE OLD COUNTRY

4

Understanding Irish History

Ireland's history is your ancestral heritage. The political decisions and social trends of the past impacted generation after generation of your Irish forebears, and learning a little of this historical context will give you more insight into their daily lives and the challenges they faced. Understanding important moments in Irish history will also help you better understand the times your ancestors lived through, plus provide a backdrop for your ancestors' decision to emigrate and, since major events often affected recordkeeping and informed how and why certain genealogical records were created, changed, or lost. In this chapter, we'll highlight the key political, social, and military events of the last one thousand years.

EARLY HISTORY: GAELIC IRELAND AND THE NORMAN INVASION

In the early medieval period, Gaelic Ireland was a unique society with a strict hierarchical structure and a highly developed (if somewhat archaic) legal code known as the Brehon Laws. It was a Christian nation (St. Patrick converted the Celts in the fifth century), and the land was divided into a handful of kingdoms ruled by dynastic lineages and their extended families. Each made a habit of invading and subjugating neighboring kingdoms. But over several centuries, political power had been dominated by a single dynasty, the

Uí Néill, who ruled great swathes of the island and founded the most prestigious kingdom of all: Tara.

The Uí Néill's monopoly of the island was broken in 1002 by Brian Boroimhe (Brian Boru; image A), whose notable defeat of Vikings and death at the Battle of Clontarf in 1014 secured him a legendary place in Irish history. Subsequent rulers tried to emulate him, but none had as much success.

By the 1100s, most of the warfare on the island was between squabbling chieftains and their dynasties: the O'Briain (O'Brien), who ruled Munster; the Ui Conchobhair (O'Connor), who ruled Connaught; the Uí Néill (O'Neill) in Ulster, which was ruled by the Mac Lochlainn (MacLaughlin); and the Mac Murchada (Mac-Murrough), who ruled Leinster.

Brian Boru was a legendary High King of Ireland and founder of the O'Brien dynasty.

The final major contest between the old Gaelic High Kings saw Rory O'Connor (from Connaught) seize the title of High King of Ireland in 1166. He then attacked the Leinster king, Dermot MacMurrough, and drove him into exile.

MacMurrough successfully appealed to King Henry II of England for help in regaining his kingdom, and he was given permission to recruit men from among his Anglo-Norman nobles. He enlisted the support of Richard fitz Gilbert de Clare (later known as Strongbow), promising him the hand of his daughter in marriage and the status of King of Leinster after his (MacMurrough's) death. The repercussions of this marriage settlement

Norman Terminology

Originally from Northern France, the Normans conquered England and took the English throne only one hundred years before their arrival on Wexford's beaches. Although they spoke French and followed French customs, they had integrated well in England and even described themselves as English. Irish historians, however, have yet to reach agreement about what to call the nobles, diplomats, and soldiers who invaded Ireland in the twelfth century. You may find them referred to as Anglo-Norman, Cambro-Norman, Anglo-French, Norman, and, as time passed and their settlement in Ireland became permanent, English.

TIMELINE Irish History

432 Saint Patrick brings Christianity to Ireland.

1170 Anglo-Normans invade Ireland.

1536 The Protestant Anglican church (called the Church of Ireland) becomes the official state church of the island.

1605 The first Scottish settlers arrive, marking the start of the Plantation of Ulster.

1649 Oliver Cromwell crushes the Irish rebellion. Over the next several decades, Parliament enacts Penal Laws designed to suppress Roman Catholics and Dissenters.

1720 The first wave of Irish-American emigration begins, with two hundred thousand Presbyterians sailing to America over the next fifty years.

1771 The Catholic Relief Acts, a series of reforms passed over the next twenty years, restore many rights suspended by the Penal Laws.

1801 The Act of Union creates the United Kingdom of Great Britain and Ireland.

1829 The Catholic Emancipation Act grants equal rights to Roman Catholics.

1845 The Great Famine begins. Millions die of starvation and disease or emigrate over the next several years.

1864 Civil registration of all births, marriages, and deaths becomes mandatory.

1870 The Church of Ireland is no longer the established church.

1914 Home Rule (Irish self-governance) is postponed as World War I breaks out. Millions of Irish sign up to fight in the British Army.

1916 Protestors take over government buildings in the Easter Rising and read the Proclamation of the Republic.

1919 The Irish War of Independence from Britain begins.

1921 The Anglo-Irish Treaty divides the island into the Irish Free State (with full self-government rights) and Northern Ireland (which remains part of the United Kingdom). The Irish Civil War breaks out between Pro-Treaty and Anti-Treaty forces over the next two years.

1949 Ireland is renamed Republic of Ireland and leaves the British Commonwealth.

1969 The Troubles begin in Northern Ireland.

1973 Ireland and the United Kingdom (including Northern Ireland) join the European Economic Community (now the European Union).

1995 Ireland's "Celtic Tiger" era begins, bringing huge economic growth and dramatically improving living standards.

1998 The Good Friday Agreement is signed, declaring peace between paramilitary groups and revising Northern Ireland's system of government.

echo down the centuries, because the subsequent invasion of Ireland by the Normans marks the start of nearly eight hundred turbulent years of English and British rule.

In the summer of 1167, the Norman adventurers landed on the Wexford coast. Just two years later, they controlled the old Viking ports of Wexford, Waterford, and Dublin, and King Henry himself visited in 1171. Strongbow had succeeded MacMurrough as king of Leinster, but he accepted Henry's superior status as Lord of Ireland. So, too, did most of the Irish kings. Even Rory O'Connor submitted in 1175, leaving no more Gaelic High Kings of Ireland and establishing the end of native-Irish rule.

Although some conflict persisted between the native Irish and the newcomers over the next two centuries, the Normans employed local peasants, introduced new agricultural practices, and built castles and towns. They were largely absorbed into Irish society, intermarrying and adopting Irish customs. This was frowned upon by England, which in 1366 enacted the Statutes of Kilkenny. This drew sharp distinctions between the Normans and the Irish, forbidding the Anglo-Normans from marrying native Irish, speaking the indigenous language, playing Irish sports, dressing in the Gaelic fashion, or riding horses bareback. It was a desperate attempt to keep the two groups separate, and it failed.

THE PROTESTANT REFORMATION AND THE FLIGHT OF THE EARLS

The fifteenth century saw Ireland enjoy a period of stability and relative prosperity, but relations with England became increasingly strained after Henry VII came to the throne in 1495 and took power back from the Anglo-Norman kings and lords. His son, Henry VIII, continued confiscating Irish lands and handing them to his followers. After his famous break from the Roman Catholic Church (in which the pope would not grant an annulment to his first marriage), Henry set up the new Church of England (also known as the Anglican Church) and made the Church of Ireland, a province, the established state church of the island. There was little opposition to Henry's Reformation; the majority of his Irish-speaking subjects continued their Catholic worship unhindered.

This changed dramatically after his death. Roman Catholics were increasingly seen as a threat to the security of the crown and state and, in 1569 during Queen Elizabeth's reign, attendance at Protestant worship was made compulsory for all. Despite fines and physical punishments for non-Conformists, the Protestant Church of Ireland failed to win over the majority Catholic population. Resentment among the Gaelic Irish lords built up, encouraged by England's archenemy, the Catholic King Phillip II of Spain. This conflict bubbled over into rebellion, and the resulting Nine Years' War continued until 1603 with defeat of the Irish chieftains Hugh O'Neill and Rory O'Donnell and their allies.

The end of the Nine Years' War coincided with the death of Queen Elizabeth and the installation of King James I, who hoped that offering favorable surrender terms would subdue O'Neill (now Earl of Tyrone) and O'Donnell (now Earl of Tyrconnell). After the Catholic-led Gunpowder Plot was exposed in 1605, the new king's attitude changed, and the Earls' prominence began a slow decline, with the English undermining their authority and confiscating their most fertile lands. Fearing imminent arrest, the two Irishmen took their families and a band of Ulstermen and set sail for the continent in what became known as the Flight of the Earls. They hoped to return with a Catholic Spanish army to rid Ireland of the English, but (though well-received by the Spanish) they neither received the commitment they expected nor returned to Ireland.

Many more Gaelic noble families followed them out of the country over the next few decades, most joining Europe's Irish Brigades as soldiers. They maintained strong links to their Irish origins and Catholicism and became known as the Wild Geese.

The Flight of the Earls and the subsequent departure of the Wild Geese were in some ways class migrations: First the aristocratic earls and their families left, followed by the gentry/middle classes. This gave rise to English propaganda that those left in Ireland were the ignorant, uneducated poor—which, unfortunately, was partly true.

THE PLANTATION OF ULSTER

Following the Flight of the Earls, King James seized the lands of Tyrone and Tyrconnell, and, in the face of less-armed opposition, set in motion an organized Protestant English and Scottish colonization known as the Plantation of Ulster, beginning in 1610.

Sending loyal, English-speaking families to Ulster was seen as a way to quell the rebellious north of Ireland. Nearly all the new arrivals came from the higher social classes in England and Scotland and brought trusted laborers and allies from their existing estates. Principal planters were known as undertakers, and they each received two thousand acres. All settlers were given incentives not to hire Irish workers, thereby ensuring jobs for more would-be colonists. Catholics were forced onto marginal, often mountainous or remote, land, condemning them to a life of poverty.

RESEARCH TIP

Read from the Best

If you're going to choose only one or two history books, seek out *The Atlas of Irish History*, edited by Seán Duffy (Gill & Macmillan, 1997), and *A History of Ireland in 250 Episodes*, by Jonathan Bardon (Gill & Macmillan, 2009). Both carry an excellent series of maps that visualize the historical information and are easy to read, written by well-regarded historians.

The Protestant Church of Ireland was granted all land formerly belonging to the Catholic Church and received a new mission: Convert as many natives as possible. This initiative was largely a failure, as most of the newly arrived clergy could not speak Irish, and the natives could not speak English!

Within only a dozen years, nearly twenty thousand British men had settled in Ulster, and the new population was growing rapidly. Sixteen new towns with predominantly Protestant populations had been established, and this tipped the balance of members of Parliament in the Irish House of Commons in favor of Protestants. With more power in Parliament, Protestants were able to legislate and execute their own agenda, often to the detriment of Catholics.

Over just one or two generations, these shifts in population had a polarizing effect, with parts of Ulster remaining Catholic and Irish-speaking and (mainly) eastern parts being English-speaking Protestant communities. The problem was compounded by a rebellion in 1641 led by Phelim O'Neill, who had retained his own land but grown dissatisfied with continual confiscation of Catholic lands. Although initially nonviolent, the Irish peasantry took the opportunity to massacre about four thousand of the new settlers, further driving a wedge between the Gaelic Catholic and the British Protestant communities.

CROMWELL AND THE BATTLE OF THE BOYNE

Meanwhile, as the Irish revolted in the 1640s, England was engaged in its own bloody civil war between the monarchy and Parliament, which wanted to curb the king's powers. King Charles I was executed by order of Parliament, and General Oliver Cromwell, a former member of Parliament and a brilliant military commander reviled in Ireland even today, transformed England into a republic called the Commonwealth of England.

As part of his efforts to consolidate power, Cromwell personally led a brutal campaign across Ireland for nine months in 1649. Driven by Puritan zeal to rid Ireland of its Catholic population, Cromwell and his men killed thousands of Irish and committed other atrocities at Drogheda and Wexford. Cromwell's followers received "Cromwellian Plantations," more than a million acres seized from the Irish by the end of the three-year conquest of Ireland. As a result, Catholic landownership dropped from 60 percent of the total acreage to just 8 percent. Parliament further oppressed the Irish by passing a series of laws restricting property ownership, the right to bear arms or hold political office, and education for Catholics and non-Church of Ireland Protestant denominations. Catholics were forbidden to celebrate mass, and priests were liable to instant execution or exile.

England's short-lived republic ended with the restoration of King Charles II in 1660, bringing a temporary reprieve from these oppressive laws. But trouble loomed again when Charles' Catholic brother James II succeeded him in 1685. Within three years,

Century Ireland

Want to learn more about Irish history? Century Ireland is an online historical newspaper, published fortnightly, that tells the rolling story of events and life in Ireland one hundred years ago through a wealth of visual, archival, and contextual material, plus modern commentary. It explores many of the domestic, social, and political challenges faced by people between 1913 and 1923—the period now known as the Revolutionary Decade.

Funded by the Irish state and hosted by Raidió Teilifís Éireann, the national public service broadcaster of Ireland, the website <**www.rte.ie/centuryireland**> is the result of a partnership between the major cultural and educational institutions in Ireland and is produced by a team of researchers at Boston College Ireland.

English Protestants had rallied behind James's Protestant daughter, Mary, and her Dutch husband, William of Orange, who were invited to rule as king and queen. James tried to regain his crown with the help of French troops and Irish supporters (called Jacobites), but he was decisively beaten by William at the Battle of the Boyne in 1690. The battle is still commemorated by Northern Ireland's Orangemen every year on July 12.

PENAL LAWS

With the Irish rebellion crushed, William III (William of Orange) passed a series of Penal Laws in the 1690s and 1700s that restricted Catholics and Protestant "Dissenters," or those who refused to join the Church of Ireland. These laws limited education, inheritance rights, ability to practice law, long land leases, public service and military employment, and the right to vote. The Catholic Church could not keep records, and both Catholics and Presbyterians were forced to marry in Protestant churches. Furthermore, upon the death of a Catholic landowner, his land was divided between all his sons, which forced successive generations to farm increasingly small plots of land that could not support them. However, if the landowner converted to the Church of Ireland, this partition was not required.

The impact of the Penal Laws on Presbyterians sparked the first of Ireland's waves of emigration: An estimated two hundred thousand Scots-Irish left Ulster in the eighteenth century and settled in rural areas of Virginia, Pennsylvania, and the Carolinas.

Following the success of the American and French Revolutions, a group called the United Irishmen mounted a campaign in 1798. Led by Theobald Wolfe Tone, the movement hoped to create a Presbyterian-Catholic alliance and demanded parliamentary reform. But, as with other Irish uprisings, the United Irishmen's efforts failed. An estimated thirty thousand people were killed in the uprising, and all the group's leaders were captured. This event (the Irish Rebellion of 1798) led to the Act of Union between Great Britain and Ireland in 1801, ending Ireland's autonomy.

Most of the Penal Laws were repealed in the late eighteenth century, but one important item remained even after the 1801 Acts of Union: the exclusion of Catholics from the House of Commons and senior political and judicial offices. In 1828, barrister Daniel O'Connell, a brilliant orator and political mastermind, ran in a by-election for a Parliamentary seat in County Clare. His decisive victory paved the way for the final repeal in 1829, and O'Connell was given the title "The Liberator." His later political years were focused on the unsuccessful repeal of the Act of Union, and he even spent a short time in prison, which weakened his health. He was also responsible for establishing a Catholic cemetery in Dublin at Goldenbridge and a nondenominational cemetery at Glasnevin, both of them firsts for Ireland. Dublin's main thoroughfare and river crossing were later renamed in his honor, and an imposing memorial to him overlooks both.

THE NINETEENTH CENTURY:
THE GREAT FAMINE AND MASS EMIGRATION

Now we reach a portion of Irish history you've likely heard of: the Great Irish Famine. While not the first famine to come to Ireland, the Great Famine became the defining event of Irish history in the nineteenth century, notable for both its magnitude and its effect on emigration.

B

THE IRISH FAMINE—SCENE AT THE GATE OF THE WORK-HOUSE

As starvation set in during the Great Famine of 1845–1849, Ireland's workhouses (designed to aid the poor) were overwhelmed.

The famine started as a natural catastrophe: A wet summer and fungal disease caused the failure of the potato crop in 1845. Potatoes were the staple diet of the poor, and crop failure was regular enough. As a result, the government was slow to respond to the crisis, and contemporary policies made the situation worse. Tenants were allowed to build up debt on their rent with the expectation that they could pay it with the following year's harvest. But when the crop failed for three of the following four years, the problem escalated enormously as tenants were no longer able to pay their latent debts.

Number of Emigrants Leaving Ireland
May 1, 1851, to Dec. 31, 1860

Province	County	Number	Percent of population*
Leinster	Carlow	10,639	15.63
	Dublin	25,196	6.22
	Kildare	12,177	12.72
	Kilkenny	33,748	21.26
	King's (Offaly)	20,867	18.62
	Longford	14,434	17.53
	Louth	16,904	15.70
	Meath	23,133	16.44
	Queen's (Laois)	19,730	17.67
	Westmeath	18,386	16.50
	Wexford	26,964	14.97
	Wicklow	11,153	11.57
	Total	**233,331**	**13.95**
Munster	Clare	49,683	23.39
	Cork	146,422	22.55
	Kerry	54,483	22.87
	Limerick	61,640	23.51
	Tipperary	80,219	24.19
	Waterford	37,962	23.14
	Total	**430,409**	**23.17**

As hunger spread, families abandoned their pathetic patches of soil or were evicted by landlords for failing to pay rent. The problem was compounded by disease, and local efforts to help the poor were unsuccessful. The Society of Friends (Quakers) set up soup kitchens to help care for the famine's victims, and workhouses (institutions set up to benefit Ireland's poor and homeless; image **B**) were overwhelmed. Meanwhile, Ireland continued to export other foods for consumption elsewhere in the British Empire.

Province	County	Number	Percent of population*
Ulster	Antrim	75,529	21.44
	Armagh	29,057	14.82
	Cavan	36,140	20.76
	Donegal	37,941	14.87
	Down	47,235	14.37
	Fermanagh	17,157	14.78
	Londonderry	27,511	14.33
	Monaghan	26,517	18.70
	Tyrone	39,178	15.32
	Total	**336,265**	**16.71**
Connaught	Galway	50,353	15.65
	Leitrim	16,428	14.68
	Mayo	28,880	10.52
	Roscommon	27,323	15.75
	Sligo	13,127	10.21
	Total	**136,111**	**13.48**
Unstated	**Total**	**27,302**	
All Ireland		**1,163,418**	**17.75**

*Percent of Ireland's population in 1851 (total: 6,552,385).
Data taken from *Thom's Alamanac and Official Directory*, 1862

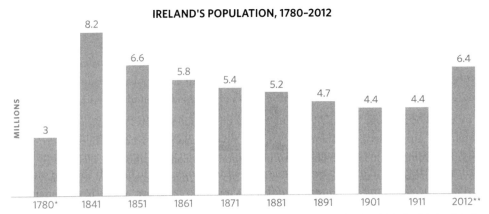

IRELAND'S POPULATION, 1780–2012

MILLIONS

| 1780* | 1841 | 1851 | 1861 | 1871 | 1881 | 1891 | 1901 | 1911 | 2012** |

3, 8.2, 6.6, 5.8, 5.4, 5.2, 4.7, 4.4, 4.4, 6.4

*Population of 1780 is estimated   **2012 population figure is the combined total of Republic of Ireland and Northern Ireland

The population of the island reached a peak in the early 1840s. It has never fully recovered from the dramatic losses of the Great Famine and the mass emigration of the following decades.

At the start of the 1840s, the population stood at 8.1 million, the highest ever recorded. By the end of the decade, it had fallen by 20 percent due to starvation, disease, and emigration. The island's population still hasn't recovered, with 4.6 million people in the Republic of Ireland and 1.8 million people in Northern Ireland (image **C**).

Though the Famine period saw the largest group of emigrants leave Ireland (see the Number of Emigrants Leaving Ireland sidebar), emigration continued throughout the century. In the first half of the 1800s, the most common destination for Irish emigrants had been Canada, mainly because it was part of Britain so fares were cheaper. During and after the Famine, the United States became the preferred destination outside the British Isles.

Once in the new country, immigrants tried to gain employment and send money back to Ireland, often helping other members of the family emigrate in turn. This process was known as chain migration, and often helped create communities of people who originated in the same part of Ireland. Many people from County Louth, for example, settled in New Brunswick, Canada, while the Beara Peninsula in County Cork experienced large-scale emigration to Butte, Montana.

In addition to sending money back home, emigrants also often stayed active in Irish politics. Some emigrants and their descendants in the United States founded the Fenian movement in the late-nineteenth century, raising funds to further their hopes of an independent Irish nation.

Back in Ireland, the new Land League, led by Charles Stewart Parnell, successfully campaigned for a reform of the land system. The Land Acts (1881, 1885, 1891, and 1903)

introduced a scheme of state-aided land purchase schemes, resulting in a mass movement of land into the hands of those who worked it (such as lower-class Irish farmers).

A cultural nationalist movement through the Gaelic Athletic Association and the Gaelic League developed alongside the land movement. As a result, the Irish language and Gaelic sport and culture experienced a revival, and a new generation set out to "de-Anglicize" the Irish people. Initially non-political, the demands of this movement inevitably led it to challenge the British government. As the twentieth century dawned, this Gaelic Revival had become an important feature of Ireland's struggle for national self-determination.

MODERN IRELAND: REVOLUTION, PARTITION, AND REBOUND

Ireland's desire for self-governance continued to grow throughout the following decades, eventually climaxing in the Revolutionary Decade, a period of civil unrest, trade union activism, and armed resistance that began in 1912 and ended in 1922/23 with the creation of two separate nations.

For years, tensions between the Irish and the British government had been growing over "Home Rule," the reinstatement of Irish self-government via a parliament based in Dublin. While Home Rule received widespread support throughout much of the island, the predominantly Protestant northern counties, whose political and religious differences had been sown by the Ulster plantation of the seventeenth century, did not wish to be governed from Dublin (which, to them, meant by Roman Catholics). In 1912, Protestants signed the Ulster Covenant, pledging to defy Home Rule by all means necessary. Despite their resolution, a Home Rule bill was finally passed by Parliament two years later, only to be shelved when World War I began in August.

Irish Nationalist groups came together to take advantage of the British government's distraction. They planned an armed uprising across the country during Easter weekend, but only the Dublin leaders and their forces went through with it. The rebels, numbering about 1,500 men and women, took several strategic sites in the capital on Easter Monday. On the steps of the General Post Office, rebels read out the Proclamation of the Republic to a largely uncomprehending and unenthusiastic audience of civilians, promising "religious and civil liberty, equal rights, and opportunities" and that the movement would "pursue the happiness and prosperity of the whole nation ... cherishing all the children of the nation equally."

The rebels held their sites for five days against a hastily deployed British Army of about twenty thousand soldiers. In the face of an insurrection that clearly had little public support, the British responded harshly, declaring martial law and arresting several thousand people. But it was the executions of fourteen of the movement's leaders in early May that

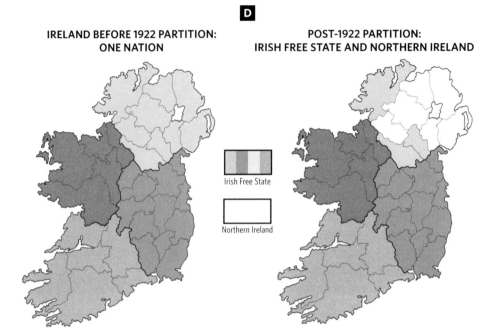

IRELAND BEFORE 1922 PARTITION: ONE NATION

POST-1922 PARTITION: IRISH FREE STATE AND NORTHERN IRELAND

Irish Free State

Northern Ireland

The Anglo-Irish Treaty was signed on December 6, 1921, and became effective from March 31, 1922. It divided the island into Northern Ireland, which remained a part of the United Kingdom, and the Irish Free State, which went on to become the Republic of Ireland in 1948.

turned the tide of public opinion, creating national martyrs and popular support for Irish independence. The Easter Rising led to Sinn Féin, a political party championing Irish independence, winning a landslide victory in the 1918 election immediately after World War I.

More conflict was to follow. The Irish War of Independence, a vicious guerrilla conflict between Irish Republican Army and British forces, raged for the next few years.

The Anglo-Irish Treaty was signed in 1921. Under its terms, the island would be partitioned into two new states: a twenty-six-county Irish Free State, and the six counties of Northern Ireland (image **D**). The latter remained part of the United Kingdom, while the Irish Free State became an autonomous dominion of the British Empire with the British monarchy as its head of state.

However, a group of Republicans were still deeply dissatisfied with the negotiated settlement, and civil war broke out in the Irish Free State between the Anti-Treaty faction (led by Éamon de Valera, an American-born secondary commander in the Easter Rising) and the Pro-Treaty faction (led by Michael Collins, who was assassinated in 1922). The conflict killed hundreds (if not thousands) and even took its toll on Irish genealogy: The shelling of the Four Courts in Dublin, the home of the Public Record Office, in June 1922 resulted in the catastrophic loss of much of Ireland's genealogical records. The civil war was over within a year, but had a lasting influence on Irish politics.

The Irish Free State remained a British dominion until 1937, when a new constitution was adopted. This new state was called Ireland (*Éire* in Irish), and was to have an elected (but non-executive) president as head of state. Its formal classification as a republic was not declared until the Republic of Ireland Act in 1948.

Living standards remained low, however, and the 1950s was an unhappy decade blighted by unemployment, economic depression, and emigration, mainly to England. But exposure to outside influences was starting to change life in the Republic. Television arrived in 1961, free secondary school education was introduced in 1967, and new modern machinery transformed industry and the countryside and industry after Ireland joined the European Economic Community (now the European Union).

As life in the Republic started to look up, the opposite was happening in Northern Ireland, where the Protestant majority continued to maintain control over Catholics (who made up one-third of their community). Civil rights issues spilled over into violence in the late 1960s, and The Troubles (a period of violent conflict between the UK government, Irish republican paramilitaries, and pro-British loyalists) dominated the next thirty years. The Good Friday Agreement of 1998 finally brought peace.

Meanwhile, the 1990s brought a boom to the Republic of Ireland. In the so-called Celtic Tiger era of the 1990s and early 2000s, Ireland's economy grew. Unfortunately, this came to a painful end with the global economic crisis of 2008. After several years in the doldrums, a recovery is now in sight.

Ireland has experienced enormous changes since the early 1900s. The country emerged from its history as one of the poorest and most undeveloped countries in Europe to become a culturally innovative island, admired for its resourcefulness and gutsy determination, and confident of its place in the world.

KEYS TO SUCCESS

Learn some Irish history to better understand your heritage and your ancestors' life and times. This chapter is a good starting point, but it's just the tip of the iceberg, as many of the terms and descriptions used in this summary oversimplify certain aspects of the island's history.

Study in some detail the period immediately prior to your ancestor's emigration. While most Irish emigrants departed for economic reasons, there may have been other social or political issues at play that influenced the final decision.

5

Understanding Irish Geography

As we discussed in chapter 3, one of the key pieces of information for successful research in Irish records is the name of the townland—the smallest land division in Ireland—where your family lived. Ireland has more than sixty-four thousand townlands, and you can locate the various administrative districts used by authorities for that precise area by linking your ancestor to a townland. In addition, knowing the relevant administrative districts for different record sets will allow you to access all surviving historical records where your ancestors may be documented.

This chapter will help you understand the administrative divisions of Ireland and how where your ancestors lived affects what record collections are available. You'll also learn about a range of tools that can help you know more about the place your ancestors called home.

UNDERSTANDING HISTORICAL BOUNDARIES

Irish genealogy is not unique in demanding that the ancestral location be narrowly pinned down. In almost all countries, the majority of records now used for family history were originally organized and administered according to the regional and local territorial divisions of the day.

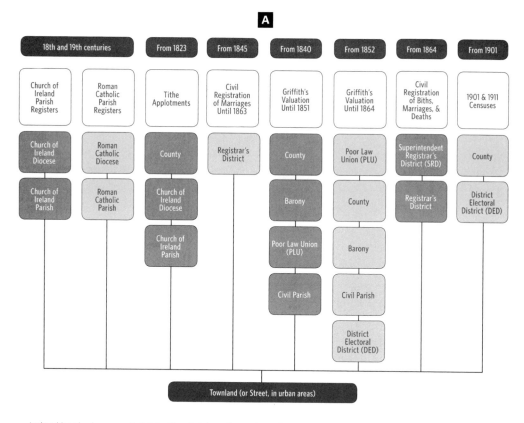

A

18th and 19th centuries		From 1823	From 1845	From 1840	From 1852	From 1864	From 1901
Church of Ireland Parish Registers	Roman Catholic Parish Registers	Tithe Applotments	Civil Registration of Marriages Until 1863	Griffith's Valuation Until 1851	Griffith's Valuation Until 1864	Civil Registration of Biths, Marriages, & Deaths	1901 & 1911 Censuses
Church of Ireland Diocese	Roman Catholic Diocese	County	Registrar's District	County	Poor Law Union (PLU)	Superintendent Registrar's District (SRD)	County
Church of Ireland Parish	Roman Catholic Parish	Church of Ireland Diocese		Barony	County	Registrar's District	District Electoral District (DED)
		Church of Ireland Parish		Poor Law Union (PLU)	Barony		
				Civil Parish	Civil Parish		
					District Electoral District (DED)		

Townland (or Street, in urban areas)

Ireland has had many administrative divisions throughout the years, each with a different purpose. This chart outlines which divisions are useful for different research purposes and across different time periods.

Over the years, new administrative boundaries carved up Ireland to serve official purposes for the central or local government, church authorities, and local landowners. As a result, the island was broken up into a series of administrative divisions (image **A**) that served specific purposes: four provinces divided into counties, then subdivided into civil parishes that are divided into townlands. With each division resulting in a smaller land area, these territories are easy enough to understand.

It gets more complicated, however, with the introduction of baronies, poor law unions, superintendent registration districts, and church parishes, which often overlap with the traditional boundaries and with one another. These other divisions were used by authorities to gather different types of information about the population.

Ireland's history (which we discussed in chapter 4) affects how some of these major divisions were set. Until 1922, the whole island of Ireland was a part of the United Kingdom, but then the island was split into two distinct entities: the Republic of Ireland (an independent country) and the province of Northern Ireland (a country within the United Kingdom). The Republic covers a little more than eighty percent of the island and includes all of the provinces of Connaught, Leinster, and Munster, plus three counties of Ulster: Cavan, Donegal, and Monaghan. Northern Ireland consists of the remaining six counties in Ulster: Antrim, Armagh, Londonderry, Down, Fermanagh, and Tyrone.

Understanding when and why Ireland's administrative divisions were created is one of the fundamentals of Irish genealogical research, and knowing which records correspond to each of these geographic divisions will save you from duplicating work searching for your ancestors in the wrong places.

The Province

The oldest of all Irish land divisions, the four provinces of Ireland (image **B**) roughly equate to the regions ruled by Gaelic kings or clans, with Connaught in the west named for O'Conor; Leinster in the east named for MacMurrough; Munster in the south named for O'Brien; and Ulster in the north named for O'Neill. They no longer serve any administrative purpose (nor do they still have an official status), but you will likely hear and see them mentioned in the course of your research.

Each province consists of counties, which will be discussed more in-depth in the next section.

- The province of Connaught is made up of Counties Galway, Leitrim, Mayo, Roscommon, and Sligo. Its flag shows an eagle and a sword.

- The province of Leinster contains twelve counties: Dublin, Carlow, Kildare, Kilkenny, Laois, Longford, Louth, Meath, Offaly, Westmeath, Wexford, and Wicklow. Its flag is a harp set on a green background.

- The province of Munster contains Counties Clare, Cork, Kerry, Limerick, Tipperary, and Waterford. Its flag shows three gold crowns on a blue background, making it similar to Dublin's flag.

- The province of Ulster is made up of Counties Antrim, Armagh, Derry/Londonderry, Down, Fermanagh, and Tyrone (which today make up Northern Ireland), and Counties Cavan, Donegal, and Monaghan (which are in the Republic of Ireland). Ulster's flag highlights a red hand on a shield set on a background of gold/orange with a red cross.

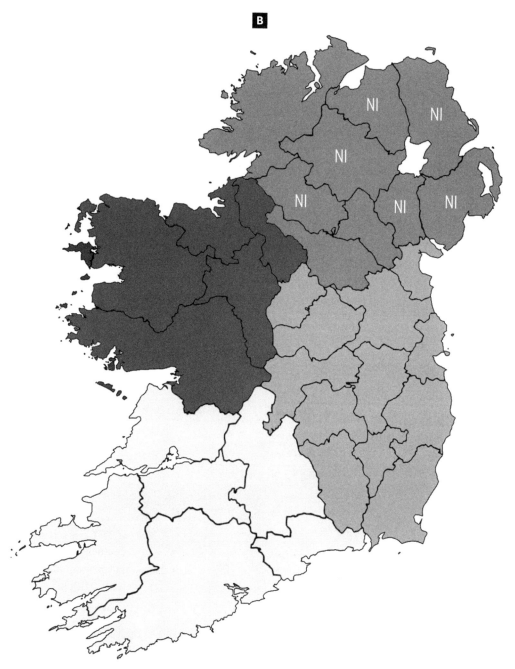

The four provinces are the oldest of all Irish land divisions and relate, loosely, to the regions ruled by pre-Norman kings or clans. Six of the counties in Ulster, identified in the map by NI, now make up Northern Ireland, which is part of the United Kingdom.

Counties of Ireland

County	Name in Irish	Meaning	Nickname of the county or its people	Province	County town	Since 1922*
Antrim	*Aontroim*	Solitary Place	The Glensmen	Ulster	Antrim	NI
Armagh	*Árd Mhacha*	Macha's Hill	The Orchard or Cathedral County	Ulster	Armagh	NI
Carlow	*Ceatharlach*	Four lakes	Barrowsiders or Scallion Eaters	Leinster	Carlow	IE
Cavan	*Cabhán*	Hollow	Blues Brothers	Ulster	Cavan	IE
Clare	*Clar*	Level piece of land	The Banner County	Munster	Ennis	IE
Cork	*Corcaigh*	Marsh	The Rebel County	Munster	Cork	IE
Donegal	*Dún na nGall*	Fortress of the foreigners	The Forgotten County	Ulster	Letterkenny	IE
Down	*Dún*	Fortress	The Mourne County	Ulster	Downpatrick	NI
Dublin	*Ath Cliath* or *An Dubh Linn*	Hurdle Ford or Black pool of water	The Dubs, The Liffeysiders, The Jackeens	Leinster	Dublin	IE
Fermanagh	*Fir Manach*	Men or tribe of Manach	Lakeland County	Ulster	Enniskillen	NI
Galway	*Gaillimh*	Stony	The City of Tribes, Galwegians, The Tribesmen	Connaught	Galway	IE
Kerry	*Ciarraí*	Descendents of the tribe of Ciar	The Kingdom	Munster	Tralee	IE
Kildare	*Cill Dara*	Church of the Oak	The Thoroughbred County, The Lilywhites	Leinster	Naas	IE
Kilkenny	*Cill Chainnigh*	Church of St Canice	The Marble County. The Cats	Leinster	Kilkenny	IE
Laois	*Laois*	Ludghaidh Laughseach (a chieftain)	The O'Moore County	Leinster	Portlaoise	IE
Leitrim	*Liatroim*	Grey Ridge	The Ridge County	Connaught	Carrick-on-Shannon	IE
Limerick	*Luimneach*	Barron spot of land	The Treaty County, The Shannonsiders	Munster	Limerick	IE

County	Name in Irish	Meaning	Nickname of the county or its people	Province	County town	Since 1922*
Londonderry	*Doire*	Oak Wood	The Oak Leaf County	Ulster	Derry	NI
Longford	*Longfort*	Ship encampment	The Slashers	Leinster	Longford	IE
Louth	*Lú*	Lugh (a heroic Celtic god)	The Wee County	Leinster	Dundalk	IE
Mayo	*Maigh Eo*	Plain of yews	The Heather or Maritime County	Connaught	Castlebar	IE
Meath	*Mí*	Middle (province)	The Royal County	Leinster	Navan	IE
Monaghan	*Muineachán*	Place of Little Hills	The Drumlin County	Ulster	Monaghan	IE
Offaly	*Ua Fáilghe*	Descendents of the tribe of Failghe	The Faithful County	Leinster	Tullamore	IE
Roscommon	*Ros Comán*	St Coman's Wood	Rossies or Sheep Stealers	Connaught	Roscommon	IE
Sligo	*Sligeach*	Shelly river	Yeats Country	Connaught	Sligo	IE
Tipperary	*Tiobraid Árainn*	The Well of Ara	The Premier County	Munster	Clonmel	IE
Tyrone	*Tír Eoghain*	The territory of Eoghan	The O'Neill County	Ulster	Omagh	NI
Waterford	*Port Láirge*	Water port or fort	The Crystal County or The Déise	Munster	Waterford	IE
Westmeath	*Iarmhí*	Western middle (province)	The Lake County, The Smokey Heads	Leinster	Mullingar	IE
Wexford	*Loch Garman*	Loch or Lake Garman	The Model County, The Yellow Bellies, The Strawberry Pickers	Leinster	Wexford	IE
Wicklow	*Cill Mhantáin*	Church of the toothless one	The Garden of Ireland	Leinster	Wicklow	IE

The thirty-two historical counties of Ireland are some of the most important geographical units for researchers.

The County

Ireland's thirty-two historical counties (image **C**) were created between the late twelfth and early seventeenth centuries, and they remain the principal unit of local government. They range in size from County Louth at 826 sq. km (319 sq. miles) to County Cork at 7,500 sq. km (2,900 sq. miles). Each county has a "capital" county town, which (confusingly) is often named after the county. For example, County Monaghan's county town is Monaghan, and County Sligo's county town is Sligo, but County Westmeath's county town is Mullingar and County Kerry's county town is Tralee.

Each county is also made up of a number of civil parishes. Roughly twenty-five of Ireland's counties each have more than one hundred parishes; County Leitrim has the smallest number, with just seventeen.

The Barony

Although its origin remains somewhat obscure, the barony used to be one of Ireland's most important land divisions and was widely used to identify property in land surveys and early censuses. For example, local taxes were set at a barony rate, and law enforcement was organized by this unit. Likewise, settlers arriving in Ireland during the Plantations (see chapter 4) were allocated land by barony. Altogether, there were about 270 of them, each composed of a number of townlands. With the introduction of poor law unions (more on these later) in 1838, baronies became less important, and the 1891 census was the last one to be organized by barony. By the end of the century, they were all but redundant. Family historians are most likely to come across them when searching Griffith's Valuation, a mid-nineteenth-century land valuation largely organized and published by barony.

The Parish

There are two types of parishes in Ireland: civil parishes and ecclesiastical parishes. The latter represents the parochial structures of the Church of Ireland and the Roman Catholic Church.

CIVIL PARISHES

From medieval times to the early nineteenth century, civil parishes were responsible for relieving poverty, collecting tithe, and recruiting young men into the army. As a result, you will find many early censuses, land and property records, and maps compiled in civil parish order.

Ireland is composed of nearly 2,500 civil parishes, spread across the island. Typically, they pre-date county and barony borders, so they frequently straddle these boundaries. Each civil parish contains an average of twenty-four townlands.

CHURCH OF IRELAND PARISHES

Following the Reformation in the sixteenth century, the Protestant Church of Ireland became the established state church of the island. It retained the old medieval (civil) parish divisions for administrative purposes. While some of these boundaries have been modified in response to population changes over the years, early Church of Ireland parishes typically follow the exact same boundaries and share the same names as modern civil parishes. However, some Church of Ireland parishes have incorporated multiple civil parishes, usually in regions where Church of Ireland congregations were small and as such a church in each civil parish could not be justified.

Church of Ireland records include christening, marriage and burial registers, marriage licenses, and vestry minutes. Most of the surviving records are held by the Representative Church Body Library (RCBL) in Dublin or by the Public Record Office of Northern Ireland (PRONI) in Belfast.

ROMAN CATHOLIC PARISHES

During the Reformation, authorities seized all the Catholic Church's assets and removed, exiled, or otherwise scattered most of its clergy. In response, the Catholic Church created much larger parishes, often containing distinct pockets of populations. County Wicklow, for example, has fifty-seven Church of Ireland parishes, but only twenty-seven Roman Catholic parishes.

While creating large parishes must have initially caused some difficulties, the Church was able to free itself from official land boundaries and be more flexible when populations grew or moved. This practice proved especially useful after the government granted full Catholic emancipation in 1829, which resulted in the creation of many new Catholic parishes.

RESEARCH TIP

Watch for Misinterpreted Answers

Where do you come from? It seems a simple enough question, but to your ancestors there were many potential correct answers. They may have responded with the name of their civil parish as a place of origin on civil documents after immigration. But they are just as likely to have recorded the name of their local Church of Ireland parish or Roman Catholic parish when completing ecclesiastical documents (e.g., noting their place of baptism or marriage, rather than their place of abode or origin). If they took the question literally, they may even have stated their Irish port of embarkation! As a result, don't assume that the town of your ancestor's origin is correct in records.

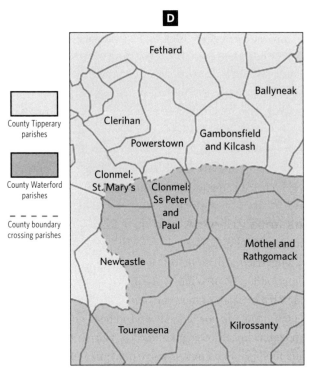

D

Legend:

County Tipperary parishes

County Waterford parishes

— — — — County boundary crossing parishes

Map labels: Fethard, Ballyneak, Clerihan, Powerstown, Gambonsfield and Kilcash, Clonmel: St. Mary's, Clonmel: Ss Peter and Paul, Newcastle, Mothel and Rathgomack, Touraneena, Kilrossanty

Many Roman Catholic parishes cross county boundaries. In this example, the parishes of Newcastle, Clonmel: St Mary's, Gambonsfield and Kilcash, and Clonmel: Ss Peter and Paul spread across the invisible border between County Waterford and County Tipperary.

Unfortunately, the result for researchers is not so favorable. Not only do some Catholic parishes share the name—but not necessarily the land—of a civil parish, but they also cover a larger population simply because the majority of the Irish was Catholic. Many of them also cross county borders (image **D**), complicating recordkeeping. Plus, the registers for a particular area may have been split between two parishes when a new parish was created; check with local clergy or the local studies library to find out if this happened in the parish your ancestors came from.

Roman Catholic Church records include baptism, marriage, and burial registers. Confirmation registers are rare. In general, the originals are held in local custody, but many have been transcribed or scanned and made available online.

The Diocese

The diocese is an old ecclesiastical unit introduced in the twelfth century. Originally, there were twenty-two dioceses, each belonging to one of four ecclesiastical provinces: Armagh, Cashel, Dublin, and Tuam. Each of the provinces was headed by an archbishop. Before 1858, the Church of Ireland diocese granted probates and issued marriage licenses, whatever the religion of the deceased or bride and groom.

CHURCH OF IRELAND

Over the centuries, the Church of Ireland chose to modify its diocesan units. It now has twelve dioceses in just two provinces, Armagh and Dublin. These two cover the whole island, as follows:

- **Armagh:** Armagh; Clogher; Connor; Derry and Raphoe; Down and Dromore; Kilmore, Elphin, and Ardagh; Tuam, Killala, and Achonry.

- **Dublin:** Cashel and Ossory; Cork, Cloyne and Ross; Dublin and Glendalough; Limerick, Killaloe, and Ardfert; Meath and Kildare.

ROMAN CATHOLIC CHURCH

The Roman Catholic Church remained faithful to the original format of the four ecclesiastical provinces, and they are divided into four archdioceses and twenty-two dioceses, each with a bishop:

Exploring the Index of Townlands

In 1861, an *Index of Townlands* (full name: *General Alphabetical Index to the Townlands and Towns, Parishes & Baronies of Ireland*) was published by Alexander Thom & Co. of Dublin, based on data from the 1851 census. It not only lists the names and acreages of all townlands existing in 1851, but also notes the county, barony, civil parish, and poor law union in which each was located.

This book is available at the National Archives in Dublin and many major libraries around the world. It has been reprinted several times by the Genealogical Publishing Company in Baltimore, Maryland.

A free online Townlands Database, created from this *Index*, can be explored at <**www.swilson.info/townlands.php**>.

The Townlands Database has three useful search options:

1. **Placename and Land Division Search** allows you to search by any place name to discover the various types of divisions and places associated with that name.

2. **Townland Database** allows you to search by townland name to reveal all the incidences of that name across the island, and provides each one's civil parish, barony, poor law union, and county.

3. **Townland Explorer** works from the opposite direction: You select a county, then drill down from the menus to find the names of all the poor law unions, baronies, civil parishes, and townlands within its boundaries.

- **Armagh:** Ardagh and Clonmacnoise; Clogher; Derry; Down and Connor; Dromore; Kilmore; Meath; Raphoe.
- **Cashel and Emily:** Cloyne; Cork and Ross; Kerry; Killaloe; Limerick; Waterford and Lismore.
- **Dublin:** Ferns; Kildare and Leighlin; Ossory.
- **Tuam:** Achonry; Clonfert; Elphin; Galway, Kilmacduagh, and Kilfenora; Killala.

You can search the National Archives of Ireland's free Roman Catholic Parish Registers collection **<registers.nli.ie>** by diocese, county, and parish.

The City and Town

Ah, the least complicated of Ireland's land divisions! Cities and towns are urban neighborhoods and should not be confused with townlands. A city or town may be made up of several townlands or, rarely, be just one part of a townland.

Fortunately, most genealogical documents for addresses in cities and towns will bear a street name and sometimes a house number or name.

A later *Index to Townlands* was published in 1904, based on data used for the 1901 census. It contains the same information but also includes the district electoral division for each townland. An online database created from this Index is freely available on the website of the Irish Genealogical Research Society at **<www.irishancestors.ie/search/townlands/index.php>**. This database also includes a note of the number of the corresponding Ordnance Survey Map for the townland and its locality.

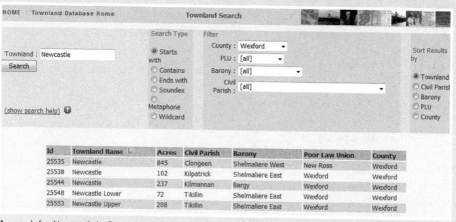

A search for *Newcastle* in County Wexford returns five options.

A Rich Landscape of Place Names

Most Irish place names refer either to permanent, visible, and easily identified features of the landscape (such as hills, rivers, lakes, and woods) or man-made features (such as farms, forts, and churches). Among the most common words used in the construction of Irish-language names are: *Cnoc*, meaning "hill"; *Cill*, meaning "church"; *Mór*, meaning "big"; *Baile*, meaning "town" or "homestead"; and *Ráth*, *Dún*, and *Lios*, all meaning "fort." The standardized spellings for these became *Knock*, *Kill*, *More*, *Bally*, *Rath*, *Dun*, and *Lis*, respectively.

While some place names were translated—"Summerbank" in County Meath, which was originally known as *Droim Samhraídh*, and "Silverwood" in County Armagh, which comes from *Coill an Airgid*—about 90 percent were Anglicized according to how non-Irish speakers thought they were pronounced. Surprisingly, the ancient pronunciation was often rather well preserved in the modernized form. Examples include *Cnoc na cille*, which means "church on the hill," being changed to "Knocknakilly" (County Kerry); *Trá Mhór*, meaning "big beach," being changed to "Tramore" (County Waterford); and *An Baile Meánach*, meaning "the middle townland," being changed to "Ballymena" (County Antrim).

The remainder of official place names are usually names bestowed by the colonists on their new settlements; examples include Bagenalstown in County Carlow, which is named after its founder Lord Bagenal (who owned an estate in nearby Dunleckney), and Draperstown in County Londonderry, a name chosen by the Worshipful Company of Drapers guild.

The Townland

The townland is the most fundamental of all Irish land divisions and is the essential ingredient for successful genealogical research in Ireland. It is the smallest official division and one of the most ancient, originally based on "ballyboes," areas of land deemed sufficient to sustain a cow. Over time, townlands varied in size; by the 1830s, some townlands comprised less than one acre, while others contained several thousand acres. (Note: The larger the size of a townland, the more likely it is that the land is of poor quality.) Land was rented out using the name of townlands, and they were used as a basis of census returns from 1821. Today, Ireland has more than sixty thousand of them across the island.

In rural areas, the townland is still used as the postal address for letters, packages, and other deliveries, and local residents have been resistant to the introduction of postcodes. Because they can cover quite small areas, townlands are not marked on road maps, but they do appear in Ordnance Survey maps.

THE STANDARDIZATION OF IRISH PLACE NAMES

In the 1830s, the Ordnance Survey dispatched teams of surveyors to visit each and every one of Ireland's townlands. In addition to mapping the landscape, the teams were required to interview locals to discover the variations in the names people called their townland, and, having consulted historical works and maps, decide on a suitable English language spelling for each name that didn't already have an acceptable English form.

The surveyors' mammoth project resulted in the names (and their spellings) of all townlands being standardized and recorded in Name Books. It was the final step in a process of Anglicization that had been going on since the Normans arrived in the twelfth century. Throughout the centuries, English, Scottish, and Welsh settlement led to even more place names changing to a version that sounded more familiar to the English-speaking settlers, or to brand-new names being bestowed by the colonists. Meanwhile, the majority-Irish inhabitants continued to use the original place names, no doubt frequently causing confusion.

While publication of the Ordnance Survey in the 1830s and 1840s may have officially consigned the old Irish names to history, they often remained in use locally, in speech, and in writing. These have become known as "unofficial place names."

The majority of researchers will not be troubled by unofficial place names. Most nineteenth-century records used by Irish genealogists use the standardized place name as published in the 1851, 1871, and 1901 *Index of Townlands*, to which officials referred (see the Exploring the *Index of Townlands* sidebar for more).

However, family historians occasionally encounter problems when an Irish immigrant has used an unofficial variation of the townland name as the ancestral place of origin in Ireland. If this should happen to you, and you cannot find the place name in the *Index of Townlands*, you will find help from the Placenames Database of Ireland at <**www.logainm. ie**>, which covers the Republic of Ireland, and the Northern Ireland Place-Name Project <**www.placenamesni.org**>. Both result from state-funded research projects to gather and study old place names, their origin, and their history. You can access them for free, and they contain a wealth of resources, including extensive glossaries of Irish topographical terms, old maps, and even useful sound files in which you can hear the correct pronunciation of the old place name. It is worth noting that the research projects explore names for all types of places, not only by townlands.

The Poor Law Union

In 1838, an Act of Parliament established a system of poor relief, designed to help Ireland's destitute. Previously, poor relief had been the Church of Ireland's responsibility, but this new system was to be delivered via a series of workhouses. Society's most unfortunate could retreat to these safe spaces when they could no longer provide themselves with basic necessities. Rather than follow the civil parish system or other traditional Irish land divisions, the government created 137 poor law unions (PLUs) across the island (image

Poor law unions (PLUs) were created by the government to administer poor relief, but they can be helpful for genealogists as well.

E), each with a local board of guardians and financed by local taxes. PLUs were focused on large market towns, where the workhouses were also built.

These PLUs varied in geographical size, with the largest in the west (where the population was more sparse) and the smallest in the east of Ulster (where the population was more dense). In 1851, the PLU system underwent changes, introducing thirty-three new PLUs and bringing the total to 163. Search an interactive map of PLUs on John Grenham's website **<www.johngrenham.com/places/plu_index.php#maps>**.

In addition, each PLU was subdivided into six or seven dispensary districts, each one headed by a medical officer. PLUs were also subdivided into district electoral divisions for census-taking (see the following section).

PLU boundaries were also used when superintendent registrar's districts were created in 1863. These, along with registrar's districts (1844), were created purely for administrative purposes, in particular to organize the civil registration of births, marriages, and deaths. They have the same boundaries as the existing PLUs and (from a genealogist's perspective) function the same as PLUs.

Confused? *A New Genealogical Atlas of Ireland* (Genealogical Publishing Company, 2009), an essential reference book for the Irish family historian, can help. Compiled by Brian Mitchell, who runs Derry City's Genealogy Centre in Northern Ireland, the book is an 178-page volume of maps showing the baronies, parishes, and PLUs of every Irish county.

The District Electoral Division

District electoral divisions (DEDs) were created in 1838. They are subdivisions of PLUs and consist of a number of townlands. Some land records—the Revision or Cancelled Land Books are the most important examples—are arranged by DED, so it is always worth making a note of the relevant DED alongside any townland name you record (see the Exploring the *Index of Townlands* sidebar).

USING MAPS, GAZETTEERS, AND PHOTOGRAPHS

While you must be familiar with Ireland's administrative land divisions to start digging into the historical records of state and local government, you will also want to explore a group of geographically related resources: maps, gazetteers, and photographs. Beyond getting the lay of the land, you can learn some basic history about a place, enjoy quaint vintage views, and add depth and color to your family history. By reviewing these materials, you can also appreciate the physical world in which your ancestors lived and how that physical world may have helped mould their characters or influence the decisions they made in life.

In addition, you will also pick up clues about where to look if your ancestors' records are hard to find. A gazetteer may provide information that allows you to pick up your ancestor's paper trail across the county border, or a photograph may tell the story of a local tragedy or other event that could have prompted a move by family members to the nearest market town or city—or even overseas.

Let's look at each of these resources in turn, and how they will help your research.

Maps

Maps come in all shapes and sizes, and each type conveys different information and serves a slightly different purpose. General political maps—the type found in most atlases—won't have the level of detail needed by a family historian who wants to become familiar with a distant area. Instead, the Irish genealogist's bookshelf needs maps that show the boundaries of the main land divisions, as these are key to identifying the administrative locations where a family's records may have been collected.

It's also worth having ready access to a good topographical map. On first exploration, you may find a town's physical surroundings cast your ancestral place of origin in a new light. You will be able to explore its relative remoteness to other pockets of civilization, discover its terrain and other natural features, and find out the names of places in the hinterland where your family may have visited or worked. For example, rather than hitting a brick wall in your research when your ancestor's marriage record isn't where you expect it to be, you can guess that your ancestor crossed the invisible parish boundary to a neighboring chapel, possibly because it was closer to the homestead or its location made for an easier journey. All kinds of clues to human behavior and lifestyle can be revealed by studying the terrain and considering its limitations and opportunities.

The Ordnance Survey has been mapping Ireland for nearly two hundred years and continues to deliver official map services to both the Republic of Ireland <www.osi.ie> and Northern Ireland <www.nidirect.gov.uk/campaigns/ordnance-survey-of-northern-ireland>. From 1833 to 1846, the entire island was surveyed at a scale of six inches to one mile, making Ireland the first country in the world to be entirely mapped at such a detailed scale. These early maps provide a full and reliable picture of the landscape in terms of roads, field boundaries, and dwelling houses just before the Great Famine.

At the turn of the nineteenth century, an even more ambitious survey mapped the island at a scale of twenty-five inches to one mile, allowing even more detail to be captured and represented more accurately. Both sets of maps are available online: <maps.osi.ie/publicviewer/#V2,578432,756724,0,10> (Republic of Ireland) and <www.nidirect.gov.uk/services/search-proni-historical-maps-viewer> (Northern Ireland). These online maps require some trial and error, but they're well worth the effort (and there are help videos on the Ordnance Survey site). These maps are fascinating to explore, as they outline and identify individual buildings and local features, and really give you a feeling of the scale of the world in which your ancestors lived, loved, and worked.

If you want to buy a paper version of an historical Ordnance Survey map from one of these websites, you should first find the correct map reference. You can do this by locating the townland of interest or a nearby town in the *Index of Townlands*.

You can also purchase paper and digital versions of modern maps from the two Ordnance Survey websites. In addition, Google Maps **<www.google.com/maps>** is worth searching, particularly for the more urbanized areas of Ireland; road maps, satellite views, and "Street View" give you an excellent picture of how your ancestral homeland looks today. All of Ireland is now covered.

Gazetteers

For contemporary descriptions of localities, as well as historical and statistical information about them, the two-volume *A Topographical Dictionary of Ireland* by Samuel Lewis (S. Lewis & Co., 1837) is an indispensable resource. Its 1,500 pages explore the cities, civil parishes, and main post towns of Ireland, describing them faithfully and carefully, often with support from data gleaned from the 1831 census. It is arranged alphabetically, and can be found in many reference libraries. It is also freely available in an online gazetteer format at LibraryIreland.com **<www.libraryireland.com/topog/index.php>**.

The Parliamentary Gazetteer of Ireland was published by A. Fullerton and Co. in 1846 and is another important gazetteer. Like Lewis's *Dictionary*, this gazetteer looks at cities

---

RESEARCH TIP

Use Gazetteers to Find Parish Names

To identify the name of a Roman Catholic parish for a specific location, search a gazetteer using the name of the civil or Church of Ireland parish, which are usually easy to find. For example, the townland of Curragh near Clonakilty is in the civil parish of Kilkerranmore. Searching this parish name in Samuel Lewis's *A Topographical Dictionary of Ireland* reveals that Kilkerranmore is "in the barony of Ibane and Barryroe, county of Cork, and province of Munster, 2½ miles (S. by E.) from Clonakilty, on the road from Cork to Skibbereen." The entry goes on to say: "In the R. C. [Roman Catholic] divisions the parish is partly in the union or district of Rosscarbery, partly in Kilmeen, and partly in Rathbarry," which means that research for Catholic ancestors in this area will need to cover three parishes: Rosscarbery, Kilmeen, and Rathbarry.

and towns, but it also ventures into small villages and records man-made structures such as bridges, river- and sea-ferry crossings, and harbors. The book presents comprehensive statistical analysis alongside topographical, historical, and (occasional) anecdotal details for some of the locations, giving you a wide variety of information. At two thousand pages total, the gazetteer is divided into ten volumes and is usually found in book format only in major references libraries and archives. Three volumes are free on Google Books **<books. google.com>**, where you can search by place name.

AskAboutIreland is a free website managed by Ireland's Library Service that has an online Reading Room **<www.askaboutireland.ie/reading-room>** and an interesting collection of local studies-themed articles and publications that you may not find elsewhere. Some of the books have to be downloaded to your device for reading, and they can be quite large files.

Photographs

The saying goes that every picture tells a story, and there's a lot of truth in that, even if the phrase may seem more naturally suited to portraits or group photos. In fact, many kinds of photos tell detailed and moving stories about the past: landscape and landmark views; photos of local events such as annual hiring fairs, monthly livestock markets, or the opening of the railway; and general shots of ordinary daily life in the streets and squares of Ireland's villages. They deliver more than whimsy: They reveal the community in which your ancestors may have lived—its apparent wealth or poverty, its relative sophistication, what clothes people wore, what services were available to them, the size of the local school, the harshness of the immediate environment, and much more.

Even if the date and location of the available resources do not exactly match the era and place when your ancestors were locals, photographs play a part in helping you develop a strong sense of time and place in the land and region your family once called home. What is more, if you are planning to write up your research for other family members to enjoy, photographs will make the finished product much more attractive than text on its own.

Increasingly, historical photograph collections of the highest quality are being made available online. The National Library of Ireland (NLI)'s free collection **<www.nli.ie/ digital-photographs.aspx>** is one of the best, with some thirty-three thousand images of places and people. The Library also maintains a photostream on Flickr **<www.flickr.com/ photos/nlireland>**, and an even larger collection remains undigitized but is cataloged on the NLI website.

Some of the NLI's Lawrence Collection is also available on Ancestry.com **<search.ancestry.com/search/db.aspx?dbid=2191>**. This collection holds twenty-one thousand images shot between 1870 and 1910, and can be searched by subject, location, or county.

Another large online collection is held by the Irish Historical Picture Company **<www.ihpc.ie>**. It includes photographic images taken in all thirty-two historical counties at the turn of the last century. This is a commercial site; while it is free to browse, you can also buy prints of the photographs.

PRONI also has a Flickr photostream **<www.flickr.com/photos/proni>**.

KEYS TO SUCCESS

- Find out the names of the various land divisions for your ancestor's townland of origin, especially county, parish, and PLU. These will help you more readily locate the records of your family across many collections.

- Consult gazetteers (geographical dictionaries) to discover historical and domestic details about your ancestor's immediate home environment and to locate the churches, schools, and markets they attended.

- Use online historical maps and atlases to familiarize yourself with the geography of Ireland and the region where your ancestor lived.

- Home in on particular locations on Google Street Map **<www.google.com/maps>** to see the lay of the land as it is today. All of the island has been captured.

6

Deciphering Irish Names and Surnames

While first names identify people as individuals, surnames indicate broader family relationships. Both are needed by genealogists to discover ancestral connections. Understanding how given names and family names developed in Ireland is, therefore, vital for any family historian of Irish heritage, besides being a fascinating subject in its own right.

In this chapter, you'll learn how Irish first names and surnames developed, how these separate histories impact your genealogical research, and how to work around some of the most common research obstacles you might encounter. You'll also discover Old Irish naming conventions that are helpful no matter the religious conviction or social standing of your ancestors.

IRISH FIRST NAMES

Unlike its Celtic neighbors—Scotland, Wales, and Brittany—Gaelic Ireland was not conquered by the Romans. This left the Celtic way of life and the Gaelic language largely undiluted by outside influence for hundreds of years. As in most other cultures, Gaelic Ireland had created its own unique names, and, by the late Middle Ages, its men were identified by wonderfully evocative names such as *Conchobhair* ("lover of hounds"), *Muirchertach*

From *Mór* to Mary

Meaning "tall" or "great," *Mór* was the most popular name for girls in the late medieval period. It had a distinguished pedigree, with two queens of Ireland bearing the name in the tenth century and other noblewomen named Mór in the fifteenth century. It was translated into Latin as *Morina*, which in turn was Anglicized as *Martha* or *Agnes*. But during the eighteenth century, it was translated directly from Irish as *Mary*.

Having been popular for so many generations, Mór continued to be widely given in its new form, and by the 1860s (when the civil registration of births was introduced), one in three female infants was named Mary.

A quirky development saw the arrival of Mary Ann and Mary Jane as standard combinations. This was unusual in Ireland because until the third or even fourth quarter of the nineteenth century, few babies received more than one Christian name.

("skilled mariner"), and *Ruadhán* ("little red one," typically bestowed on a red-haired infant). Women, too, had delightful names such as *Gormlaith* ("splendid sovereignty"), *Maedhbh* ("intoxicating"), and *Duibheasa* ("lady of the waterfall"). For lists of Old Irish names and their meanings, see NameNerds.com **<www.namenerds.com/irish/tradXY.html>** for boys' names and **<www.namenerds.com/irish/tradXX.html>** for girls' names.

With the arrival of the Anglo-Normans in the twelfth century, continental names were added to the mix and given an Irish flavor: *Émann* (Edmond), *Cóilín* (Nicholas), *Uilliam* (Willhelm), *Síban* (Johanne), *Sibéal* (Isabelle), and *Ailis* (Alice).

It wasn't until the end of the 1600s that English domination and influence started to impinge on the Gaelic way of life, and English speakers attempted to respell the locals' traditional names so they'd be easier to read and pronounce. Some names were translated when spelling alterations didn't achieve this goal, and many of these were decidedly odd and differed from place to place. Men called *Áedhán*, *Cóilín*, *Domnall*, *Émann*, *Eógan*, and *Uilliam* would become Aidan, Colin, Daniel, Eamonn, Owen, and William. These Anglicized translations have at least some connection to the original, but that can't be said for all the translations. For example, how the Celtic *Finnguala* became Penelope, *Calbhach* and *Cormac* became Charles, and *Tairdelbach* became Charles or Terence remains a mystery. The same lack of explanation applies to the Anglicization of *Síban* (*Siobhán* in modern Irish), which was Anglicized as Susan or Judith in the north of Ireland, but as Susanna, Julia, Jude, and Nonie in the south and west.

This period of contraction in the variety of Irish names across Ireland coincided with a new Catholic decree that only saints' names should be bestowed at baptism. Many of these (such as *Pátraic*, *Micheál*, and *Tomás*) had been in popular circulation since Christianity came to the island, but were now Anglicized (to Patrick, Michael, and Thomas).

Towards the end of the 1800s, the Gaelic League was set up in Dublin amid concerns that the Anglicization would cause the Irish to completely lose a sense of their separate nationality. The group generated a renewed interest in the Irish language and in traditional Irish names. Initially, this manifested itself in the widespread reattachment of the surname prefixes *O'-* and *Mac-/Mc-*, but it also resulted in the return of names such as Kevin, Brendan, and Rory in the first half of the twentieth century. Although Anglicized versions of Irish names, these names were a step in the right direction of reviving Irish culture.

The re-emergence of traditional names didn't really take hold until the 1960s and 1970s, when many people whose names had been Anglicized for generations started to discover and even adopt the original Irish form. This process sped up towards the end of the century, and the music of traditional Irish names can be heard once again in school classrooms across Ireland. In 2015, the top names for newborn boys in the Republic of Ireland included Conor, Seán, Oisín, Cian, Fionn, Liam, Darragh, and Cillian, while the top names for infant girls included Aoife, Saoirse, Caoimhe, and Roisin.

First-Name Research Basics

Irish first names were used in specific ways, and these patterns may impact your research. The following explanations highlight some of the challenges you may encounter. Remember to be flexible (especially in regards to spelling) when searching for your ancestors both online and offline:

- **One name was the rule:** Before the third quarter of the 1800s, it was rare for an Irish infant to be given more than one name. The most frequently encountered exceptions are Mary Ann and the slightly less popular Mary Jane, both of which are usually treated as one name (although some databases will only respond to Mary).

RESEARCH TIP

Note the Second Name

It is only in the last century that the giving of two names (a first name and a middle name) has become more commonplace in Ireland. If your eighteenth- or nineteenth-century Irish immigrant appears in North American records with a second name, he or she may have left you an important clue: These names were often those of a parent, grandparent, or sibling.

RESEARCH TIP

Check Each Database for a Soundex System

Before searching an online database, find out if it has a Soundex system, which allows the search engine to return results that have similar spelling and pronunciation to your search terms. If it doesn't, you may need to search for all alternative spellings of first names, surnames, and place names.

- **Families re-used the names of dead children:** If a child died, his or her first name was often given to the next-born child of the same sex. This practice, which seems emotionally cold to modern sensibilities, was widespread, and sends a strong hint to the researcher that the re-used name was an "important" name within the family (e.g., the name was chosen to honor a parent, grandparent, or another close relative).

- **Officials loved abbreviations:** Some first names have acquired a standard written form of abbreviation, and you will often encounter these in registers and other documents completed by various officials. Fortunately, most modern databases are able to translate the shortened version into the long form, but it's a good idea to be aware of them anyway. The General Register Office for Northern Ireland provides a free list of the most common abbreviations used during the nineteenth century **<www.nidirect.gov.uk/articles/search-gronis-online-records>**.

- **Names were often Latinized:** Until the tail end of the nineteenth century, Catholic priests tended to enter forenames in Latin in their parish registers. The repetition of the same names, particularly *Brigida* for Bridget, *Maria* for Mary, *Margarita* for Margaret, *Gulielmus* for William, *Jacobus* for James, *Joannis* for John, and *Patricius* for Patrick, is indicative of how limited the palette of names had become in Ireland since the old Gaelic names had fallen out of favor. See appendix A for more examples of Latinized names.

- **Irish spellings are rare in records before 1900:** Although not a widespread practice, some families registered a newborn with a saint's Anglicized name but would use an Irish version of a name at home. If you can't finding an elusive ancestor, try searching for the Irish version of his or her name (e.g., *Seamus* for James, *Aileen* for Eileen, *Seán* for John or Jack). After 1900, Irish appears in formal documentation much more frequently, but the correct spelling may not always be transcribed or recognized by the search engine software. Try wildcard searches to get around this.

- **Look for nicknames and diminutives:** Until fairly recently, full standard names would have been used in formal or official records, such as for baptisms and civil birth registers. However, your ancestor may have been known by a nickname or diminutive that was recorded in later records, such as trade directories, newspaper reports, or marriage, death, military, and court records. Most of these nicknames are well-known and not exclusive to Ireland, but some might trip up researchers (for example, *Delia* for Bridget and *Darby* for Dermot).

Traditional Naming Patterns

Most families in the eighteenth and nineteenth centuries, regardless of religion or social status, followed a well-worn naming convention for new babies, with the result that the same names tend to be repeated generation after generation (see image **A** for an example). While this can cause some confusion when researching your ancestors, recognizing a likely pattern to your family's names can be useful when you're faced with numerous families with the same surname in a small geographical area.

The trick is to not be too rigid, as not all families adhered to tradition all the time—and by the second half of the twentieth century, the naming convention had all but disappeared. So while naming patterns can be helpful directional guides during research, they should not be taken as conclusive proof of family connection without documentary evidence to support such a verdict.

FOR SONS

- The first son was named after the father's father.
- The second son was named after the mother's father.
- The third son was named after the father.
- The fourth son was named after the father's eldest brother.
- The fifth son was named after the mother's eldest brother.

RESEARCH TIP

Familiarize Yourself with Variants, Nicknames, and Interchangeable Names
See *A Rose By Any Other Name* by Judith Eccles Wight (self-published, 1985) for a handy overview of the variant spellings, nicknames, Latin and Irish versions, and interchangeable options of Irish first names. It's free and can be downloaded from the Family History Library at **<dcms.lds.org/delivery/ DeliveryManagerServlet?dps_pid=IE105460>**.

A

Superintendent Registrar's District of *No. 8 South*   08067944

18__. Marriage solemnized at the Roman Catholic Chapel of *St Finbar* in the Registrar's District of *8 South* in the Union of *Cork* in the County of *City of Cork*

No.	When Married.	Name and Surname.	Age.	Condition.	Rank or Profession.	Residence at the Time of Marriage.	Father's Name and Surname.	Rank or Profession of Father.
81	19th May 1878	Denis Santry	full	Bachelor	Carpenter	Straw Hall	Denis Santry	Carpenter
		Ellen Santry	full	Spinster		St Finbarr Place	Denis Santry	Farmer

Married in the Roman Catholic Chapel of *St Finbarr* according to the Rites and Ceremonies of the Roman Catholic Church by me, *J. McMahony C.C.*

This Marriage was solemnized between us { *Denis Santry* / *Ellen Santry* }   in the Presence of us, { *John Santry* / *Kate Leary* }

No prizes for guessing what the bride and groom, who were second cousins, named their first son.

FOR DAUGHTERS

- The first daughter was named after the mother's mother.
- The second daughter was named after the father's mother.
- The third daughter was named after the mother.
- The fourth daughter was named after the mother's eldest sister.
- The fifth daughter was named after the father's eldest sister.

IRISH SURNAMES

The use of personal, given, or first names is an ancient practice found among nearly all cultures throughout recorded history, but the use of surnames or family names is much more recent. In fact, Ireland is thought to have been one of Europe's oldest adopters of surnames, and possibly even the first. They were in widespread use by the early twelfth century, but they were not hereditary.

Instead, they lasted just one or two generations, and they used the prefixes *Mac-/Mc-* (the latter merely an abbreviation of the former) and *O'-*. The prefix *Mac-* or *Mc-*, meant "son of." So the name *Dermot mac Fiachra* meant "Dermot, the son of Fiachra," and Dermot's son might be *Darragh mac Dermot* ("Darragh, the son of Dermot"). Similarly, the prefix *O'-* (or the older form *Ua-*) was used to mean "grandson of" or "from." So *Ciaran O'Conor* was the grandson or descendent of Conor, while *Oisín O'Laoghaire* was a descendent of Laoghaire. This echoing of the first name can still be heard today in many of the most instantly recognizable Irish last names, with or without *Mac-* or *O'-* prefixes: Connor/O'Connor, Cormack/MacCormack, Dermot/MacDermot, and Leary/O'Leary.

Norman Influence on Irish Last Names

Following the Norman invasion of 1169, a large number of Anglo-French first and last names appeared in Ireland. Many, such as Burke, Costello, Nagle, Nugent, Power, Roche, and Walsh, are nowadays considered exclusively Irish. So, too, are those with the *Fitz-* prefix such as Fitzhenry, Fitzgerald, or Fitzsimon—names most people would regard as Irish as a shamrock.

However, these names have richer histories than you might think. Over the early medieval period, most Norman names evolved into an Irish form, which were then Anglicized in the seventeenth and eighteenth centuries into the versions we now recognize. Many of them have their origins in continental words: Burke from *de Burgh*, Roche from *de Roiste*, Power from *de Paor*. Likewise, *Fitz-* is a continental version of "Mac," derived from the Latin/French *fils de*, meaning "son of." (Fitzpatrick is an exception to the latter; it's a Gaelic-Irish adaptation meaning "follower of Saint Patrick.")

Other introductions from this period came from the mercenary soldiers who accompanied the Norman invasion; Walsh (meaning, and pronounced, "Welsh") and Joyce and Flemming (from Flemish mercenaries) are examples, as are many of the trades of the early medieval period (such as Archer, Butler, Carpenter, Draper, Skinner, Tanner, and Woodman).

The non-hereditary arrangement was considered entirely satisfactory until the twelfth century, when the tradition began to evolve into the one we recognize today: fixed names being handed down from one generation to the next. Most of the practice's early adopters were at the top end of the social ladder, as those on the bottom rungs had no real need of surnames until the sixteenth century.

In exactly the same way as happened with first names, Irish surnames started to be translated into English in the late medieval period. A new wave of newcomers, this time from England and Scotland, did not assimilate themselves into Gaelic society as the Normans had done five hundred years earlier. Rather than translate their own surnames into Irish, they forced English translations onto the Irish.

This is where a lot of confusion arises about the origin of Irish last names. The name Smith or Smyth is a perfect example. It was already the most common surname in England and widespread in Scotland, too, so there were many Smiths among the new Protestant settlers who arrived in Ireland during the sixteenth and seventeenth centuries. For this reason, many descendants of Smiths from Ireland imagine they are descended from English or Scottish Smiths. However, this isn't necessarily the case. The Irish word for a blacksmith was *gabhann*. As an occupation, it had long been adopted as a surname, and one of the largest indigenous groups of MacGabhanns was based in County Cavan. Their name was translated to Smith/Smyth despite not being related to English or Scottish

TABLE showing One Hundred of the principal Surnames in Ireland (including varieties) taken from the Births Index of 1890, together with the Estimated Population bearing each Surname.
Population of 1890, estimated at 4,717,959 persons.

No. on List.	SURNAMES.			Estimated Population bearing each Surname.	No. on List.	SURNAMES.			Estimated Population bearing each Surname.
1	Murphy,	.	.	62,600	51	Sweeney,	.	.	12,500
2	Kelly,	.	.	55,900	52	Hayes,	.	.	12,300
3	Sullivan,	.	.	43,600	53	Kavanagh,	.	.	12,200
4	Walsh,	.	.	41,700	54	Power,	.	.	12,100
5	Smith,	.	.	33,700	55	McGrath,	.	.	11,900
6	O'Brien,	.	.	33,400	56	Moran,	.	.	11,800
7	Byrne,	.	.	33,300	57	Brady,	.	.	11,600
8	Ryan,	.	.	32,000	58	Stewart,	.	.	11,400
9	Connor,	.	.	31,200	59	Casey,	.	.	11,300
10	O'Neill,	.	.	29,100	60	Foley,	.	.	11,200
11	Reilly,	.	.	29,000	61	Fitzpatrick,	.	.	11,100
12	Doyle,	.	.	23,000	62	Leary,	.	.	11,000
13	McCarthy,	.	.	22,300	63	McDonnell,	.	.	11,000
14	Gallagher,	.	.	21,800	64	McMahon,	.	.	10,700
15	Doherty,	.	.	20,800	65	Donnelly,	.	.	10,700
16	Kennedy,	.	.	19,900	66	Regan,	.	.	10,500
17	Lynch,	.	.	19,800	67	Donovan,	.	.	9,900
18	Murray,	.	.	19,600	68	Burns,	.	.	9,800
19	Quinn,	.	.	18,200	69	Flanagan,	.·	.	9,800
20	Moore,	.	.	17,700	70	Mullan,	.	.	9,800
21	McLaughlin,	.	.	17,500	71	Barry,	.	.	9,700
22	Carroll,	.	.	17,400	72	Kane,	.	.	9,700
23	Connolly,	.	.	17,000	73	Robinson,	.	.	9,700
24	Daly,	.	.	17,000	74	Cunningham,	.	.	9,600
25	Connell,	.	.	16,600	75	Griffin,	.	.	9,600
26	Wilson,	.	.	16,300	76	Kenny,	.	.	9,600
27	Dunne,	.	.	16,300	77	Sheehan,	.	.	9,600
28	Brennan,	.	.	16,000	78	Ward,	.	.	9,500
29	Burke,	.	.	15,900	79	Whelan,	.	.	9,500
30	Collins,	.	.	15,700	80	Lyons,	.	.	9,400
31	Campbell,	.	.	15,600	81	Reid,	.	.	9,200
32	Clarke,	.	.	15,400	82	Graham,	.	.	9,100
33	Johnston,	.	.	15,200	83	Higgins,	.	.	9,100
34	Hughes,	.	.	14,900	84	Cullen,	.	.	9,000
35	Farrell,	.	.	14,700	85	Keane,	.	.	9,000
36	Fitzgerald,	.	.	14,700	86	King,	.	.	9,000
37	Brown,	.	.	14,600	87	Maher,	.	.	9,000
38	Martin,	.	.	14,600	88	McKenna,	.	.	9,000
39	Maguire,	.	.	14,400	89	Bell,	.	.	8,800
40	Nolan,	.	.	14,300	90	Scott,	.	.	8,700
41	Flynn,	.	.	14,300	91	Hogan,	.	.	8,600
42	Thompson,	.	.	14,200	92	Keeffe,	.	.	8,600
43	Callaghan,	.	.	14,000	93	Magee,	,	.	8,600
44	O'Donnell,	.	.	13,900	94	McNamara,	.	.	8,600
45	Duffy,	.	.	13,600	95	McDonald,	.	.	8,500
46	Mahony,	.	.	13,500	96	McDermott,	.	.	8,400
47	Boyle,	.	.	13,000	97	Moloney,	.	.	8,300
48	Healy,	.	.	13,000	98	Rourke,	.	.	8,300
49	Shea,	.	.	13,000	99	Buckley,	.	.	8,200
50	White,	.	.	13,000	100	Dwyer,	.	.	8,100

This list of Ireland's top one hundred surnames was published by the Registrar General of Marriages, Births, and Deaths in Ireland and is based on the 1890 birth index.

settlers. Outside of County Cavan, other MacGabhanns preferred to Anglicize the spelling, becoming Mac/McGowans.

Many other mistranslations and changed spellings occurred during this time period, but perhaps the greatest casualty of the period was the discarding of the traditional Gaelic *Mac-* and *O'-* prefixes.

As laws against Catholics relaxed in the early 1800s, a small number of families started to readopt their surname prefixes. Daniel O'Connell, the champion of Catholic emancipation, was a high-profile example, but significant numbers of Irish folk didn't readopt the traditional forms of their family names until the Gaelic League began the revival of Irish culture towards the end of the century. Other surnames have chosen to reject their prefix permanently. Murphy (the most common Irish family name; see image **B**), Connolly, Donnelly, Doyle, Foley, Hogan, Kelly, Kennedy, Nolan, Quinn, and Sheridan are rarely seen with an *O'*. The *Mac-/Mc-* prefix has not been returned to its rightful place at the same rate as the *O'*. This is rather camouflaged by the existence of Scottish *Mac-* names that had never dropped the prefix, especially those in Ulster.

The name Sullivan/O'Sullivan is a useful example of the *O'* debate. In the 1860s, only 4 percent used the *O'*. The proportion had risen to 13 percent by 1890 and climbed again to 20 percent by 1914. But after independence, nearly 60 percent of Sullivans were using their prefix, and the figure had reached more than 80 percent by the twenty-first century.

Surname Research Basics

All Irish researchers can follow some best-practice techniques when studying surnames:

- **Search for your immigrant ancestor's name, both with and without a prefix:** If your ancestor's family name is one that historically attached a prefix, don't assume your family has always spelled it only one way. For example, if your ancestor left Ireland in the early 1800s with a prefix, he or she may have discarded it on or shortly after arrival. The prospect of a new life in a new home saw many discard their prefix as too fussy or "too Irish." Others took the opposite view, proud to reattach a prefix that restored their Irish identity. There was no one-size-fits-all approach.

- **Use wildcards when searching online databases:** If you use wildcards (characters like question marks and asterisks), you'll usually receive a broader set of results. These are handy and simple devices for finding variant spellings of names. For example, if you type *M*cGowan*, the search engine will find both "MacGowan" and "McGowan" entries. This is a good starting point for your research and may reveal some interesting new surname variants. Wildcards can also be revealing because they allow you to search using the phonetic sounds of your name. For example, type

Dunn* and the search engine will return both "Dunn" and "Dunne." Learn more about wildcards in chapter 9.

- **Discover the regional spread of your surname:** Many Irish family names are identified with specific areas of Ireland. Some continue to be found only in tight geographical areas. If you know your ancestor's surname but not where your immigrant ancestor came from, focus on the area that's closely tied to your surname. Genealogist John Grenham has created a wonderful tool to help you research your Irish surname's origins, variant spellings, and geographical occurrences across the island in the mid-nineteenth century <www.johngrenham.com/surnames> (image **C**). You can use the software to identify parishes where two surnames appear. It is free to "light" users.

C

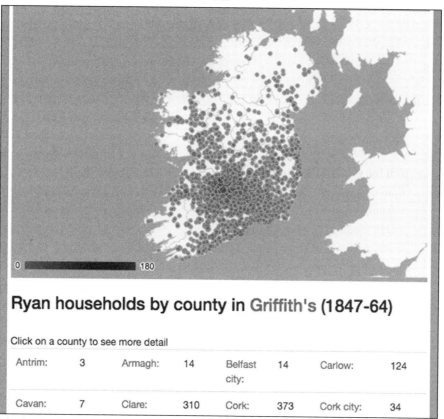

Ryan households by county in Griffith's (1847-64)

Click on a county to see more detail

Antrim:	3	Armagh:	14	Belfast city:	14	Carlow:	124
Cavan:	7	Clare:	310	Cork:	373	Cork city:	34

John Grenham's website features a helpful tool that allows you to visualize the numbers of households in Griffith's Valuation with a particular surname.

- **Indexes don't all follow the same alphabetical system:** *Mac-* and *Mc-* are interchangeable (don't believe any stories about one being Irish and one being Scottish), but some indexes and databases treat them separately. Similarly, O Kelly (or Ó Kelly) and Kelly are the same surname, but you may find one is located alphabetically under *O* (or *Ó*) and the other is found under *K*.

For a more in-depth review of the history of Irish family names, right up to recent times, see *A Survey of Irish Surnames, 1992–97*, by Seán J. Murphy. It's free to download at Academia.edu **<www.academia.edu/9204227/A_Survey_of_Irish_Surnames_1992-97>**. *Irish Names and Surnames* by Rev. Patrick Woulfe is a standard work, published in 1923, and a searchable online version is available free of charge at LibraryIreland **<www.libraryireland.com/names/contents.php>**. For the bookshelf, try Edward MacLysaght's acclaimed *The Surnames of Ireland* (Irish Academic Press, 1989), a guide to more than four thousand Irish surnames.

KEYS TO SUCCESS

Be flexible with the spelling of names, both given and family names. They were not standardized until the early twentieth century, and prior to this were typically recorded by officials with their own ideas about how certain sounds should be written down.

Find out all you can about your ancestors' first names. If they are traditional Irish names, explore their meanings, spellings, and pronunciations. Discover their Irish, Latin, and English translations (if any) and see if there were any nicknames commonly attached to people with such names.

Apply the traditional naming pattern to ancestral stories handed down to discover any possible research directions. Remember to be flexible in your findings, because the custom was not universally followed.

Learn the history of your ancestral name, its variant spellings, and whether it is identified with a specific location in Ireland.

7

Civil Registrations

Our ancestors' lives were bookended by important events that left traces: births, marriages, and deaths. The documents created to record these major milestones are known as vital records. In Ireland, they are known as civil registration records, making the distinction between the mandatory registration demanded by civil authorities and church records. (We'll discuss the latter in chapter 8.)

While Irish civil registration records are not perfect (they don't contain all the genealogical information we would like them to), the collections provide the building blocks of all genealogical research and help us to work back in time, generation by generation. There are some differences in the types of information recorded on each side of the Atlantic, but the basic research techniques used by family historians are the same.

This chapter will set out the background and development of the system over time, direct you to where you can access the records, and provide information that will help you solve any problems you may encounter.

THE CIVIL REGISTRATION SYSTEM

Civil registration began in Ireland more by chance than by design. After a spate of bigamy cases went before the courts in the 1830s, an 1842 case went all the way to the House of

Lords in London. There the government established that all marriages of Protestant Dissenters (mostly Presbyterians) in Ireland were invalid. Couples in Ulster, where most of the Dissenters resided, were outraged at the suggestion that so many had been living in sin and that their children were, by extension, illegitimate.

The Marriages (Ireland) Act was passed in 1844 and came into force on April 1, 1845. It created a centralized civil registration system for all non-Catholic marriages. It had been intended that the Act would embrace all Christian and Jewish religious denominations, but the Catholic Church, concerned that civil registration would detract from the religious nature of the marriage ceremony, resisted what it saw as interference. For this reason, Irish marriage registrations from 1845 to 1863 (inclusive) recorded non-Catholic unions only.

During this time, demand grew for a compulsory registration system for births, deaths, and marriages (performed by all religious denominations). Employment laws in England and Wales required Irish migrants to produce documentary evidence of age; rights of inheritance needed to be supported with proof of legitimacy; and vaccination programs demanded reliable statistical information about the population. Finally, the law was changed on January 1, 1864, when registering births, deaths, and *all* marriages became required.

The new system divided Ireland into approximately 160 superintendent registrar's districts (SRDs), comprising exactly the same boundaries as the poor law unions. Each SRD comprised several registration districts (or dispensing districts, which you can identify online <www.swilson.info/regdistmap.php>; see image **A**), each with its own registrar.

At the end of each quarter of the year, each registrar copied out the details of all the births, marriages, and deaths (BMDs) he had registered. These quarterly returns—effectively duplicates of the originals that remained in local custody—were sent to the General

Impact of the 1922 Partition

Following the Partition of Ireland in 1922, the historical BMD registers for the entire island remained in the GROI in Dublin, but copies of the records for Counties Antrim, Armagh, Down, Fermanagh, Londonderry, and Tyrone were sent to a new General Register Office for Northern Ireland (GRONI) in Belfast. See below for a breakdown of where you can find BMD certificates based on when they were taken.

- BMDs from the whole island, 1845/1864–1921: GROI in Dublin and Roscommon
- BMDs from the six Northern Ireland counties, 1845/1864–present: GRONI in Belfast
- BMDs from the Republic of Ireland, 1922–present: GROI in Dublin and Roscommon

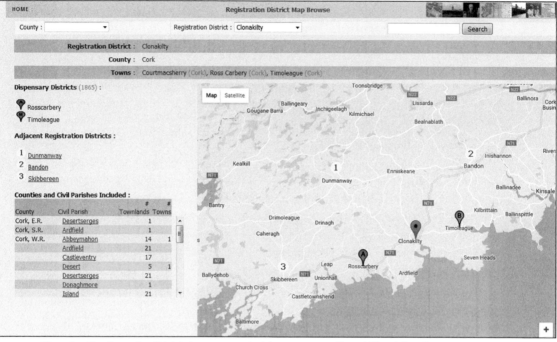

To explore the dispensing districts for your ancestor's home area, see Shane Wilson's free Registration District Map Browse tool, which highlights all the districts within and adjacent to a selected SRD.

Register Office (GROI) in Dublin, where they were arranged into bound volumes and compiled into indexes. Until 1877, these indexes were arranged alphabetically for the entire year, but from 1878 they were divided by quarter.

An increased interest in Gaelic began to emerge in the 1890s, but it was not until the mid-twentieth century that registrations began to be recorded in the Irish language. Most of these entries were registered in the Gaeltacht (Irish-speaking areas of Ireland). If you have been unable to find a registration for an ancestor using his or her name in English form, it may be worth searching the records using the Irish form. (See chapter 6 for advice on the Irish form of names.)

Unusually for Ireland, the civil registration collection is considered complete—in the sense that records have survived intact. Having said that, not every BMD was recorded. Even though the system was compulsory, up to 15 percent of such events are thought to have gone unregistered, at least in the early years.

Non-registration was particularly a problem in the more rural, western seaboard: Counties Clare, Cork, Donegal, Galway, Kerry, Mayo, and Sligo. In the minds of ordinary folk, this new registration system was simply redundant given similar records were

Playing the Generation Game

Family historians move backwards in time, one generation at a time, by using the records of one generation to locate the records of the previous one. Civil registration records demonstrate this technique. For example, starting with a known person (let's call her Mary), you can locate her birth certificate and note the names of her parents. Other details such as occupation may also come in handy. Then search for a marriage certificate for Mary's parents; this will provide the names of the bride's and groom's fathers, plus their occupations. You now have information about Mary's grandfathers.

Now search for Mary's father's birth record. You already know his father's name and possibly his occupation, and this will help you identify the correct birth record. The birth certificate will give you his mother's first and maiden names. You can use that to find marriage certificates for Mary's paternal grandparents and discover the names of *their* fathers (Mary's great-grandparents).

Working this way, from birth record to marriage record to another birth record, provides the documentary evidence needed for building a solid family tree.

maintained by the church parish. What need was there to give information about a birth to the authorities, when the infant's baptism had been recorded in the church register?

Baptisms were much less likely to go unrecorded than were civil registrations of birth, so family historians can usually find a secondary source to support a date and place of birth for an ancestor. Missing death registrations, however, can be problematic, as few Roman Catholic parishes maintained any sort of burial registers.

Overall, marriages were less likely to be registered late, but there were some teething problems when Roman Catholic marriages were added to the compulsory system in 1864. While Anglican parishes and Presbyterian congregations had been issued a printed register that they had to copy and submit to Dublin every quarter, responsibility for the registration of Catholic marriages landed on the bride and groom. It apparently wasn't a priority for most young couples; many marriages failed to be registered in the early years. Beginning in 1880, this responsibility shifted to the parish priest.

RESEARCH TIP

Add a Couple Years to Your Search Criteria

Search at least two years wider on either side of an approximate date of birth or marriage. Stated ages and recollections of time were not always accurate, so you'll want to widen your search to capture any mistakes.

Registration of Births

Registration of births began on January 1, 1864. The information recorded in each registration included (when known) the date and place of birth; the name and sex of the child; the father's name and address; the mother's name and maiden surname; the father's profession or rank; the informant's name, qualification, and address; the date of registration; and the registrar's signature.

To encourage timely registrations, especially for births, a late-registration penalty or fine was imposed on tardy parents. To avoid the fine, some parents gave an incorrect, later date of birth for their child. This happened with my grandfather in Clonakilty, County Cork. He celebrated his birthday on January 20 every year, but his birth certificate (image **B**) states he was born on February 13. Sure enough, the church register (image **C**) shows he was baptized on January 21, nearly four weeks before his "official" birth. In fact, the

B

The date of the my grandfather's birth was officially registered as February 13, but other evidence suggests he was born earlier. Were his parents trying to avoid the late-registration fine by lying?

C

Baby Timothy had been baptized on January 21, more than twenty-eight days before his father went to register his birth.

law allowed twelve weeks to elapse before a penalty was imposed, so there would not have been a price to pay for registering baby Timothy's correct birth date, anyway. As he was their first child, perhaps the new parents were not aware of the long lead time allowed.

Either parent could register the child, and a number of others were also qualified to attend the registrar and provide the information: various relatives, an occupier of the house in which the child had been born, a midwife, and even neighbors. When a child was born out of wedlock, only the mother's details were recorded unless the father also attended the registrar's office. The register books did not necessarily provide the home address of a single mother; whether or not to include this was at the registrar's discretion.

Registration of Marriages

Registration of marriages began in April 1845 and included all (non-Roman Catholic) Christian, Jewish, and civil marriages. Roman Catholics were excepted because (as briefly discussed earlier in this chapter), the Church, the majority in much of Ireland, initially refused to engage with the new system. It was not until 1864, when the civil registration of births and deaths also took effect, that Catholic marriages were included in the compulsory system.

The information recorded on marriage certificates is similar and sometimes more detailed than that required by some early US marriage registrations. For each marriage, the date, place, and denomination is recorded, along with both parties' names, ages, marital statuses, occupations, home addresses, and fathers' names and occupations. Two witness names are also noted. In practice, ages are rarely noted other than whether or not the parties were "full age," meaning twenty-one or older. If one (or both) of the parties' fathers was deceased, this was supposed to be noted but often was not. As you can see in image **D**, illiteracy was noted by an *X* in the middle of a "signature," usually with *his mark* or *her mark* added.

Marriage registrations in the Republic of Ireland didn't record birth dates for the bride and groom and the names of both parents until 1956. At the same time, the father's occupation ceased to be requested.

RESEARCH TIP

Don't Assume Who's Living
The marriage certificate was supposed to note if the fathers of the bride and groom were deceased, but this requirement was often overlooked. If there is no reference to the father being either alive or deceased, don't assume he was still living on the day of the wedding.

SCHEDULE G.]	Registrar's District of *Banbridge*							
1883. Marriage solemnized at *Banbridge* in the *Parish* of *Seapatrick* in the *Co. Down.*								
No.	When Married.	Name and Surname.	Age.	Condition.	Rank or Profession.	Residence at the Time of Marriage.	Father's Name and Surname.	Rank or Profession of Father.
143	April 7. 1883.	Sarah Elizabeth Shanks	20	Spinster	Yarn worker	Edenderry, Parish of Seapatrick	David Shanks	Weaver
		Samuel Wright	24	Bachelor	Yarn-man	Banbridge	John Wright	Yarn-man

Married in the *First Presbyterian Church* according to the Form and Discipline of the Presbyterian Church, *by Licence* by me,

T. M?arumon

This Marriage was solemnized between us, { Sarah Elizabeth x Shanks (her mark) / Samuel Wright } in the Presence of us { Jessie Kidd / James x Wright (his mark) }

On April 7, 1883, yarn-makers Sarah Elizabeth Shanks and Samuel Wright married in the First Presbyterian Church in Banbridge, a major linen-producing area in County Down. This marriage register entry is unusual only for the order in which it records the couple; it was more typical to record the man first, then the woman.

Registration of Deaths

Of the three forms of registration, deaths were the most likely to fall through the system and fail to be registered, a surprise to many researchers who imagine that a death certificate would be required in order to bury a body. But when compulsory registration of deaths began on January 1, 1864, the deceased's family and/or community had up to twelve months to register the death before receiving a penalty for late notification. Even today, the Republic allows three months, while in Northern Ireland, deaths must be registered within five days and the body cannot be disposed of until the certificate has been issued.

Death certificates are also the least informative vital record, genealogically speaking. The details included were the date and place of death; the name of the deceased; and the deceased's sex, marital status, age, and occupation. In addition, the record listed a cause of death and the informant's name, qualification, and address. The registrar was required to note if the deceased's home address was different from the place of death, but in practice this instruction was not consistently followed. Note that Irish death registrations do not record how and where the body was disposed.

While official responsibility for registering a death laid with the next of kin, it was often registered by an official when a death occurred in a hospital or other institution. Given this, details should be treated with caution because too often information was guessed: home addresses were omitted, ages were rounded up or down, occupations were given

No. (L)	Date and Place of Death. (2.)	Name and Surname. (3.)	Sex. (4.)	Condition. (5.)	Age last Birthday. (6.)	Rank, Profession, or Occupation. (7.)	Certified Cause of Death and Duration of Illness. (8.)	Signature, Qualification and Residence of Informant. (9.)	When Registered. (10.)	Signature of Registrar. (11.)
4	18*91* Twelfth April Gobnascale	Isabella Barr	F	widow	94 yrs	widow of a labourer	Senile decay not certified no medical attendant	Mary Barr Her mark present at death daughter Gobnascale	Twenty fifth April 18*91*	W. H. Elliott Registrar.

This death certificate records the passing of Isabella Barr of Gobnascale in County Londonderry on April 12, 1891, aged ninety-four.

simply as laborer even when they were more trade-specific, and marital statuses were noted as "married" even if the deceased was actually widowed.

The death certificate for Isabella Barr, who died in Gobnascale in County Londonderry is reasonably informative (image **E**). It shows that her unmarried, illiterate daughter Mary was present at the death and registered it, and she stated her mother was ninety-four years old. The relationship between Mary and her mother is close enough to consider this age a reasonable approximation, but you should not rely upon it alone. Isabella died of "senile decay," a non-specific ailment generally meaning "old-age decline," for which no medical attention had been sought. Isabella's husband predeceased her and was a laborer. Unfortunately, church records for this area do not start until the 1860s, so neither baptism nor marriage records are going to provide additional details about Isabella. It is quite possible this death certificate is the only surviving documentary evidence of this woman's life.

Such little information is recorded in Irish death registrations that it can often be impossible to correctly identify a relevant record for individuals with common names (John Murphy, for instance). Dates, places of birth, and parents' names were not recorded in the Republic of Ireland until as late as December 2005. In Northern Ireland, while date and place of birth have been recorded since 1973, death records didn't note parents' names until 2012.

HOW TO ACCESS CIVIL REGISTRATION RECORDS

Over the last few years, records offices have been scrambling to improve traditional hard copy and microfilm access to BMD records. The result is a rather confusing muddle of records being available across a number of state-run, commercial, and not-for-profit sites. Some of them use the same data set but have made various enhancements, some having full transcriptions while others have images. In addition, they have myriad start and end dates and different geographical coverage. Yes, it really is a mess.

In this section, I'll outline what sources to consult if you're seeking a particular kind or format of record, from indexes to transcriptions.

Indexes and Images: GROI and GRONI

Until fairly recently, the only way to access Ireland's BMD records was to search through a set of annual indexes, one for each event, created by GROI in Dublin or GRONI in Belfast. As finding aids, the indexes include only nominal information, presumably enough for searchers to identify a relevant record. In practice, the information is often insufficient. Even so, the vast majority of searches for Irish BMDs are going to be made from either the pay-to-view GRONI site or GROI's free IrishGenealogy.ie site as they develop (image **F**).

GRONI raised the bar in online record access when it launched an online database <https://geni.nidirect.gov.uk> in 2014, complete with images of the register entries. It covers BMDs for the six counties of Northern Ireland back to 1845/1864 and includes births that are at least one hundred years old, marriages that took place at least seventy-five years ago, and deaths that occurred more than fifty years ago. This is known as the "100-75-50 year" rule. A basic search of the GRONI database is free of charge and provides just a little more information than the indexes provided, but you'll have to pay a small fee to

Personal Searches in Dublin and Belfast

Both GROI and GRONI have public research rooms (in Dublin and Belfast, respectively), which allow family historians greater access to indexes and copy certificates since the 100-75-50-year rule does not apply to personal searches.

In Dublin, GROI is based at Werburgh Street and is open Monday through Friday. Only paper indexes are available, each index covering either a year or quarter and bound into large and often heavy volumes. When you find an indexed entry of interest, you can purchase a "research copy" (photocopy of the respective register entry). These copies are usually available within fifteen to thirty minutes, depending on how busy the office is at the time.

In Belfast, GRONI is based at Stranmillis and is open Monday to Friday. It has computerized indexes only, right up to current registrations, and these are linked to a digital image of the BMD register entry. Fees apply.

F

GRO databases for Indexes and Images

HTTPS://CIVILRECORDS.IRISHGENEALOGY.IE

INDEXES

Births: 1864 to 100 years ago. All-island.

Marriages: 1845 to 75 years ago. All -island to 1921. Republic only from 1922.

Deaths: 1864 to 50 years ago. All-island to 1921. Republic only from 1922.

IMAGES OF BMD CERTIFICATES

Births: As indexes

Marriages: Since 1882 only

Deaths: Since 1891 only.

Note: Images download as pdf files and show full register page. Phase 3 of the digitization project (probable completion 2017 or 2018) will add images for pre-1882 marriage and pre-1891 deaths.

Costs

All free of charge.

Access

Pop-up box requires you make an 'application'. Type your name, type your initials… anything. It makes no difference. No data is collected!

HTTPS://GENI.NIDIRECT.GOV.UK/

INDEXES

Births: 1864 to 100 years ago. Northern Ireland counties only

Marriages: 1845 to 75 years ago. Northern Ireland counties only.

Deaths: 1864 to 50 years ago. Northern Ireland counties only

IMAGES OF BMD CERTIFICATES

Births: As indexes

Marriages: As indexes

Deaths: As indexes

Note: You need a minimum of one credit in your account before you can search the records. You cannot save or download images; use screengrab.

Costs

Basic search is free. Small charge to view 'enhanced' transcriptions. Additional charge to view image of full register entry.

Access

You have to create an account and purchase credits.

This image summarizes the civil registration coverage and availability at both the Republic of Ireland's GROI and Northern Ireland's GRONI.

receive more details or to view an image of the register entry (e.g., a partial copy of the official certificate).

The Republic's GROI met these developments with its own plan. Phase One saw the online launch of an "enhanced" database of the historical (100-75-50 year rule) indexes at <www.irishgenealogy.ie>. The civil records' enhancements include the mother's surname in birth indexes from 1900. Phase Two involved uploading downloadable PDF images of register entries for all birth certificates from 1864, all marriage certificates since 1882, and all death certificates since 1891. Both the indexes and certificates are provided free of charge. Phase Three will add images of all remaining historical records to the site.

Online Indexes: FamilySearch.org, Ancestry.com, and Findmypast

Sometimes, your only option will be to search the original indexes and make a physical application for a BMD certificate, such as for all births, marriages, and deaths that took place outside the years available on the GROI and GRONI public databases. But there may also be times when you simply can't find an event in those two databases, no matter how many surname variants you used or how flexible you are about dates. Like all databases, GROI and GRONI are not perfect, with missing records, misindexed entries, and links to incorrect entries. The GROI site, in particular, can be fussy about surname spellings and wildcards. If you can't find the entry you want, try another database.

So what are your alternatives? Back in the late 1950s, the Church of Jesus Christ of Latter-day Saints (LDS), which now operates the FamilySearch organization, microfilmed GROI indexes up to 1958 (these indexes did not include entries for events in the six counties of Northern Ireland from 1922). More recently, volunteers transcribed these microfilms and uploaded these index transcriptions to a free searchable collection: "Ireland Civil Registration Indexes 1845–1958" <www.familysearch.org/search/collection/1408347>. This database includes many additional variant spellings of surnames, making it extremely useful as an alternative search aid. The database has been shared with Ancestry.com <www.ancestry.com> and Findmypast <www.findmypast.ie> (subscription required). Merging it with the search engines of these sites has resulted in more refinements, particularly with locating marriage records.

Register Transcriptions: RootsIreland

The Irish Family History Foundation's islandwide network of county-based genealogy and heritage centers has been busily transcribing parish and civil registers for many years and now holds more than twenty million records on its website <www.rootsireland.ie>. Being locally based, these transcriptions are made from the locally held BMD registers,

Searching the Indexes

As stated earlier, civil registration indexes are finding aids. As such, they include only enough information for the searcher to identify a relevant record, then order a certificate that will provide additional details about the person's birth, marriage, or death.

Ireland's indexes include the year of registration (and quarter for some years), the first name and surname, the superintendent registrar's district, and the volume and page number of the register. Death indexes also note the age of the deceased.

If you are able to identify an entry of interest in the index, create a reference that contains: full name, year (and quarter), registration district, volume number, and page number—for example: *John Deasy, 1909 Q2, Naas 2.275.* (If you're using the IrishGenealogy.ie database, you can also use the group registration ID for some records.) Then, order a "research copy" (photocopy) of a BMD certificate (for a fee), quoting your reference number. You can only apply by post or fax. Request

SR District/Reg Area - Donaghmore	
Death of **PHILIP TIERNEY** in **1868**	
Back to search results	
Name	PHILIP TIERNEY
Year of Death	1868
Group Registration ID	N/R
SR District/Reg Area	Donaghmore
Deceased Age at Death	50
Returns Year	1868
Returns Quarter	3
Returns Volume No	13
Returns Page No	317

Each registration entry has a unique reference. In the case above, the death registration reference is *Philip Tierney, 1868 Q3, Donoghmore, 13/ 317.*

e-mail delivery for a digital copy; otherwise a paper copy will be sent to you by post. You can find full details at IrishGenealogy.ie <**www.irishgenealogy.ie/en/civil-records/help/i-want-to-get-a-copy-of-a-certificate-what-do-i-do**>.

If you are unable to identify an entry of interest in the index (but are confident there should be one), you can request GROI to make a search for a small fee. You can apply by post or fax only.

Note that you do not need an index reference for BMD events that took place in Northern Ireland counties since 1922. See GRONI's website for more information <**www.nidirect.gov.uk/articles/ordering-life-event-certificates**>.

rather than the copies sent to Dublin, making it a unique database and worth checking if you cannot find a particular entry where you think it should be.

At least fifteen of the centers have collections of civil BMD register transcriptions. Some have the full mix of BMD records, while others have only marriage records. You should search the detailed list of the records in the database for each county **<ifhf. rootsireland.ie/generic.php?filename=centres/ifhf/sources.tpl>** before you decide to purchase a subscription. See appendix E for more on the Irish Family History Foundation and genealogy and heritage centers.

KEYS TO SUCCESS

- Depending on where your ancestors lived, familiarize yourself with GRONI's "Geni" database for Northern Ireland events and the GROI IrishGenealogy database for events in the Republic. These have very simple interfaces and will help you become acquainted with the civil registration system.

- Take advantage of GROI's "research copy" service (by post or e-mail) for copies of BMD certificates that are not online.

- BMD certificates often have more information in them than is obvious at first glance. Scrutinize the date, the residences, and the informant details carefully. How do these details fit with what you already know about the ancestor?

8

Church Records

reland's church registers form a large and vital part of the family historian's tool kit. With civil registration of non-Catholic marriages beginning in Ireland in 1845 (and given registration of birth, deaths, and Catholic marriages didn't begin until 1864), parish registers are often the only source of records relating to an ancestor's life before these dates. Some of them even date back to the 1600s, but unfortunately, most don't!

Two pieces of information are crucial before you can realistically hope to trace your family in Irish church records: your ancestors' religion and their place of origin to a civil parish, town, or townland. (See chapter 5 for details about these land divisions.) If their surname is not too common, you might be able to locate them if you are confident about a county of origin and are prepared to put in a lot of hard work. Parish registers were collected locally and remain, to a large extent, accessible at a local level.

The good news is that digitization and online availability have improved dramatically in recent years and are expected to continue, even if the rate of new collection launches may slow. Some clergy remain reluctant to hand over their private registers (all of which are private records, save for those of the ex-established/state church) to commercial enterprises, but easier access to records has largely prevailed, usually through an archive.

For researchers whose earlier work has unearthed both the geographical and religious details of their ancestors, the biggest issue will be whether or not the relevant parish records survive. Regardless of denomination, Ireland's historical church records suffer gaps. For example, the Church of Ireland parish of Emlafad and Kilmorgan in County Sligo has baptism, marriage, and burial registers that date back to 1762, which is obviously excellent news for anyone trying to trace their Protestant family from near Ballymote. But the prognosis is completely different if those ancestors were instead Roman Catholic, as baptism and marriage records for this district survive only from 1824—and no Catholic burial records for the region survive at all. And it could be even worse: In the neighboring parish of Achonry, no registers for either religion survive prior to the introduction of civil registration in 1864, seriously limiting deeper family history discoveries in the area.

With this is in mind, this chapter will give you an understanding of the issues affecting the survival and availability of records and where you might find them in Ireland and online. It will also explain the type of information gathered by the clergy or ministers of the main denominations, and why you may not find records of your ancestors where you would expect them to be.

ROMAN CATHOLIC RECORDS

Catholicism's roots in Ireland run deep. Saint Patrick converted the pagan Celts of Ireland to Christianity in the fifth century. Within another century, the island had been organized into a basic diocesan structure, and its landscape transformed with monasteries, libraries, schools, and skillfully carved high crosses. This Catholic Ireland was known throughout Europe as the "Island of saints and scholars."

The arrival of Catholic Anglo-Normans in 1167 did not much disturb religious practice in Ireland, even if Roman practices started to reform the Gaelic Catholic practices that had dominated the island.

But King Henry VIII's break with Rome in 1534 caused more than a ripple. The king demanded his subjects to pledge loyalty to him and not the pope; those that sided with the pope and remained Catholic were accused of being disloyal. Priests were banished, and church land was confiscated and passed to the newly established (1536) Protestant Church of Ireland.

The lives of Irish Catholics became severely restricted under a series of Penal Laws. The Penal Laws, which made proper recordkeeping difficult and potentially dangerous for priests and their congregations, are the primary reason for the patchy coverage and poor survival of Ireland's baptism, marriage, and burial registers. Only a small proportion of pre-1820 Roman Catholic registers survive, and (while the laws were relaxed in the second half of the eighteenth century) Catholic emancipation was not achieved until 1829.

As with many kinds of Irish records, some Catholic records from this period are exceptions and still survive. Among them are the registers for St. Mary's in Limerick City (which date from 1745), St. Catherine's in Dublin (from 1740), Wicklow (from 1747) and Nobber (from 1754) in County Meath, and (the very oldest) for Wexford Town from all the way back to 1671. In general, the oldest records hail from the more prosperous and Anglicized eastern half of the island. Registers for poorer and more densely populated parishes in the west and north usually do not start until the mid-nineteenth century. Sadly, these poorer areas were also those that supplied the greatest numbers of passengers on emigrant ships, so their descendants in the United States may have trouble finding records of them.

Most Roman Catholic registers are recorded in Latin, but don't let this overly concern you. While first names usually appear in a Latinized form, surnames do not, and priests tended to repeat the same format for all entries on a page, making them easy to scan. (See appendix A for more about Latin in church registers.)

Surviving Roman Catholic baptism records usually record the ceremony date, the child's name, the father's full name, the mother's first name and (in a departure from Church of Ireland standards) maiden name, the names of any godparents (sponsors, usually indicated by an *SS*), and the parents' residence. These facts are a huge boon to Irish genealogists, because they allow you to match all the children of a couple with some confidence once you know their home parish. In theory, at least, it also means your maternal line should be as easy to trace as your paternal line.

A marriage entry typically includes the bride's and groom's first names, surnames, and places of residence, as well as (usually) the names and occupations of the bride's and groom's fathers. In addition, the register also includes names of the officiating priest and two witnesses, the latter of whom were often related to the couple. The place of residence was sometimes omitted in earlier registers, but became more regular after the 1860s as priests were provided with new registers that included a section for addresses for both

RESEARCH TIP

Extend Your Search to Adjacent Parishes

In the nineteenth century, new Catholic parishes were created, and the boundaries of many parishes changed. As a result, you may find earlier records for your ancestors' locality in the registers of an adjoining parish.

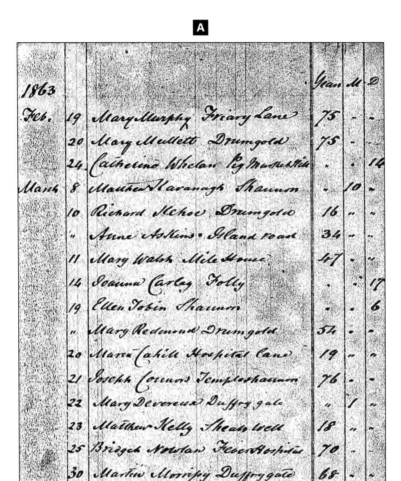

Historical Roman Catholic burial registers are rare. This 1863 example comes from Enniscorthy parish in County Wexford.

the couple and the witnesses. Note: Most Catholic marriages took place in the bride's "mother church," or the place where she was baptized. Even if the couple moved to another parish, the first child (at least) was often baptized in the mother church.

Compared to the Church of Ireland's records, historical Roman Catholic burial registers (image A) are a rarity. They are also patchy in geographical spread (e.g., while all of County Longford's parishes have surviving burial records, those of County Cork have none) and tend to convey little of genealogical interest. A typical entry would provide only the name of the deceased and date of interment. See the Burying the Dead sidebar for more.

In modern times, Church authorities provide their clergy with blank registers that have printed headings and columns in which the priest is obliged to record details of the ceremonies performed in his church. Such registers were often available to larger churches and cathedrals in the late nineteenth centuries, so you may find relatively neat register entries if your ancestors lived in urban areas.

Unfortunately, it was a case of "anything goes" in poorer rural areas where priests seem to have been told what details to record but not necessarily how to record them. They seem to have decided on their own individual structure of presentation, but didn't always demonstrate much discipline in following it. Some drew ruled lines to create columns. Some did not and instead recorded the formula information across the page. Some wrote legibly, while others did not. Some noted the townland of the people recorded, and some noted personal views and observations (usually derogatory) about them, too. It was a free for all. Family historians need to be prepared to encounter some difficulty in deciphering some of the earlier register entries, but (after reviewing the record types over a period of time) can usually identify a pattern.

Where to Access Roman Catholic Records

In one of the major (and most controversial) Irish genealogy developments in recent years, the National Library of Ireland (NLI) digitized and released its collection of microfilmed Roman Catholic baptism and marriage registers online <registers.nli.ie>. Covering

Burying the Dead

Until the 1820s, only the Church of Ireland could own burial grounds. Its clergy were allowed to charge for burial in its churchyards, and (until 1871) had responsibility for the decent burial of the poor or those with no family.

It is therefore worthwhile checking local Church of Ireland parish registers to find your deceased ancestors, even if your family was of another religion. The entry in the register will not usually acknowledge the individual's alternative beliefs.

After the 1820s, you may still find headstones erected to Catholics, Methodists, and other Protestant groups in Church of Ireland graveyards. In most such cases, the burial was transferred to the Church of Ireland grounds because the graveyards of these congregations were full and more land had yet to be purchased. While Church of Ireland papers recorded a grave, the burial site would not usually be in the official registers.

The creation of municipal cemeteries on the outskirts of towns in the late nineteenth and early twentieth centuries reduced the number of such anomalies. With separate sections for different faiths, these cemeteries were run by county or local councils.

The NLI's database of Catholic baptism and marriage register images is arranged by county or diocese and parish. This screenshot shows parishes in County Waterford and parts of adjoining counties.

events up to 1880 only, it is an unindexed, image-only collection, arranged by parish and covering all but fifty-six parishes across the island (image **B**). When you select a parish, you begin viewing individual pages of the registers. Filters allow you to enhance the image or select a specific date. It is a user-friendly site and highly efficient, and the FAQs page provides additional guidance.

Ancestry.com and Findmypast created an index to this digitized collection in a joint project, and both sites link to the images on the NLI site. The websites hold identical indexes, but each site handles variant spellings differently (and Findmypast's index is free for registered users, while you'll need a subscription to view Ancestry.com's index). If you strike out searching one website's index, try the other.

Another extensive collection of Roman Catholic records is held by RootsIreland **<www.rootsireland.ie>**, a subscription-only site. This database holds records for almost all of the island; the most notable areas of non-coverage are Dublin City, County Kerry, and southwest County Cork. Its records are transcriptions of locally held registers, nearly all of them exceeding the NLI cutoff date by at least a few decades (e.g., to 1899); some even extend well into the twentieth century. RootsIreland links to the NLI images where relevant, and you should check the detailed parish-by-parish list of sources available for each county before you commit to a subscription.

If you have ancestors from Dublin City, County Kerry, or southwest County Cork, you have some extra help: Catholic records from these areas are available, free of charge and complete with images, on the free, state-managed Irish Genealogy website **<civilrecords.irishgenealogy.ie/churchrecords>**. A detailed list of the parishes and dates of its registers is found at **<churchrecords.irishgenealogy.ie/churchrecords/parishes.jsp>**. This site recognizes both Latin and English versions of names, regardless of the language used in the register.

CHURCH OF IRELAND RECORDS

Founded in 1536 by King Henry VIII of England, the Anglican Church of Ireland was imposed on the overwhelmingly Roman Catholic population of the island as its state (or established) church. As such, it was obliged from the seventeenth century to keep records of baptisms and burials of Irish Protestants. This process began with urban areas and gradually spread out to the surrounding countryside, but it was more than one hundred years before some rural parishes were created. As a result, the majority of registers don't begin until the late eighteenth or early nineteenth century.

On January 1, 1871, the Church of Ireland ceased to be the established church, and a few years later its registers—considered state records—were ordered to be sent to the Public Record Office (PRO) in Dublin for safekeeping, unless the local clergy could demonstrate they had suitable, safe storage for them. Nearly one thousand parishes complied with the order, and all these registers were lost when the PRO, housed within the Four Courts complex alongside the River Liffey in Dublin, was ravaged by fire in 1922 during the Irish Civil War.

Fortunately, some clergymen had made transcripts of their registers before sending them to Dublin, and these transcripts—and the registers belonging to 637 other parishes that had not surrendered their records—are all that survive. Post-1900 registers are in local hands, but the majority of the historical records are now in the care of the Representative

RESEARCH TIP

Identify Pretenders

You may be able to trace your ancestors in Church of Ireland registers even though they were not practicing Anglicans. The Penal Laws made compliance with the established church a sensible move for many Irish men and women, even if their true beliefs were practiced in private elsewhere.

C

Church of Ireland baptism registers rarely provide the mother's surname. Note how this 1880 entry shows the child's baptism date as nearly four months after his birth date.

D

Marriage registers are one of the most useful sources of genealogical information. This 1900 entry records a Society wedding in the Church of Ireland.

Church Body Library (RCBL) in Dublin following a concerted campaign to gather these documents into one place. A long-term project is underway to digitize the collection.

Church of Ireland baptism registers (image **C**) usually state the child's name, the father's full name, and at least the mother's first name. (In most cases, the mother's maiden surname is not provided.) After 1820, the clergy more commonly recorded the father's occupation and the child's date of birth. The latter can be an important addition because some families waited several months to baptize their infants. Sometimes a townland or urban street name is also included.

Marriage and burial registers were less thorough. A typical entry in a marriage register (image **D**) would record the full names of the bride and groom, the date of the wedding, the name of the officiating clergyman—and that's it. Likewise, burial registers usually give the name of the deceased and date of burial, sometimes with the deceased's residence (townland or street name) and, occasionally, age.

As a general observation, Church of Ireland registers are more clearly organized and easier to decipher than their Roman Catholic counterparts. This may be because they are written in English and contain less information. In addition, the widespread introduction of pro-forma registers after the 1820s helped keep the presentation of entries legible and more consistent, even if some parishes did not start using them until a few decades later. Prior to the 1820s, however, Church of Ireland clergyman adopted and followed their own formats.

Where to Access Church of Ireland Records

The RCBL publishes a free list of all historical Church of Ireland registers, detailing which records were lost and where surviving records can be accessed. It is regularly updated, and you can view or download the current list from the RCBL website **<www. ireland.anglican.org/about/rcb-library/list-of-parish-registers>** (image **E**).

PRESBYTERIAN RECORDS

The Irish Presbyterian Church was established in the early seventeenth century by Scots who had settled in Ulster, especially in Counties Antrim and Down. By 1861, the numbers of Presbyterians across the thirty-two historical counties had risen to 650,000 (roughly 8 percent of the population), and they formed more than four hundred congregations.

Like Roman Catholics, Presbyterians suffered severe restrictions under the seventeenth- and eighteenth-century Penal Laws. Their ministers had to perform marriage under Church of Ireland ceremonial rites. If they didn't, the union could be declared invalid, and any children might be declared illegitimate and have their rights of inheritance adversely affected. In response to the law, Presbyterian ministers often performed

RESEARCH TIP

Locate Records for Your Ancestor's Church in Ulster
Download a copy of the Public Records of Northern Ireland (PRONI)'s comprehensive guide to its holding of records from all religious denominations **<www.nidirect.gov.uk/sites/default/files/publications/Guide_to_church_records.pdf>**. The majority of parishes listed are located within the six counties of Northern Ireland, but also some from parishes in the Republic of Ireland, particularly the border counties of Donegal, Cavan, Leitrim, Louth, and Monaghan.

E

Parish, Church/Chapel	Diocese	County	Baptisms	Marriages	Burial	Key	Comments
Derrylane	Kilmore	Cavan	1831-1840	1846-1956	-		Some earlier records destroyed in 1922.
Derryloran	Armagh	Tyrone	1796-1875	1796-1845	1796-1875	T	Transcripts available online as part of the Anglican Record Project, see http://ireland.anglican.org/about/179
Derrynahinch	Ossory						see Knocktopher
Derrynoose	Armagh	Armagh	1822-1875	1822-1845	1835-1875		Some coverage at RootsIreland.ie.
Derver	Armagh	Louth	1832-1876	1836-1837	-		
Dervock							see Derrykeighan
Derryvullan North	Clogher	Fermanagh	1803-1909	1803-1934	1804-1902		
Derryvullan South	Clogher	Fermanagh	1803-1877	1814-1845	1803-1877		
Desartlyn	Armagh	Derry	1797-1871	1797-1845	1797-1876		Some coverage at RootsIreland.ie.
Desartmartin	Derry	Derry	1797-1875	1797-1845	1797-1875		There are earlier entries in a Vestry Book, commencing 1751. Some coverage at RootsIreland.ie.
Desartoghill	Derry	Londonderry	1806-1873	1839-1845	1835-1877		
Desert	Ross						see Kilgariffe
Desertcreat	Armagh	Tyrone	1812-1873	1812-1845	1812-1875		
Desertegny	Derry	Donegal	1790-1877	1813-1831 & 1843-1845	1803-1804 & 1832-1877		Some coverage at RootsIreland.ie.
Desertmore	Cork	Cork	1817-1876	1817-1852	1819-1876		
Desertmore	Cork	Cork	-	1847-1972	-		
Desartserges	Cork	Cork	1811-1986	1812-1956	1822-1999	M	Existence up to 1952 of a copy register, 1811-1837, noted
Devenish	Clogher	Fermanagh	1800-1873	1800-1837	1801-1939		Some coverage at FindMyPast.ie
Diamond, The	Armagh	Armagh	1848-1877	-	-		Some coverage at RootsIreland.ie.
Diamor	Meath						see Loughcrew
Dingen Donovan	Cloyne						see Killeagh
Dingle	Ardfert	Kerry	1707-1997	1707-1943	1708-1993		Some coverage on IrishGenealogy.ie
Disert	Ardfert						see Killentierna
Disert	Ardfert						see Listowel
Disert	Elphin						see Tessaragh
Disertmore							see Rosbercon
Doagh, Grange of,							see Kilbride and Donegore
Dogstown	Cashel						see Knockgraffan
Donabate	Dublin	Dublin	1811-1897	1814-1848	1817-1850		Some coverage at RootsIreland.ie.
Donacavey	Derry	Tyrone	1800-1878	1800-1850	1800-1874		
Donacavey	Derry	Tyrone	1878-2000	1845-2007	1878-1999		see also Findonagh
Donadea	Kildare	Kildare	1890-1968	1846-1939	1892-1920		Registers are too fragile for use. Some coverage at RootsIreland.ie.
Donagh	Clogher	Monaghan	1796-1876	1796-1845	1796-1875		Some coverage at RootsIreland.ie.
Donagh	Derry	Donegal	1836-1877	1837-1851	1836-1876		
Donaghadee	Down	Down	1771-1819	1772-1815	1771-1886		PRONI also holds indexes for baptisms up to 1900; marriages to 1921 and burials to 1923. Some coverage at RootsIreland.ie.

The RCBL's color-coded and annotated List of Church of Ireland Registers details which records have been lost; specifies where any transcripts, originals, and online copies can be accessed; and links to additional parish information.

marriage ceremonies in secret. Similarly, their funeral services could take place only if a Church of Ireland minister was also present, and Presbyterian churches were not allowed to have their own graveyards.

A gradual reform of the Penal Laws in the early nineteenth century saw Presbyterian ministers maintaining their own registers from about the 1820s, with a few earlier exceptions. In 1845, Presbyterian marriages were recognized by the state, but it was not until the disestablishment of the Church of Ireland in 1871 that complete freedom of worship was guaranteed.

Presbyterian registers are similar to those of other denominations in that they were not standardized in format or content, and they sometimes have huge gaps in the years recorded even in a single congregation. This inconsistency means you might find significant changes in the information recorded even by the same minister.

This 1821–1822 marriage register from the First Armagh Presbyterian Church provides the names and townlands of the bride and groom, the date of the wedding, and the names of witnesses. It does not, however, include any parental information.

The contents of baptism records differ from parish to parish. Some contain only the child's name, the father's full name, and the mother's first name. Some provide a little more detail, recording the parents' residence, the mother's maiden name, and the name of godparents (sponsors). The date of birth may also be given, especially if it was significantly before the baptism.

Early Presbyterian marriage registers (image **F**) usually provide only the names of the couple and the father of the bride, while later ones—certainly from 1845—provide the names and residences of the bride and groom, their marital status, ages and occupations, and the names and occupations of their fathers. Advance notice of weddings had to be sent to the Kirk Session (the governing religious authority), and these notices were then recorded in the Session Minute Book. These books survive (most are at PRONI; a smaller number are held by the Presbyterian Historical Society of Ireland's library) and are worth checking for additional details of your family.

Presbyterian burial registers are uncommon, as few churches had burial grounds.

Where to Access Presbyterian Records

The only significant online source of Presbyterian records is the subscription site RootsIreland. Its transcription-only database holds records for all nine counties of Ulster, in addition to smaller collections for congregations in other provinces. The free Irish Genealogy website holds baptism records for Lucan in County Dublin, and the Irish Genealogical Research Society has a members-only database of ten thousand Presbyterians living in Dublin in 1875 <www.irishancestors.ie/?page_id=6861>.

Offline, PRONI has microfilmed nearly all surviving Presbyterian registers, and the Presbyterian Historical Society of Ireland's library <www.presbyterianhistoryireland.com/collections/library/guide-to-congregational-records> holds a small but exclusive collection of baptism and marriage registers, plus some early Session Minute Books. Local ministers also hold a small number of pre-1900 registers and other records.

OTHER DENOMINATIONS

Historically, Roman Catholic, Church of Ireland, and Presbyterian congregations made up all but a tiny proportion of the religious mix of Ireland. Statistics from the 1831 census, for example, show they represented 80.5 percent, 10.5 percent, and 8 percent of the population, respectively. The followers of other faiths (i.e., the remaining 1 percent) were clearly not numerous, but you may still have Irish Methodists, Quakers, or Jews amongst your ancestors.

Methodist Records

Until the second decade of the 1800s, Methodists usually had dual membership with their local Church of Ireland parish church, and their baptisms, marriages, and funerals will be recorded in the registers of that church. The earliest Methodist-only registers date from 1815/16, but most of them started in the 1830s/1840s. They contain the same information as Church of Ireland records.

PRONI has a large collection of Methodist records on microfilm, and local chapels hold most of the remainder. See the websites of the Methodist Church in Ireland <irishmethodist.org> and Methodist Historical Society of Ireland <methodisthistoryireland.org> for contact details. RootsIreland also has some transcribed records from Methodist registers.

Society of Friends (Quaker) Records

Happily for genealogists with connections to the Society of Friends, the majority of Quaker records of births, marriages, and deaths go back to the 1670s or even to 1655, a year after the group opened its first meeting house in Lurgan, County Armagh. On the downside, the registers do not usually contain much more detail than the names and addresses of the parties concerned.

The records of the Society of Friends are online at Findmypast, with some privacy restrictions; you can't access records of birth within the last one hundred years or marriages within the last seventy-five years. For more information about the extensive Quaker archives, see the Quakers in Ireland website <quakers-in-ireland.ie/historical-library>.

Jewish Records

The Irish Jewish Family History Database <irishjewishroots.com> holds records of more than fifty-seven thousand individuals who lived in Ireland between 1700 and the present. The website also includes details of publications useful to further research.

KEYS TO SUCCESS

Identify the correct ecclesiastical parish for your ancestors' home area. See chapter 5 on Irish geography for more guidance.

Always check the applicable dates for record sets, especially in online collections. Many have gaps in coverage, and the name of the collection may not reflect this. Additionally, the dates for surviving records are often not the same for baptism, marriage, and burial.

As always, be flexible with spellings of your ancestor's surname. The priest or officiating minister would have recorded the name how he thought it should be spelled, and this may not match its modern spelling.

If the records you seek are not online, consider commissioning a professional researcher in Ireland to visit the archive or library where they are held and carry out a specific register search. Set your search criteria and budget in advance. The National Archives of Ireland presents a list of researchers at <www.nationalarchives.ie/genealogy1/genealogy-researchers-nationwide>.

9

Census Records

For government agencies, the purpose and value of conducting censuses is obvious: gathering information on the social, economic, and demographic characteristics of society to assist with local, state, and national planning and development. For the genealogist, the value of census returns lies in the presentation of family groups in one place at one point in time: the relationships between family members and their ages, places of birth, social statuses, and housing conditions.

Unfortunately for genealogists, Ireland has a spotty record of safeguarding its census manuscripts, so most researchers exploring pre-twentieth century ancestors have to rely on a swathe of genealogical resources known as census substitutes, a disparate group of records scattered across many repositories that you can piece together to provide at least some of the same information as would the missing census.

This chapter will guide you through this maze of resources, setting out what survives and where records can be consulted, plus how each collection might help your research.

IRISH CENSUSES

Ireland's first attempt at a national census was in 1813, surprisingly early compared with other parts of the United Kingdom. It was, though, a failure, and the paperwork was discarded shortly afterwards. The government then took islandwide decennial national censuses from 1821 to 1891, but only a few fragments have survived fire, dynamite, and short-sighted decisions by government administrators. Only the 1901 and 1911 censuses are available in their entirety.

Over the years, the information requested in these censuses varied slightly but always included at least the names of the individuals, their ages, and their relationships to the head of household, plus some basic data about their land or dwelling.

In this section, you'll find details of each census, including the specifics of who and what was recorded, and which records survive. You'll also learn some detailed tips to avoiding the most common problems encountered by researchers when searching these records.

Nineteenth-Century Records

Over the course of the century, the personal details requested by the census changed. In the earliest years, only the names, ages, and relationships of people within individual households were asked. But by the end of the century, the census forms asked about each individual's place of birth, occupation, marital status, and literacy levels. Some even asked for marriage dates, causes of death for recently deceased members of the household, or places of residence for absent family members.

1821–1851

In the first four islandwide censuses, the information requested varied slightly but always included at least the names of the individuals, their ages, and their relationship to the head of household, plus some basic data about their land or dwelling. For administrative purposes, they were all organized by county, barony, parish, and (in rural areas) townland or (in urban areas) street.

Sadly, these priceless records were almost completely lost in the 1922 explosion and fire at the Public Record Office (PRO) in Dublin during the Irish Civil War. The small number of originals or transcripts that survive are widely referred to as census fragments. Some notable fragments for this period include:

- **1821:** Every member of the household present on the night of May 27, 1821, was identified by name, age, occupation, and relationship to the head of household. In addition, the land acreage held by the head of household was noted, as was the number of stories of the dwelling. Fragments survive for small areas of counties Cavan, Fermanagh, Galway, Meath, and Offaly (then called King's County).

- **1831:** Officially, this census was taken on June 6, 1831. In practice, visits by enumerators to the households in their designated locales took place over several months. Every member of each household was identified by name, age, occupation, reli-

2ND TABLE.—Return of the Members of this Family now Alive, and whose Home is in this House, but who were Absent on the night of **SUNDAY, the 30th MARCH, 1851.**

NOTE.—*This Table is necessary in order to ascertain the number of persons belonging to each Family, whether present or absent on the said night.*

NAMES.		AGE.		SEX.	RELATION.	RANK, PROFESSION, OR OCCUPATION.	
Christian Names.	Surnames.	Years.	Months, for Infants under one year.	Whether Male or Female?	Of each to the Head of the Family, whether Wife, Son, Daughter, or other relative, Servant, &c?	State the particular Rank, Profession, Trade, or other Employment of each person; or, if a child, whether attending school?	In what Country, County, or City at present Residing?
Susan	McGlaughlin	25	—	Female	Sister	House Servant	America
Catharin	McGlaughlin	19	—	Female	Sister	Dressmaker	America

3RD TABLE.—Return of the Members, Visitors, and Servants, of this Family, who have **DIED** while residing with this Family, **since the 6th JUNE, 1841,** the date of the last Census.

NOTE.—*The necessity for this Table is caused by the want of a General Registration of Deaths in Ireland.*

NAMES.		AGE.		SEX.	RELATION.	RANK, PROFESSION, OR OCCUPATION.	CAUSE OF DEATH.	TIME OF DEATH.	
Christian Names.	Surnames.	Years.	Months, for Infants under one Year.	Whether Male or Female?	Of each to the Head of the Family, whether Wife, Son, Daughter, or other relative, Visitor, Servant, &c?	State the particular Rank, Profession, Trade, or other Employment of each person?	Disease or Accident which caused Death?	Season—as Spring, Summer, Autumn, or Winter?	In what Year?
Owen	McGlaughlin	70	—	Male	Father	Farmer	hurt in the breast	Summer	1850
Ann	Mullen	50	—	Female	Step mother	Flax Spinner	Liver Complaint	Spring	1842

I believe the foregoing to be true Returns concerning all the Members of this Family.

(Signature of Head of Family) _Owen McGlaughlin_

Affirmed by _____ before me, the _____ day of _____ 1851.

In conformity with Act 13 & 14 Vict., cap. 44.

I hereby affirm that the foregoing Returns are correct, according to the best of my knowledge and belief.

Signature of Enumerator. _____

Magistrate.

Both the 1841 and 1851 censuses asked about family members who were absent on census night or who had died in the preceding decade. In this example, Ann McGlaughlin of Clonee, Lurg, County Fermanagh, recorded the absence of her sisters who were in America. She also noted the deaths of her seventy-year-old father and her fifty-year-old step-mother, Ann Mullen.

gion, and relationship to the head of household. In addition, the census noted the respondent's land acreage. Most of the original returns (or transcripts made in 1834) survive for County Derry. Offline, these records can be searched by personal visitors to the Public Record Office of Northern Ireland (PRONI) in Belfast and the Genealogical Centre in Derry City.

- **1841:** Every member of the household was identified by name, age, sex, relationship to the head of household, occupation, literacy, birthplace, marital status, and date of marriage. In addition, members of the family who were not at home on census night (June 6, 1841) were included, as were those who had died since the 1831 census (with cause of death noted). The only original returns that survived are those for Killeshandra in County Cavan. A number of transcripts of originals also survive, most of them for locations in the south of County Kilkenny and Monaghan, plus random households in the counties of Cork, Fermanagh, and Waterford.

- **1851:** Each member of the household was identified by name, age, sex, relationship to the head of household, occupation, literacy, birthplace, marital status, and date of marriage. In addition, heads of household were asked to record members of the family absent on census night (March 30, 1851), as well as those who had died since the 1841 census (with cause of death noted; image **A**). Acreage of the household's land was noted, and the dwelling was rated according to a grading system. While most of the surviving fragments or transcriptions relate to parts of County Antrim, fragments survive—sometimes for only one or two households—from all other

1901 and 1911 Census Forms

Census-takers used a number of different forms when compiling census returns. While most were completed by the head of household of each individual home or by the person responsible for an institution or ship, three statistical returns (Forms B1, B2, and N) were completed on a townland or street basis by the enumerator. Here's a breakdown of all the census forms:

Ordinary households

- **Form A:** The standard Form A recorded each member of the household and any visitors who happened to be staying overnight on census day. These forms were collected by an enumerator, typically a local police constable, who would fill in the forms if the head of household was illiterate.

- **Form B1:** The House and Building Return was filled in by the enumerator as he went from house to house, recording the number of rooms occupied by each household; details of how the walls and roofs were constructed (e.g., mud, stone, or thatch); the number of rooms; the number of windows at the front of the house; how many families lived in each property; and the name of the landholder. In addition, the enumerator graded the house as first-, second-, or third-class. In addition to providing details of your ancestor's living conditions, the completed Form B1 delivers an at-a-glance summary of all the heads of household in the townland or street. This can be useful for identifying relatives living nearby.

- **Form B2:** The Return of Out-Offices and Farm-Steadings form records additional buildings or features of a property, such as cow sheds, barns, pig sheds, forges, and stables.

counties except Cork. Fragments and copies relating to counties now in Northern Ireland are available to in-person visitors to the PRONI in Belfast.

1861-1891

Manuscripts from the 1861 and 1871 censuses were intentionally destroyed by government administrators some time after all the required statistical information about population and society had been extracted from them. Only two transcriptions, made from the originals before they were pulped, survive:

- **1861:** Enniscorthy Parish, County Wexford. Only the details of Roman Catholic families were transcribed. These transcriptions form part of the National Library of Ireland (NLI)'s free online Roman Catholic Parish Registers Collection **<registers.nli.ie>**.

- **1871:** Drumcondra and Loughbracken parish, County Meath. Details of all families in the parish, regardless of religion. These transcriptions form part of the NLI's free online Roman Catholic Parish Registers Collection **<registers.nli.ie>**.

- **Form N:** The Enumerator's Abstract provides a summary of the total number of houses within the townland or street, together with the total number of occupants of each household and their religions.

Institutions, ships, and the sick

Individuals who were living in something other than an ordinary household or who were crew on ships in port had to be recorded on one of the following forms:

- **Form B3:** Ships
- **Form C:** The sick living in their own homes
- **Form D:** "Idiots and lunatics" not living in institutions
- **Form E:** Workhouses
- **Form F:** Hospitals
- **Form G:** Students living at colleges and boarding schools
- **Form H:** Policemen living in barracks
- **Form I:** "Idiots and lunatics" living in institutions
- **Form K:** Prisons

Rather than using the full names, most policemen and asylum inmates were recorded by their initials. You may find that the details given for birth county, occupation, and marital status will help you identify these individuals with some certainty.

In a similar vein, the paper returns for the 1881 and 1891 censuses did not survive World War I. No documented instructions have been discovered, but it is widely assumed that an order was issued to pulp the manuscripts during a paper shortage.

Twentieth-Century Records

With census records from the 1800s so few and far between, census records from the 1900s ought to be one of your first ports of call if your ancestors left Ireland in the past one hundred years and you have some dates and a rough location to work from. You should be able to find your ancestor's close family—parents, grandparents, and siblings—plus their ages and residence. These should quickly direct you to the parish and civil registration records that will help you move back to earlier generations.

Even if your immigrant Irish ancestor departed earlier than 1900, you should still make an early investigation into these records. The census will hold details of the family your ancestor left in Ireland (parents, siblings, nieces, nephews) and their descendants. If you can identify these relatives, you will have at your disposal names and ages that can help you bridge the gap of time and ultimately rebuild the family unit that your ancestor may have known.

1901 AND 1911

The 1901 census was taken on March 31 and recorded the following:

- Name
- Relationship to the head of household
- Religion
- Literacy level (read and write/read only/cannot read)
- Occupation
- Age
- Marital status
- Irish county of birth (country, if born abroad)
- Irish language ability (Irish only/Irish and English)
- Disabilities (Deaf and Dumb/ Deaf only/ Imbecile/Idiot/Lunatic)

The 1911 census was taken on April 2. It requested the same details as the 1901 census, but with one extremely useful addition: Married women were asked to state how many years they had been married, the number of children they had borne, and how many of these children were still living. (Widows were not asked to provide this information, nor were men. Even so, it is not uncommon to find they have answered these questions.)

Don't Rely on Ages Quoted in the Census

When only a minority of the population had a birth certificate, few people knew (or cared about) their precise age. As a result, census respondents gave their best guess about their ages, some of which have been rounded up or down to the nearest five or ten years. Consistency is also an issue; you may find your relatives aged more or less than ten years between the 1901 and 1911 census! Ages quoted in census returns (and in many other records) should always be treated with some caution and backed up with other sources.

Both censuses were organized by the simple hierarchical structure of county, district electoral division, and townland (in rural areas) or street (in urban areas). The worksheets at the end of this chapter will serve as templates for you to record census entries.

Let's look at these records in practice to see what they can tell us. According to the 1901 census (a completed Form A; image **B**), Daniel O'Brien was a sixty-eight-year-old Roman Catholic farmer living with his family in the townland of Farrihy in the district electoral division of Broadford in County Limerick. He was a native of Limerick while his sixty-year-old wife, Catherine, was from the neighboring county of Cork. The four children living with them were all born in County Limerick. Form B1 (not shown) details that the family's two-room home was made of stone, brick, or concrete construction and had four windows at the front. According to the form, Mathew O'Brien was Daniel's neighbor; although O'Brien is a common surname (especially in the province of Munster, which includes Limerick) it is possible Daniel and Mathew are related—a lead worth exploring.

The same family's 1911 census return (another completed Form A; image **C**) provides further evidence. According to the record, he and Catherine still lived in Farrihy, and they now had a domestic servant. Two of their children are living with them, but only one of those who was sharing the family home ten years previously. Catherine is recorded as giving birth to fourteen children, but only six have survived. (Across the two censuses, we now know the names of five of them.) She and Daniel have been married for fifty years, according to the return. While this may not be completely accurate, it provides a good starting point for a search of parish marriage registers.

And while viewing multiple years' census returns for the O'Brien family gives us a fuller picture of the family's history, we also notice a peculiarity often encountered by Irish researchers: Both Daniel and Catherine appear to have aged more than ten years during the intervening decade. Daniel has aged an impressive seventeen years (sixty-eight in 1901 to eighty-five in 1911) and his wife thirteen years (sixty in 1901 to seventy-three in 1911). Such discrepancies reflect a time when age mattered little and few people

CENSUS OF IRELAND, 1901.

(Two Examples of the mode of filling up this Table are given on the other side.)

FORM A.

No. on Form B. 6

RETURN of the MEMBERS of this FAMILY and their VISITORS, BOARDERS, SERVANTS, &c., who slept or abode in this House on the night of SUNDAY, the 31st of MARCH, 1901.

NAME and SURNAME	RELATION to Head of Family	RELIGIOUS PROFESSION	EDUCATION	AGE		SEX	RANK, PROFESSION, OR OCCUPATION	MARRIAGE	WHERE BORN	IRISH LANGUAGE	If Deaf and Dumb
				M	F						
Daniel O'Brien	Head	R. Catholic	Read & write	68		M	Farmer	Married	Co. Cork		
Kate O'Brien	Wife	do	Read & write		60	F		Married	Cork		
Jeremiah O'Brien	Son	do	Read. Write	24		M	Farmer's Son	Not married	Co. Cork		
Timothy O'Brien	do	do	Read & write	22		M	A. Scholar	do	do		
Kate O'Brien	Daughter	do	Read & write		20	F	Farmer's Daughter	do	do		
Maggie O'Brien	Daughter	do	Read & write		16	F	Farmer's Daughter	do	do		

I hereby certify, as required by the Act 63 Vic, cap 6, s 6 (I), that the foregoing Return is correct, according to the best of my knowledge and belief.

James McCarthy _____ *(Signature of Enumerator.)*

I believe the foregoing to be a true Return.

Daniel O'Brien _____ *(Signature of Head of Family.)*

The 1901 census is an invaluable resource for Irish researchers. Note the ages provided here for the O'Brien family; they'll be inconsistent with the ages listed in the 1911 census.

CENSUS OF IRELAND, 1911.

Two Examples of the mode of filling up this Table are given on the other side.

FORM A.

No. on Form R. ___

RETURN of the MEMBERS of this FAMILY and their VISITORS, BOARDERS, SERVANTS, &c., who slept or abode in this House on the night of SUNDAY, the 2nd of APRIL, 1911.

Name and Surname		Relation to Head of Family	Religious Profession	Education	Age (last Birthday) and Sex		Rank, Profession, or Occupation	Particulars as to Marriage				Where Born	Irish Language	If Deaf and Dumb; Dumb only; Blind; Imbecile or Idiot; or Lunatic.
Christian Name	Surname				Age of Males	Age of Females		Whether "Married," "Widower," "Widow," or "Single."	Completed years the present Marriage has lasted	Total Children born alive	Children still living			
Daniel	O'Brien	Head of Family	Roman Catholic	Read & Write	85	—	Farmer	Married	53	8	8	Co. Limerick	Irish & English	—
Catherine	O'Brien	Wife	Roman Catholic	Read & Write	—	73		Married	54	14	6	Co. Cork	Irish & English	—
Matthew	O'Brien	Son	Roman Catholic	Read & Write	40	—	Agricultural Labourer	Single				Co. Limerick		—
Kenneth	O'Brien	Son	Roman Catholic	Read & Write	37	—	Farmer's Son	Single				Co. Limerick		—
Mary	Daly	Servant	Roman Catholic	Read & Write	—	16	General Domestic Servant	Single				Co. Limerick		

I hereby certify, as required by the Act 10 Edw. VII, and 1 Geo. V., cap. 11, that the foregoing Return is correct, according to the best of my knowledge and belief.

_____ Signature of Enumerator.

I believe the foregoing to be a true Return.

Daniel O'Brien Signature of Head of Family.

The O'Brien family seems to have aged more than ten years in the decade since they appeared in the 1901 census. Rather than superhuman abilities, this discrepancy is likely due to the family's lack of birth certificates/precise dates of birth.

genuinely knew or cared about their date of birth; in 1911, no adults over the age of forty-seven would have had birth certificates. See the Don't Rely on Ages Quoted in the Census tip box for more about this phenomenon.

1921 TO 1946

While the 1901 and 1911 censuses survive more or less intact, many other twentieth-century records were either never taken or are still under privacy restrictions. No census was taken in Ireland in 1921 due to the War of Independence, which was raging across the island in the first half of the year. Following the Partition in 1921, when the island was split into Northern Ireland and the Irish Free State, no more islandwide censuses were taken. Each entity now had responsibility for setting up its own census and distinct administrative arrangements.

Whichever side of the border your ancestors hailed from, however, the records are not yet available to the public. While the United States releases census records seventy-two years after their compilation, both the Republic of Ireland and Northern Ireland operate a one-hundred-year closure period for census records.

Although these records are not yet accessible, a summary of the post-Partition censuses will show you what to anticipate:

- **1926:** Censuses were taken on both sides of the border. Northern Ireland's returns have been completely lost, but those for the Irish Free State (as the Republic was then called) survive and will be released to the public on January 1, 2027. The Council of Irish Genealogical Organizations and others are campaigning for them to be released early.
- **1931:** No censuses were taken either in Northern Ireland or the Irish Free State.
- **1936:** A census was taken in the Irish Free State. Records will be released on January 1, 2037.

RESEARCH TIP

Check Out the Irish Free State Military Census 1922
Following the Partition of Ireland, the Irish Free State carried out a census of all soldiers in barracks on the night of December 12, 1922. In addition to their names, ranks, and corps, the census recorded each soldier's home address, age, marital status, and religion, as well as the date and place of their attestation and the name and address of their next of kin. It is free to access at **<census.militaryarchives.ie>**.

- **1937:** A census was taken in Northern Ireland. Its questions were of limited scope, diminishing its value to family historians. Records will be released on January 1, 2038.
- **1941:** The census was canceled in Northern Ireland due to World War II.
- **1946:** A census was taken by the Republic of Ireland. Records will become available for public inspection on January 1, 2047.

COMMON PROBLEMS WITH IRISH CENSUS RECORDS

While Ireland's surviving census returns can be found on a number of commercial databases, the only free and complete collection is held by the National Archives of Ireland (NAI) **<www.census.nationalarchives.ie>**, where it can be explored by name using the Search Census menu option and by location via the Browse menu option. The site has a simple interface, and most family historians will readily find records of their ancestors or extended family.

However, both the records and the database have some idiosyncrasies that you need to be aware of. The following sections will help you troubleshoot five issues Irish researchers frequently encounter and save you valuable research time.

Personal details were not validated.

In preparing the database's index, transcribers were required to record the details provided on the census returns as they were written. Spellings of names and place names have not been corrected, so you may have to be imaginative in your searches. In addition, respondents' ages and marital statuses have not been corroborated. For example, if your ancestor said he was a seventy-five-year-old bachelor at the time of a census, his online entry for that census will be based on these statements—even if you have documentary evidence that he was eighty-four and the form shows him as living with a wife. Additionally, some census entries were illegible and some of the paper returns have been so damaged that the writing is incomplete or cannot be deciphered, leading to further indexing errors.

Some census returns are missing.

The census returns for a number of townlands/streets do not appear in the online versions of the 1901 and 1911 censuses. In some cases, this is because the paper returns were not available at the time the returns were originally microfilmed. And since the microfilmed images were used for the subsequent digitization project, these returns were never digitized or transcribed. But there is another group of returns, relating to 1911 and from at least forty-five villages, that were microfilmed but accidentally omitted from the transcription project. In other words, while the images of the returns are online, the inhabitants cannot be found via the search page.

If you are confident of the location where your ancestors lived and suspect it may be one of these "missing" villages, follow John Grenham's instructions in his *Irish Times* blog <www.johngrenham.com>.

Nicknames and shortened first names were transcribed as written.

Names recorded on the census returns were transcribed as written, so any of your ancestor's pet names, nicknames, or abbreviated versions of their first names will have been faithfully transcribed. Among the most common are: *Maggie* and *Peggy* for "Margaret"; *Danl* for "Daniel" or "Donal"; *Jno* for "John"; *Lizzie* for "Elizabeth"; *Geo* for "George"; *Jerry* for "Jeremiah"; *Mick*, *Mike*, or *Ml* for "Michael"; *Kate* for "Catherine"; and a whole raft of possibilities for "Patrick"—*Paddy*, *Pat*, *Patsy*, *Patty*, and *Packie* (nevermind the Irish versions, *Pádraic* and *Pádraig*, and all their variations). You can either search using all the alternative versions and spellings of your ancestor's name, or try searching with a wildcard character (asterisk *) when you're not sure of the spelling that might have been used. For example, searching *Cat*rine* will return Catherine, Catharine, and Cathrine, but not Katherine, Kate, etc.

Some search software is better than others.

All search engines are not created equal! Some have much better name-recognition software than others. Depending on which database you're using, the search facility may "instinctively" recognize *Pat* as a shortened form of "Patrick" or *Nellie* as a form of "Ellen," while others will require you to click a variants box to indicate that you want it to extend the standard search parameters. Similarly, surname variants are accommodated if you select the variants option. Or, depending on the surname, you could try using an asterisk to return results with multiple spellings: *Cr*wley* should find "Crawley" and "Crowley," while *M*Carthy* will return "MCarthy," "MArthy," "Maccarthy," "Mc Carthy," "Mac Carthy," and many more of that surname's many spelling options. If you are using the NAI's Census search engine, be aware that the software does not include automatic recognition software, but you can use wildcards.

The correct name order may have been reversed.

When filling in their paper census returns, people sometimes entered their entire name in either the surname or forename column, or transposed their names (i.e., placing their forename in the surname column and the surname in the forename column). Again, these

Exploring the NAI Census Database

The NAI free census database <**www.census.nationalarchives.ie**> can be interrogated in all kinds of ways. In addition to searching by name, you can search by religion, occupation, relationship to head of family, literacy status, county or country of origin, Irish-language proficiency, specified illnesses, and child survival information.

Although it can be quite unforgiving (especially with spellings), the search engine can be surprisingly flexible. For example, you may assume that finding your Murphy family without an exact address will be impossible. You may well be right: More than fifty-six thousand Murphys were recorded in the 1901 census. However, other clues revealed through your earlier research may guide you. Was there a story about your ancestor's father being a blacksmith? Or the family hailing from Mayo? Or having an older brother called Jeremiah who inherited the farm? You can dive into the database with these queries by using the often-overlooked More Search Options button on the main search page. You can also use the More Search Options button if you're doing some social history research. If you've always wanted to know how many people spoke Irish in Ballyshannon in 1901, or how many Presbyterians there were in County Roscommon in 1911, this is the place to find out.

While there is no guarantee of a "eureka!" moment, digging deep into the census may reveal some worthwhile lines of enquiry.

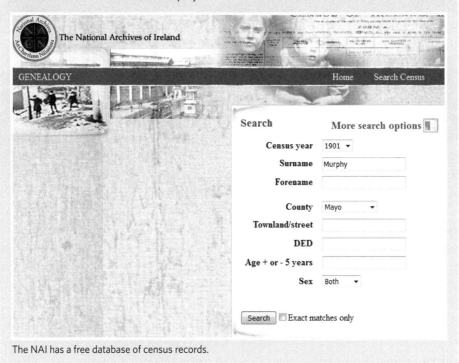

The NAI has a free database of census records.

Locating Census Returns

The NAI **<www.census.nationalarchives.ie>** and FamilySearch.org **<www.familysearch.org>**, both free resources, hold the 1901 and 1911 census returns, all the 1821 to 1851 census fragments mentioned in this chapter, and the NAI collection of Census Search Forms.

Findmypast **<www.findmypast.ie>** holds the same collections but offers an improved search facility that can, not only pick up name variants, but also search by year of birth and for more than one family member at a time. The latter can be particularly useful when you are searching for ancestors with a common surname. While you need to have registered with Findmypast, you do not need to have a subscription to search and view these collections, which link to images of the census returns on the NAI website.

Ancestry.com offers a free Web Search **<www.ancestry.co.uk/websearch>** allowing researchers to search the 1901 and 1911 census and link to images on the NAI's site. You don't need to subscribe or even register with Ancestry.com to use Web Search collections.

The PRONI holds a microfilmed collection of Census Search Forms relating to people living in Antrim, Armagh, Cavan, Derry, Donegal, Down, Fermanagh, Monaghan, and Tyrone at the time of their pension applications and include those who had been born or spent their childhood in other counties. This microfilmed collection is also available via the FamilySearch Library. Its contents have additionally been published in two books by Josephine Masterson: *Ireland 1841/1851 Census Abstracts* (Republic of Ireland) and *Ireland 1841/1851 Census Abstracts* (Northern Ireland). You can find these on Ancestry.com.

entries have been transcribed and indexed in the same order as they appear on the paper return. This is why, for example, the 1901 census database holds more than five hundred people recorded with the surname Patrick, even though probably fewer than 120 are correct. So you won't find "Patrick De Courcy" of Blackmore Lane in Cork in the 1901 census unless you search for him as "De Corcy Patrick," nor "Patrick O'Dwyer" in County Limerick without searching for "O'Dwyer Patrick," and so on.

CENSUS SUBSTITUTES

Ireland's so-called "census substitutes" are a miscellaneous collection of surveys and name lists compiled on a national level or across either a localized geographical area or a distinguishable group of people. They were created for various reasons, and many of them would not have become genealogically significant had it not been for the destruction of nearly all of Ireland's nineteenth-century national population censuses.

You will find the scope and content of these substitutes vary considerably. Nonetheless, even the least detailed may be helpful in pinpointing your ancestor to a given place and time period, and this may open up new directions of research.

The two most important census substitutes are the Tithe Applotment Books and Griffith's Valuation, which we'll explore in more detail in chapter 10. Census substitutes dating from the eighteenth and nineteenth centuries and of regional or island-wide coverage are listed in the sections that follow, along with brief descriptions and an indication of where they can be accessed:

- **The 1740 Census of Protestant Householders:** For local tax reasons, a census of Protestant householders was compiled in 1740. It was organized by barony and parish, and transcripts survive for parts of Counties Armagh, Antrim, Derry, Donegal, Down, Longford, and Tyrone. Hard copies are held by the Public Record Office (PRO) in Dublin, PRONI in Belfast, and the NLI in Dublin. It is not available online.

- **Catholic Qualification Rolls and Convert Rolls, 1700–1845:** To avoid the restrictions of the Penal Laws, Roman Catholics could take an oath of allegiance to the king of England or renounce their religion for that of the Protestant Church of Ireland. The collection of about sixty thousand records is free on the NAI's website **<www.genealogy.nationalarchives.ie>**.

- **The 1749 Census of Elphin:** Authorized by the Bishop of Elphin, the 1749 Census of Elphin diocese was designed to discover the ratio of Protestants to Catholics in the diocese. Considering its simple statistical aim, this census is wonderfully detailed, and you can count yourself lucky indeed if your ancestors hailed from the covered area. Names, addresses, and occupations of householders, together with the numbers and genders of all children and servants, are listed by townland. It covers fifty-one parishes in County Roscommon, eight parishes in County Galway, and thirteen parishes in County Sligo. The returns are arranged by parish and townland, and give names of heads of household (some also include the first name of the householder's wife), religion, profession, number of children, and number of servants. The Irish Manuscripts Commission published a transcription of the census in 2004; this is available on Findmypast and on microfilm through the FamilySearch Library. You can also view an alternative index form on the Irish Genealogical Research Society's website **<www.irishancestors.ie/?page_id=1688>**.

- **The Religious Census of 1766:** Authorized by the Irish Parliament, the Church of Ireland instructed its rectors to compile a snapshot view of their parishes. Clergy members gathered records of all householders, indicating occupants' religion as either Church of Ireland (Episcopalian), Roman Catholic (Papists), or Presbyterians (Dissenters). They also recorded details of any Catholic priests operating within the parish. Unfortunately, the instructions did not explain how this detail was to be provided, so rectors interpreted them differently. Some listed every townland and

Record Alternatives: Census Search Forms

In January 1909, the Old Age Pensions Act introduced a non-contributory pension for eligible individuals aged seventy and over. To be eligible, applicants had to have an income of less than thirty-one pounds and tens shillings per annum (£31.50), and had to "be of good character." They also had to prove they met the age requirement; this immediately presented a problem because anyone of that age and older would have been born before 1840. Since civil birth registration was not introduced until 1864, how could would-be pensioners prove when they were born?

An administrative solution involved a search for documentary evidence of the claimant's age in the 1841 and 1851 census returns, which survived until 1922.

There were two routes claimants could follow:

- **Form 37s:** Most claimants submitted a claim at a local Pension Board office by providing details of their parents' names and their residence in March 1841/1851. These particulars were noted on a Form 37, and sent to the PRO in Dublin where the census returns were held. Officials checked the census returns for the relevant townland or address provided and returned their findings to the Pension Board.
- **Green Forms:** Some claimants chose to directly commission (and pay) the PRO in Dublin to search the old censuses. In these cases, the particulars were noted on Search/Extract of the Census 1841/51 forms, which came to be known as Green Forms. Officials checked the census returns for the relevant townland or address provided, noted the details discovered, and returned their findings directly to the claimant.

Many of the early claimants would have been children or young adults at the time the 1841 and 1851 censuses were taken, so it is not surprising that their memories—especially of the address—often proved to be hazy or incorrect. As a result, many of these applications were noted as "not found" and rejected. Even so, some of the data provided by the applicant, especially names of parents and siblings, may be useful to researchers.

Fortunately, the memories of many claimants held up, and their eligibility for the pension was confirmed. Successful searches often provide outstanding genealogy material because some officials transcribed from the census return the names and ages of every person living in the claimant's household. Others, sadly, merely confirmed the recorded age of the claimant.

Let's look at an example of a census search form. Michael Nash's pension claim was submitted in September 1910 on a Green Form. He believed his parents to be Edward Nash and Jane Foran who lived in the town of Rathkeale in County Limerick. After checking the census returns in several townlands in Rathkeale, the PRO clerk located the five-year-old Michael in Rathkeale Hill and noted his parents as Edmond and Jeney Nash. Although superfluous to the pension claim, the clerk has additionally noted that Michael's parents married in 1815 and his father died in 1837. Regardless of whether Michael's claim was successful, the record provides several key details about Michael's life and family.

Surviving census search forms are split between the NAI in Dublin and the PRONI in Belfast.

Cen S/17/85

Application No. D. 17.928
10.

Date of receipt, 2 Septr 10   Disposed of,

SEARCH IN CENSUS OF 18 41.

Full Name of Applicant, Michael Nash

Address,

Officer of Customs and Excise. Limerick 1/2.

Full Names of Father and Mother of Applicant, Edward Nash Jane Foran

Name of Head of Family (if other than Father)
with which Applicant resided in 18

Residence in 18 54 :

Tt of Rathkeale

Lynches Lane

Rathkeale Square

County,   Limerick   Boherbuoy street
                               Bourhean Road
Barony,   Connello Lr.   Thomas street
                               Pipards Lane
Parish,   Rathkeale   Riches street
                               Pound Lane
                               Chapel Lane   (15)
Townland,   Rathkeale   Well Lane
                               Church Street
Street (if in a town),   High Street
                               Main Street
                               Rathkeale Hill X

Place in Record Treasury, 62 23 6 63 - 30 89

Return searched by GB 8/9/10 GB 9/9/10
                    (died 1837)   married 1835
Particulars found, Edmond & Jesey Nash with son Michael 5 yrs

Sheet 45 Rathkeale Hill x

Form replaced by

Result despatched to Officer,

Please state which year is to be Searched (1841)

Census search forms, like this one for Michael Nash, can fill in gaps left behind by the missing 1841 and 1851 censuses.

householder within it; others made a simple numerical record. Ancestry.com has the only online collection of this census, an index of about eleven thousand names of parishioners in the north of Ireland. For details of where to find surviving returns for the whole of Ireland, download the NAI's Guide to the Religious Census of 1766 <www.nationalarchives.ie/PDF/ReligiousCensus.pdf>.

- **The Spinning Wheel Entitlement List:** Also known as the Flax Growers Bounty or the Irish Flax Growers List, this list was published in 1796 by the Irish Linen Board. It names some sixty thousand people who were granted free spinning wheels or looms as part of a government program to encourage linen production. Since most of the flax required for linen was produced in the north of the island, the majority (but not all) of those named hail from parishes in Ulster. The List is free to search at Fáilte Romhat <www.failteromhat.com/flax1796.php>.

- **Pigot's Commercial Directory, 1824:** This publication provides brief details of towns across the island, and lists the names of the local gentry, merchants, and artisans by profession and trade. It is free to download at Fáilte Romhat <www.failteromhat.com/pigot.php>. See chapter 11 for more about directories.

- **Tithe Applotment Books, 1824–38:** This collection consists of a manuscript book for almost every civil parish across the island. Each book lists the names of each townland's occupants, the amount of land held, and the sums to be paid in tithes to the Church of Ireland. Because the tithes were levied only on agricultural land, urban areas were not included. See chapter 10 for more details.

- **Lord Viscount Morpeth's Testimonial Roll, 1841:** This roll contains the signatures of some 160,000 people. The 412-meters-long scroll was presented to Morpeth as he left office as Chief Secretary for Ireland. Most of the signatories were politicians, clergy, and other members of the establishment, but some merchants and non-nobility supporters also signed. Unfortunately, the residential address of the signatories is provided in only a relatively small percentage of instances. The indexed collection is free at Ancestry.com.

- **Slater's Commercial Directory of Ireland (1846, 1856, 1870, 1881, 1894):** Slater's directories followed a similar format to Pigot's, but expanded the number of towns and provided additional details. The 1846 version is available free to download at Fáilte Romhat <www.failteromhat.com/slater.htm>. See chapter 11 for more about directories.

- **Griffith's Valuation, 1848–64:** In the absence of mid-nineteenth-century census records, this taxation survey has become Ireland's top census substitute and one of the major record collections used by Irish genealogists. It is examined in detail in chapter 10.

- **Valuation Revision Books, 1860s to 1970s:** Also known as Cancelled Land Books, these books are extensions of Griffith's Valuation and note changes of ownership since the original survey. You'll find more about them in chapter 10.

- **Landowners of Ireland Survey, 1876:** This was an islandwide survey of those landowners who held more than one acre. Some thirty-two thousand landowners are listed, along with the acreage and value of their landholdings. County-by-county transcriptions can be downloaded free from Fáilte Romhat **<www.failteromhat.com/lo1876.htm>**.

Earlier census substitutes also survive. So, too, do a number of more tightly localized surveys. See the Irish Genealogical Research Society's free Irish Census Substitutes, 1630–1875 for a detailed list of census substitutes arranged chronologically and by county **<www.irishancestors.ie/?page_id=7937>**.

KEYS TO SUCCESS

Know which census resources are available for your ancestor's county of origin. They are extensive for some (Londonderry, for example) but sadly limited for others (Mayo, for example).

Don't disregard the 1901 and 1911 censuses just because your ancestor had left Ireland by those dates. These records could hold the details about the descendents of your ancestor's extended family. They may yield valuable information, especially if you are hoping to trace living relatives.

Search all census resources using a variety of name spellings as database search engines differ in their abilities to recognize variants.

Be creative when searching for census substitutes. Directories, census search request forms, and various religious censuses can help you find information that has been lost in destroyed census records.

1901 CENSUS WORKSHEET

Townland: _____   Union: _____   County: _____

DED: _____   Number on Form B: _____

Christian name(s)	Surname	Relation to head of household	Religion	Education	Age at last birth-day	Age months (for infant)	Sex	Rank, profession, or occupation	Marital status	Where born	Irish language	Infirmity

1911 CENSUS WORKSHEET

Townland: _____ Union: _____ County: _____

DED: _____ Number on Form B: _____

Name and surname	Relation to head of household	Religion	Education	Age at last birthday		Rank, profession, or occupation	Marital particulars				Where born	Irish language	Disability
				M	F		Married, single, widow, or widower	No. of years married	No. of children born	No. still living			

10

Land and Property Records

D ue to the loss of nearly all nineteenth-century censuses and the relatively late introduction of civil registration of births, marriages, and deaths, Irish family history research is surprisingly reliant on property and land records. These records are contained in a number of different resources, many compiled for tax and legal reasons and some more accessible than others. They won't answer your genealogical questions as readily as records showing family units and relationships, but they may help you to pinpoint your family and tell you more about your ancestral story.

To make best use of the resources, learn the controversial history of land ownership in Ireland (see chapter 4 on Irish history). As early as the sixteenth and seventeenth centuries, English authorities confiscated most of the land owned by Roman Catholics and gave it to rich and well-connected Protestant families and settlers. Since the island's population was predominantly Roman Catholic and/or poor, most researchers of Irish descent won't find their genealogies written up in some resources such as *Burke's Landed Gentry of Ireland*, 1855 edition at Ancestry.com **<search.ancestry.com/search/db.aspx?dbid=35030>**, nor the 1899 edition at Findmypast **<www.findmypast.ie/articles/world-records/full-list-of-the-irish-family-history-records/newspapers-directories-and-social-history/burkes-landed-gentry-of-ireland-1899>**). Likewise, impoverished ancestors' names don't appear in early lists of landowners or in the deeds and leases of Ireland's great country houses and estates.

Where the majority of the Irish middle and lower classes do appear, however, is in records designed to facilitate tax collection. In this chapter, you'll learn about each of the major property and land collections, but I'm going to concentrate on Griffith's *Primary Valuation of Ireland* as it is, in some ways, the most important and relevant for nearly all researchers.

GRIFFITH'S *PRIMARY VALUATION OF IRELAND*

Despite its rather uninspiring title, the *Primary Valuation of Ireland* (Griffith's Valuation for short) is one of Irish genealogy's greatest treasures: a nationwide survey of property and land carried out between 1847 and 1864 to determine the rate each household should pay towards supporting the poor and destitute within the local poor law union. It was supervised by Sir Richard Griffith, a Dublin-born geologist, whose large team of surveyors and valuers traveled across the island, county by county, assessing the value of each property and the names of those responsible for paying the tax on it. Given its thoroughness, the Valuation is considered the best of Ireland's census substitutes, as it names nearly all heads of households across the island.

The Valuation was published in a series of three-hundred-plus volumes, arranged by county (see image **A** for dates the survey was conducted), barony, poor law union, civil parish, and townland. The first installment (for parts of County Dublin) was published in 1847. Within each county, the Valuations are arranged by union, then by parish. The townlands of each parish are then listed alphabetically.

You can access the Valuation from a number of online sources—see the Griffith's Valuation Online sidebar for more information. Remember: The object of your search is to find the land where your ancestral family resided in the mid-nineteenth century, which may be where they had been living for many previous decades.

All the individuals named in the Valuation were considered heads of their household and responsible for paying the tax levied on the property and land they were occupying. The head of household was rarely a woman; where women do appear, they are usually

RESEARCH TIP

Make an Exception for Urban Ancestors

While Griffith's Valuation records almost all heads of households, your ancestor may not be included if he lived in a street tenement with other families. Usually, only one head of household per house was named in cases of high-density shared occupancy in urban areas.

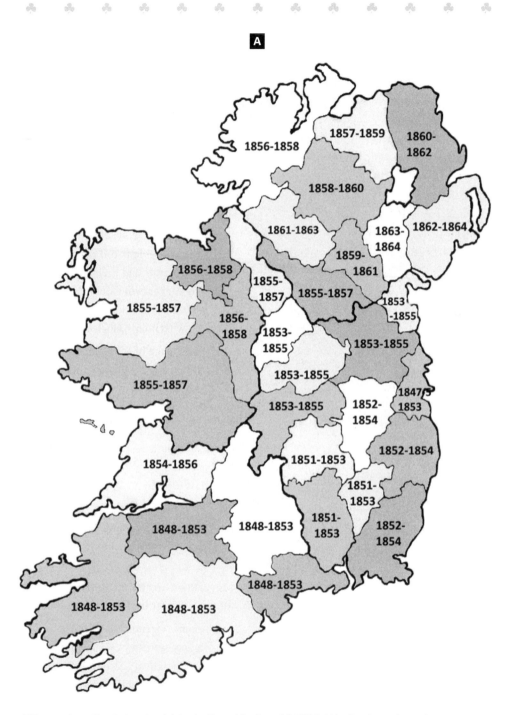

This map shows the start and end dates for the publication of Griffith's Valuation for each county.

widows with no resident adult son. It is unlikely many of the heads of household would have been under age twenty-one, but many could have been in their sixties or older. Use image **A** to check when Griffith's Valuation was carried out for your ancestor's area, if you know it, and relate the date to the age and era of your known ancestor. The person you see named may be the brother, father, uncle, nephew, or even grandfather or grandson of your ancestor.

Cracking the Code

Griffith's team of valuers listed and briefly described every plot (or lot) of land within a townland, recording the names of both occupier and landlord, the acreage of the land, and a calculation of the annual tax rating. While it may not at first look too promising, the Valuation can reveal remarkable details about how your ancestors and their communities lived. The secret lies in understanding the "code" used by the team of valuers.

To crack the code, take a look at the sample first page of the Valuation for the poor law union of Castlerea in County Roscommon and note the following points, labeled in image **B**:

1. The header (or masthead) announces this as the first page of the Valuation for the [Poor Law] Union of Castlerea. As discussed in chapter 5, a poor law union was a local administrative area, usually centred on a market town, set up to administer the poor relief and provide a workhouse, while a barony was a wider administrative area that started to become obsolete after the 1850s.

2. In Griffith's Valuation, the term *parish* refers to civil parishes, usually identical or similar to Church of Ireland parishes. If your ancestors were Roman Catholic, you can identify the corresponding Roman Catholic parish, then search for baptismal and marriage records. See the Gazetteer section of chapter 5 for more details.

3. Plot numbers and letters relate to individual lots within a townland. The references also appear on the corresponding Valuation maps, allowing you to see exactly where each lot of land and buildings was situated.

4. Land was uniformly measured by (Statute) Acre, Rood and Perch (or ARP). See the Nineteenth-Century Land and Money Values sidebar later in this chapter for more.

5. Property descriptions hint at the occupier's economic circumstances, but you can more precisely gauge an individual occupier's financial status by comparing how his accommodation and property rated compared to his neighbors'. Households with a rateable value of only a few shillings, such as the one Mary Cunniff and Michael Grogan of Ballyfinegan live in (circled in the image), would have been struggling to survive. Note: The "garden" mentioned in this description would have been a vegetable

[11]

❶ UNION OF CASTLEREA.

COUNTY OF ROSCOMMON.

BARONY OF CASTLEREAGH.

❷ PARISH OF BALLINTOBER.

❸ No. and Letters of Reference to Map.		Names.		❺ Description of Tenement.	❹ Area.			Rateable Annual Valuation.			Total Annual Valuation of Rateable Property.		
		❻ Townlands and Occupiers.	Immediate Lessors.		A.	R.	P.	Land. £ s. d.			£ s. d.		
								Land.		Buildings.			
		❼ ARDNAMULLAGH. (Ord. S. 27.)											
1	a	Michael Carty, .	William R.W.Sandford,	House, office, and land,	19	3	30	15 10 0		1 5 0	16 15 0		
2		James M'Loughlin, .	Same, .	Land,	49	3	0	32 15 0		—	32 15 0		
—	a	Vacant, .	James M'Loughlin, .	House, .	—			—		0 10 0	0 10 0		
3	a	Francis Linn, .	Same, .	House and land,	0	2	10	0 10 0		0 15 0	1 5 0		
4 A		James M'Loughlin,	William R.W.Sandford,	Land, }	4	1	10	3 10 0		—	} 8 0 0		
— B					4	3	25	4 10 0					
5	a b	John Madden, .	Same, . {	House and land, Pound (no value), }	2	0	0	2 0 0		0 10 0	} 2 10 0		
—					0	0	5	—					
				Total, .	81	2	0	58 15 0		3 0 0	61 15 0		
		❽ BALLINTOBER. (Ord. S. 27.)											
1		John Mahon, .	Henry Sandford Pack-enham Mahon,	Land, . . .	45	0	31	57 0 0		—	57 0 0		
2	a	James M'Loughlin, .	Same, .	House, offices, and land,	8	0	8	7 10 0		6 0 0	13 10 0		
—	b	Martin Duffrey, .	Free, .	House and forge,	—			—		1 0 0	1 0 0		
3		James M'Loughlin,	Henry Sandford Pack-enham Mahon,	Land, . . .	2	2	20	3 5 0		—	3 5 0		
4	a	. . . .	. . .	R.C. Chapel & grave-yd. (see Exemptions).									
5		James M'Loughlin, {	Hen. Sandford Pack-enham Mahon, {	Fair-green, . . Tolls & customs of fair,	1	3	37	—		—	12 0 0		
					—			—		—			
				Total of Rateable Property, .	57	3	19	67 15 0		7 0 0	86 15 0		
				EXEMPTIONS:									
4	a	. . . .	. . .	R.C. Chapel & grave-yd.	1	0	20	0 10 0		10 0 0	10 10 0		
				Total, including Exemptions, .	58	3	39	68 5 0		17 0 0	97 5 0		
		❾ BALLYFINEGAN. (Ord S. 34 & 27.)											
1	a	Patrick Tighe, .	Wm. R. W. Sandford,	Ho.,offs.,herd's ho.&ld.,	160	3	0	109 0 0		11 10 0	120 10 0		
—	b	Thomas Reddy, .	Patrick Tighe, .	House and garden, .	0	1	17	0 5 0		0 10 0	0 15 0		
2	a {	Patrick Concannon, } Michael Lyons, }	Same, .	House and land, .	1	1	20	{ 0 10 0		} 0 10 0	{ 0 15 0		
								0 10 0			0 15 0		
3	a	Patrick Cryan, .	Wm. R. W. Sandford,	House, office, and land,	14	0	0	5 15 0		0 10 0	6 5 0		
—	b	Bridget Cryan, .	Patrick Cryan, .	House, . .	—			—		0 5 0	0 5 0		
4	a { b	Patrick Kilbride, Michael Kilbride,	Wm. R. W. Sandford, {	House and land, } House and land, }	12	1	13	{ 3 5 0		0 10 0	3 15 0		
								3 5 0		0 5 0	3 10 0		
5	a	Michael Fynns, .	Same, .	House and land, .	6	1	5	3 5 0		0 5 0	3 10 0		
6	{ A B	James M'Loughlin, .	Same, .	Land, . .	10	0	20	7 5 0		—	} 16 15 0		
					10	3	29	9 10 0		—			
—	a	Patrick Hanlon, .	James M'Loughlin, .	House and garden, .	0	1	37	0 10 0		0 10 0	1 0 0		
—	b	Michael Grogan, .	Same, .	House & small garden, .				—		0 5 0	0 5 0		
—	c	Mary Gunniff, .	Same, .	House and garden, .	0	0	24	0 5 0		0 5 0	0 10 0		
7	{ A B	Patrick O'Connor,	Wm. R. W. Sandford, {	Land, . . {	2	0	15	1 0 0		—	} 4 15 0		
					4	0	20	3 15 0		—			

Griffith's Valuation is one of the most valuable resources for Irish researchers. To dissect this sample page of the Valuation, see the numbered notes in the Cracking the Code section. Source: AskAboutIreland.com.

patch rather than an expanse of lawn with flower beds and shrubs. Tenants and owners with a landholding of twenty acres or more would have been quite prosperous.

6. "Immediate Lessor" refers to the landlord or middleman from whom the occupier is leasing the property. If you can identify the "ultimate" landlord, you may be able to locate and explore estate papers (which we'll discuss in more detail later) for more information about how the land was used and how the estate developed. The stated lessor does not necessarily live in the area. In the three townlands featured on this page, we can see William R. W. Sandford has sizeable holdings in Ardnamullagh and Ballyfinegan, but he isn't a resident.

An entry contains a wealth of information. Let's use the first on this page, Ardnamullagh, as an example. William Sandford is the townland's dominant landlord, but he does not live here. The lowercase *A* in the first column reveals that only three of the occupiers reside here: Michael Carty, Francis Linn, and John Madden.

At Plot 1, Carty's house has an annual rate value of one pound and fifteen shillings and includes "offices." These could have been any buildings not used permanently as dwellings or for public purposes, and they would have been farm buildings in most rural areas. In more built-up areas, they might be a shop, mill, or factory.

Another of Sandford's tenants is James McLoughlin, who rents the land on Lot 2. Although this lot includes a house, it is currently vacant; McLoughlin himself lives in the adjoining townland of Ballintober. McLoughlin is shown as the lessee for the vacant house, as well as for the Plot 3 house in which Francis Linn lives. It is likely he is renting these lots from Sandford. Further investigation through any surviving Valuation Office books (see the next section) or estate papers may be able to clarify if this was the case.

Lot 4 is a land-only plot divided into two "quality" lots, labeled A and B. These references relate to the quality of the soil, with A being of poorer quality than B. This has an impact on the rateable value of the two parcels of land. In this case, the values are not markedly different. Again, a study of the Valuation Office books may provide an explanation.

The second entry (for Ballintober) is another example. The valuers' use of the term "house" could denote any dwelling, from a stone-built mansion with a slate roof to a one-room mud-walled cabin. Size and quality differences are reflected in the rateable value of the property. Here, we can see James McLoughlin lives in a house with a rateable annual valuation set at six pounds, which would have been a comfortable home.

Sharing Ballintober's Lot 2 is Martin Duffrey, who's presumably the local blacksmith (his plot includes a forge). The description "Free" in the Immediate Lessor column makes an infrequent appearance in the Valuation. It means the occupier was not paying rent to anyone and usually indicates he or she owned the land or property. Such ownership might have dated back many generations.

The page's last entry, for Ballyfinegan, provides much more information about the community. The first entry (1a) for this townland shows Patrick Tighe renting a swathe of land measuring 160 acres, complete with his house, outbuilding, and a herdsmen's house (probably little more than a shed or hut). The annual value of his house makes it considerably superior to all the others in the three townlands featured on this page. At 1b is Thomas Reddy, probably a laborer, who rents a small dwelling and a half acre of land; if he had a family to support, this would not have provided even a subsistence-level existence.

Lot 4 has two households (a and b) on a twelve-acre plot. Patrick and Michael Kilbride reside in separate dwellings, but they hold the land "in common," as denoted by the brackets. Under this "in common" system, each occupier worked his own part of the land but was financially responsible for the full rent. In this case, if Patrick Kilbride fell ill and couldn't pay his share of the rent, Michael would have to pay both shares of the rent. A

Griffith's Valuation Online

The *Primary Valuation of Ireland* is online at Findmypast (for a fee) **<www.findmypast.com/ articles/world-records/full-list-of-the-irish-family-history-records/census-land-and-substitutes/griffiths-valuation>**, Ancestry.com (for paying subscribers) **<search.ancestry. com/search/db.aspx?dbid=1269>**, or at AskAboutIreland (free) **<www.askaboutireland. ie/griffith-valuation>**, where you can search by the name of your ancestor or by place. While the search engines at Ancestry.com and Findmypast can be instructed to search for variant spellings of surnames, AskAboutIreland's surname search is more limited, so you may have to search for the alternative spellings individually.

The free AskAboutIreland site includes links, not only to the original Valuation, but also to zoomable maps showing the boundaries of each numbered plot of land and the location of each property in a townland. One complication: The maps on this site—and there are often several options for a given area—are revised versions of the original valuers' maps. Some were annotated a few decades after the originals, by which time some properties had been renumbered. You may, therefore, find the plot numbers do not always correspond with the printed Valuation's numbers.

If you know where your ancestors lived, either precisely or roughly, you should be able to locate them quite readily in one of the online versions of Griffith's Valuation. When you've done that, take a look at their neighbors in the same townland. Are there other households with the same surname, or whose surnames are familiar—perhaps as baptism sponsors or the maiden names of female ancestors? Study a good map (you can screenshot a zoomed map directly from AskAboutIreland.ie) that includes all the adjacent townlands, too, and note where the surname occurs in this wider area. These households may well be related to your ancestors, and it's worth saving these details for further investigation.

similar arrangement applies to Patrick Concannon and Michael Lyons, although they share one property and just over one acre of land.

Valuation Revision or Cancelled Land Books

Griffith's Valuation did not begin and end with publication of each volume. Inevitably, land changed hands, families emigrated or simply moved, and parcels of land were sold off for building purposes or as wedding settlements. The details of such changes, and any adjustment to the rateable value of a plot, were recorded in annual revision books, with each volume typically covering a ten-year period.

The changes were recorded in these books using different colors of ink, one color for each year. While this may sound complicated, it was actually a clever visual device. If, for example, the name of the previous occupier of Plot 1 has been crossed through in red ink and another name inserted above, also in red, you should find a date (usually just the year)

Without a fairly precise location for your ancestor's place of origin, Griffith's Valuation is not going to be of much help to your research. However, if you are searching for an unusual surname, its index may help you narrow down the possibilities. This can be freely searched at Fáilte Romhat <**www.failteromhat.com/griffiths.php**>.

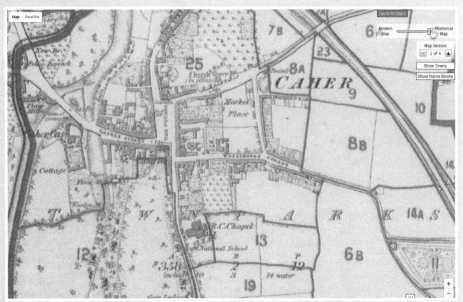

Griffith's Valuation maps, like this one from County Tipperary (viewed on AskAboutIreland), marked allocated plots. Source: AskAboutIreland.com.

in the "Observations" column, written in the same color ink. This would indicate that in the given year, Plot 1 changed hands.

These annual revisions may be useful clues to significant dates in your family's history, such as dates of emigration or death. If the surname of both old and new occupier is the same, the change may have been due to the death of the former occupier (a possibility worth checking in civil registration records). They may also show that your family purchased their plot from their landlord (see the Land Act Purchases sidebar), divided it, sold it, or built new properties on it. Using each revision book volume as a stepping stone through time, you may also find clues to help you locate living descendents.

Land Act Purchases

In the latter part of the nineteenth and early-twentieth centuries, tenants were given assistance by the government's Land Commission to buy the plots they occupied. By 1915, nearly 75 percent of land had moved into the hands of those who worked it through such agreements.

You'll see many entries in the revision books marked as "In Fee," which meant that the named tenant had become the owner. You may also see noted (often by a stamp) the letters L.A.P.; this means the occupier had received a long-term low-interest government loan under a Land Act Purchase arrangement.

For example, the 1899–1914 revision book for the townland of Benagh Upper in Kilkeel, County Down, shows that six plots of land previously owned by the Earl of Kilmoney had been bought by his ex-tenants.

Some revision books, like this one from County Down (courtesy of Deputy Keeper of the Records, Public Record Office of Northern Ireland, reference number: VAL/12B/19/13D), shows if tenants acquired the land they worked on via a Land Act Purchase agreement.

In the six counties of Northern Ireland, the revision book system continued until the 1930s. The Public Record Office of Northern Ireland (PRONI) has digitized the books, and they can be viewed free of charge online on a dedicated PRONI database <www.nidirect.gov.uk/services/searching-valuation-revision-books>.

For reasons lost to time, the revision books are called the cancelled books or cancelled land books in the Republic of Ireland. They are not online, and an in-house digitization project is progressing very slowly. The books can be viewed by in-person visitors only at the Valuation Office in the Irish Life Building in Dublin. A postal or e-mail research service is available for a fee <www.valoff.ie/en/Fees>.

Valuation Office Notebooks

Not to be confused with the revision/cancelled books, the Valuation Office books collection is a selection of notebooks used by Griffith's valuers as they went from townland to townland recording land features and buildings, measurements, ownership, names of occupiers, soil quality, etc. This fieldwork was then continued in the Valuation Office and translated into the format used in the published *Primary Valuation of Ireland*.

While most of the notebooks relate to preparatory Valuation work carried out in the 1840s, others were taken during unsuccessful attempts at uniform valuation in the 1830s and even the 1820s. Survival of all these Valuation Office books is inconsistent (as it is for so many Irish records), but the National Archives of Ireland (NAI)'s free Genealogy website <census.nationalarchives.ie/search/vob/home.jsp> has collected all extant books. Detailed descriptions of the books and the types of information they hold are provided on the site.

The collection holds more than two million names and consists of the following four types of notebooks:

- **Field books** recorded information about the size and quality of the soil of an individual holding.
- **House books** were compiled between 1830 and roughly 1844, recording the occupier's name and details of his living conditions, so you may find an earlier generation of your family recorded. Some even include sketches of the property, barns, and outbuildings.
- **Tenure books** recorded the legal basis of the property or land holding and the starting date of the lease/will, plus the annual rent paid. These date from 1844 only.
- **Quarto books** covered small and medium-sized towns from 1844.

Since the NAI's digitization project has been completed, more notebooks have been discovered and will eventually join the online collection.

TITHE APPLOTMENT BOOKS

Among Ireland's earliest land records are the Tithe Applotment Books, which record a tax levied to support the clergy in the state's Protestant Church of Ireland. The burden of payment fell mostly on the Roman Catholic peasantry, and it was, understandably, hugely unpopular. It was introduced in 1823 and suspended in 1838. Over this fifteen-year period, valuers went from parish to parish to determine how much each land occupier had to pay, calculated by the number of acres, the quality of land, and the types of crops produced. Their findings were written up in notebooks that became known as the Tithe Applotment Books (TABs).

The TABs are not as comprehensive as Griffith's Valuation because the Tithe was levied only on certain types of agricultural land. Urban dwellings were excluded, as were Church of Ireland holdings ("glebes") and land historically settled by monasteries ("granges"). Landless labourers obviously don't feature in these books, either. Estimates suggest 40 to 50 percent of total households do not appear.

Despite these limitations, you should consult the collection to place your family in a known location in the early decades of the nineteenth century. If your ancestors emigrated prior to the Great Famine of the late 1840s, this collection may be the only source that will identify your family's original home in Ireland. Those researchers who have

Nineteenth-Century Land and Money Values

Land measurements

Griffith's *Primary Valuation of Ireland* shows land measurements in English acres, roods, and poles (or perches):

- An English acre is 4,840 square yards.
- A rood is one-quarter of an acre (1,210 square yards); four roods make one acre.
- A pole (or perch) is one-fourtieth of a rood (30.25 square yards); forty poles make one rood.

Money

All monetary values in these land and property records used the currency circulating in Britain and Ireland in the nineteenth century, known as the pre-decimal British Sterling:

- The pound (£)
- The shilling (s), one-twentieth of a pound; twenty shillings equal one pound.
- The pence (d), one-twelfth of a shilling; 12 pence equals one shilling (240 pence makes one pound).

Money values using multiple units were written with a dash between each denomination; for example, £2-9-3d indicates two pounds, nine shillings, and three pence.

already found an ancestral connection in the later Griffith's Valuation collection should search the TABs for the same townland. This may reveal a different land occupier with the same surname, indicating a family connection, possibly father and son. Such a relationship may be endorsed by entries in local parish registers, if they survive for the period.

The NAI's online database <**titheapplotmentbooks.nationalarchives.ie**> is shared with FamilySearch.org <**www.familysearch.org/search/collection/1804886**>. Both cover all counties now in the Republic of Ireland, plus some cross-border areas in the north. (TABs for the six counties of Northern Ireland are not online as of this book's publication.)

The database is free, but it has serious shortcomings. Townland names (which weren't standardized until 1837) were inconsistent, so the books use various local names and spellings for them. Further, record-keepers often mis-transcribed names, resulting in two or three versions of one place name—and NAI's lack of a spelling-variant function in search means you'll have no way of easily combing these records. Some townlands have even been "attached" to the wrong parish, often many miles away. Those who know the townland and parish where their family lived can get around this by using the database's Browse function.

Offline, the islandwide records can be accessed on microfilm at the NAI in Dublin and also through Family History Centers. The original TAB notebooks for the six counties of Northern Ireland, plus a microfilm of TABs for all nine counties of Ulster, can be searched at PRONI in Belfast.

ESTATE RECORDS

During Ireland's turbulent sixteenth and seventeenth centuries, much of the land was confiscated from Roman Catholics and given to Protestant followers of the British Crown. This process created huge estates. Most of the new owners had no interest in managing the estates themselves, so they divided their land into small holdings and leased or rented them to tenants. Many of these tenants, in turn, divided up their land parcels and sublet them to smaller farmers. At the end of the chain, the plots could be so small that the tenants could barely eke out a living and would have to provide additional labor or other services to their immediate landlord.

The archives of such estates can be useful because the owners employed vast numbers of retainers—domestic staff, farm laborers, stonemasons, and other craftsmen—and kept records such as leases and rentals concerning their tenant farmers, as well as letters, reports, receipts, and maps. They can provide stunning details about the place where your ancestor lived and toiled.

They are, however, time-consuming to explore, requiring personal visits to the holding archive. In addition, they come with no guarantee that you'll find any mention of an ancestor. As such, estate records are usually of most interest to the more advanced researcher.

They can also be difficult to track down, as they are private records. Some collections remain in the archives of the estate owner's family; some have been deposited with solicitors. Substantial collections are available through the major repositories of the United Kingdom and Ireland, and an increasing number are being deposited in local archives and are slowly being cataloged. Others have not survived.

Once, you've identified your ancestor's landlord, find out where such records might be accessible. The NAI has a helpful overview at **<www.nationalarchives.ie/genealogy1/ genealogy-records/estate-records>**, and PRONI offers practical advice for exploring paper collections **<www.nidirect.gov.uk/sites/default/files/publications/08%20%20Landed%20 Estates.pdf>**. You should also consult the NLI's Sources catalog **<sources.nli.ie>**

Landed Estate Court Rentals

With the Great Famine starving Irish laborers or forcing them to emigrate, many landowners were left with mounting debts and little rental income. To help them dispose of these bankrupt estates, Parliament set up the Encumbered Estates Court in 1849 to administer the sale of the insolvent estates. Detailed sale catalogs were drawn up to attract prospective buyers, and some of these survive today.

Within these sale catalogs are details of the landlord's tenants, together with the value and terms of their lease agreements or rental commitments, precise locations and descriptions of the land parcels, and (in rare cases) personal details such as the extended family's emigration information, the tenant's health, or the size of the tenant's family.

The Landed Estate Court Rentals collection covers the entire island, with more than five hundred thousand tenants from the roughly eight thousand estates that had changed hands by 1877. It is online at Findmypast and can also be accessed at LDS Family History Centers.

REGISTRY OF DEEDS

The Registry of Deeds was established in 1708 and details deeds recording transfers of land, mortgages, marriage settlements, financial arrangements for illegitimate children, and transactions related to legal cases. About one million memorials of deeds were registered by 1835, the vast majority of them involving wealthy landlords, farming gentry, professionals, and merchants. While many deeds provide little (if any) genealogical information, others may supply family particulars for up to three generations.

Copies of signed deeds were created, witnessed, and legally verified, and these "memorials," as they were known, were then registered and bound into transcript books. Surname and land indexes were created of the transcript books, and these are now available for public inspection at the Registry of Deeds in Dublin. You can view grantor and land indexes from 1703 to 1929 on microfilm from the Family History Library, or search microfilms of memorials transcripts dating from 1708 to 1929 at PRONI and Family History Centers. A volunteer-led Registry of Deeds Index Project <irishdeedsindex.net> is the only online offer available to researchers. See a more detailed overview of this resource <www.johngrenham.com/browse/retrieve_text.php?text_contentid=89#Deeds>.

Note that, because of the Penal Laws restricting land ownership by Roman Catholics and (to a lesser extent) Presbyterians, nearly all those recorded in early deeds were adherents of the Church of Ireland. Of course, there were a small number of Roman Catholics who found a way around the rules, and certainly some non-Church of Ireland families climbed far enough up the social ladder to have register deeds recorded after the Penal Laws were relaxed. But these were very much the minority. For most of us descended from Roman Catholics who had little to sell or bequeath, the Registry of Deeds is not going to be a priority resource.

KEYS TO SUCCESS

- Invest time in gaining a deep understanding of Griffith's *Primary Valuation of Ireland* in order to extract every possible detail about your ancestor's townland and local neighborhood.

- Explore households with your ancestral surname in adjacent townlands. If the name is not too common, these households are probably related, and so further investigation may reveal more helpful details.

- Concentrate on Griffith's Valuation at the early part of your research before moving onto TABs and revision books. The notebooks, estate records, and landed estate court records can be saved for a later phase of research.

- Develop a strong sense of place for your ancestral homeland by bringing together land record details with historical information from gazetteers and directories and try to "walk the landscape" using some of the exceptionally detailed historical and modern maps now online (see chapter 5).

Printed Records

S tate and church organizations may have deliberately and formally created most of the records consulted by family historians, but a distinct group of incredibly useful genealogical material was created for very different reasons. Newspapers, trade directories, gazettes, and other printed sources can help fill in gaps between the official records, as well as provide leads for future research.

In this chapter, we'll be looking at what these sources offer, where to access them both in the United States and in Ireland, and how to take advantage of the rich detail they may hold.

NEWSPAPERS

Historical newspapers can help you gain an insight into the times and places your ancestors lived in. Reading between the lines of the international, national, and local news reports, you can understand the issues that affected and motivated them, and you can also discover much about the daily routines of their communities. They are also valuable sources of direct genealogical details.

For all this obvious value, newspapers were (until recently) a largely untapped source of family history research, mainly because they were just too unwieldy due to their size and lack of an index. Researchers could spend hours and days poring through bulky volumes of broadsheet editions or whirring through reel after reel of microfilmed copies. Digitization has largely overcome these hurdles, with genealogists able to access entire decades of publications with relative ease. However, many titles have yet to make their way online and may still be worth tracking down through local and county libraries.

Stateside Resources

The most obvious genealogical value of newspapers is in its collection of obituaries, funeral notices, and various announcements: births, engagements, marriages, deaths. But the careful researcher can find much, much more within their pages, especially in the pages of smaller community-oriented papers where the joys and tribulations of the local residents are the editor's prime focus.

These smaller-circulation newspapers often published "society news," short notices recording visits by residents to a place in Ireland where they had a connection, or to extended family elsewhere in the United States. These names and locations may be priceless clues. Journalists on these papers also reported accidents, crimes, elections to local committees and societies, church and school events, neighborhood events, job appointments and promotions, divorces, bankruptcies, probate, letters to the editor ... almost anything that happened within the distribution area was considered noteworthy.

The newspapers most likely to yield fruit for Irish researchers fall into three categories:

- **nineteenth-century newspapers for Irish immigrants:** The names of these publications usually clearly identify their target audience (e.g., *Kentucky Irish American*; image **A**).

- **Catholic titles:** These had significant circulations among the Irish and their descendants. Most of these niche or ethnic papers were published in New York City and Boston, and many were short-lived. Those that bucked this trend were *The Pilot* or *Boston Pilot*, 1829–present (see Missing Friends/Information Wanted Advertisements sidebar); *New York Freeman's Journal and Catholic Register*, 1840–1918; *Irish American*, 1849–1915; *Irish World and American Industrial Liberator*, 1878–1944; *The Chicago Citizen*, 1882–1928; and *Kentucky Irish American*, 1898–1968.

- **local general-interest papers:** These may not have specifically targeted the Irish reader, but were published in areas with large Irish populations. The *Brooklyn Daily Ledger* and *New York Herald* are among many that fall into this group.

A bibliography of all US newspapers can be found at Chronicling America <chroniclingamerica.loc.gov>, a joint project of the Library of Congress and the National Endowment for the Humanities. Its database holds not only the names and dates of publication for the newspapers, but also guides to the repositories where all or parts of

A

RECENT DEATHS.

The sad intelligence has been received in this city of the death of Dennis Hines, which occurred at his home in Kil, parish of Drom, County Tipperary, Ireland, on July 10. Mr. Hines was eighty years old and a farmer by occupation. He leaves a son and daughter in Ireland and a son and daughter in Louisville, Thomas Hines, of the Courier-Journal, and Mrs. Michael Barry.

Daniel R. McCarthy, a respected citizen, died at the residence of his niece, Mrs. Thomas McGuire, 3118 Fourth avenue, last Wednesday evening. The funeral took place from the Church of the Holy Name at 9 o'clock Thursday morning. The deceased was a brother of Dennis McCarthy, the well known marble cutter, and had many friends in this city.

Mrs. Sarah Lee O'Connell, a well known lady, died at her home, 126 Bullitt street, on Tuesday evening. The funeral took place from the Cathedral of the Assumption at 9 o'clock yesterday morning. Mrs. O'Connell was born in the County Galway, Ireland, sixty-eight years ago. She is survived by her husband, Andrew O'Connell, and two children, Dominic O'Connell and Mrs. John F. Gilhooley.

Like many newspapers targeting the Irish community, the *Kentucky Irish American* published death notices that often held detailed genealogical information, including a place of origin.

the paper's run may be accessed in paper format or on microfilm. Another database that tracks newspaper digitization projects is hosted by the University of Pennsylvania's library <libraries.psu.edu/about/departments/preservation-conservation-and-digitization/pa-newspaper-project/free-historic>.

Several subscription-based online collections of Irish-American, local, regional, state, and national newspapers are now available to researchers. Among the best are:

- GenealogyBank.com <www.genealogybank.com>: Gives access to eight Irish-American titles dating from 1810 to today, in addition to more than seven thousand fully searchable county, city, and community papers from all fifty states (1690–2010).

- Newspapers.com <www.newspapers.com>: A sister company to Ancestry.com that holds more than 4,300 mostly US papers (but also some Canadian and Irish papers), spanning 1700 to present.

- NewspaperArchive.com <www.newspaperarchive.com>: Contains some eight thousand titles, spanning 1753 to present.

- Ancestry.com <www.ancestry.com>: Regular US collection package includes about 1,400 titles spanning

Missing Friends/Information Wanted Advertisements

Many Irish-American papers published advertisements placed by people looking for immigrant friends and relatives with whom they had lost contact. Some carried succinct but heartbreaking tales of women with several mouths to feed reaching out for news—any news—of their husbands who had left Ireland in search of work to support their families, or orphaned youngsters arriving in America with no means of support who were hoping to find older siblings, aunts, or uncles who had immigrated years before. The lives behind the placing of some of the advertisements would have been in turmoil, while others may have been motivated by the possibility of recovering a debt or chattels.

Whatever the original motive behind the placements, the Information Wanted columns continue to help families find their relatives. Each advert typically refers to the town or townland of origin of the seeker and/or the "lost" immigrant. In just a few column lines, the details may also include the route taken by the immigrant, including the name of the ship, known employment, or temporary places of residence.

More than forty-five thousand of these advertisements were transcribed and published in the multi-volume *Searching for Missing Friends: Irish Immigrant Advertisements Placed in "The Boston Pilot" 1831-1920*, edited by Ruth-Ann Harris, Donald M. Jacobs, and B. Emer O'Keeffe (New England Historic Genealogical Society, 1989). The publication is available in major reference libraries and can be searched or for free at the NEHGS website **<www.americanancestors.org>**.

The *New York Irish American* also published significant numbers of these classified ads. It can be accessed at both GenealogyBank and Ancestry.com.

---

60   *Missing Friends*

Of GEORGE DUFFY, who left St. John, N. B. in August, 1841, and when last heard from lived with the Doctor of the Naval Hospital Chelsea. Any information respecting him will be thankfully received by his father, Patrick Duffy, of Portland, St. John, N. B.

Of MARTIN DYER, a native of the parish of Killoran, co. Sligo, Ireland, who left his wife in St. John, N. B., about 13 months ago, and came to Providence, R. I. and stopped about 6 months. When last heard from was on the York and Erie Rail-road. Any information respecting him will be thankfully received by his wife, who is now in Providence, R. I.

5 November 1842   *INFORMATION WANTED*

Of JOHN HEALY, of Ballywiniter, Parish of Mallow, county Cork, when last heard of was in Albany, N. Y. Any information respecting him will be thankfully received by his sister, Johannah Healy, care Rev. Mr. O'Sullivan, Bangor, Me.

If you're lucky, you can find your ancestor listed in the Missing Friends or Information Wanted sections of an Irish-American newspaper.

the last four centuries, while its All Access subscription additionally includes the basic Newspapers.com collection.

While each of these commercial online newspaper databases delivers an outstanding amount of research material to family historians, you need to choose wisely to avoid an expensive mistake. Make sure the site has publications for the area you're interested in, and for the time frame you're researching. Some have only a short run of editions for some of the titles in their database, while others may have significant gaps between editions. Spend time exploring the details of each database's holdings. If you're still unsure, take them up on their free trial offers—they all have one.

Also make sure you exhaust the growing number of opportunities to explore newspaper databases free of charge. Ancestry.com's collection is free at any county public library, and many city or county libraries also hold their own, more localized newspaper databases and have microfilm collections. Another trend in recent years is for state historical societies to partner with local universities to digitize their newspaper holdings and place them online. Some examples include North Carolina Newspapers <www.digitalnc.org/collections/newspapers>, Nebraska Newspapers <nebnewspapers.unl.edu>, and Utah Digital Newspapers <digitalnewspapers.org>.

The online *Your Guide to Using Newspapers for Genealogical Research* <www.barbsnow.net/Newspapers.htm> contains links to articles and a list of books about newspaper research, links to digitized historical newspapers (both free and fee-based), and useful tips on finding offline publications. Cyndi's List <www.cyndislist.com/newspapers/general> also has lists of online newspapers.

Irish Resources

Irish newspapers date to the 1650s, but they did not publish any reports of genealogical relevance until *Faulkner's Dublin Journal* (1725), *Belfast Newsletter* (1737), and the *Freeman's Journal* (1763) were launched. Other cities and provincial towns started publishing somewhat later: *Corke Journal* (1765), *Limerick Chronicle* (1768), and *Londonderry Journal* (1772). These earliest papers tended to concentrate on national and international news with just a sprinkling of birth, marriage, and death announcements—nearly always limited to the aristocracy and land-owning gentry.

Newspaper publishing didn't spread to market towns and start reporting events and concerns from their circulation area until the very late 1700s and early 1800s. Initially, these reports were confined to the lives and deaths of the local gentry and the merchant and middle classes. But with literacy rates in Ireland growing dramatically from the 1840s, even those lower down the social ladder began to be represented in the birth, marriage, and death announcement columns. As the century progressed, editors filled more and more of their publications with news from their local communities, and these pages can tell you about your ancestor's involvement with social, financial, or church committees; business success; bankruptcy or brush with the law; sporting prowess, or ownership of the community's prize heifer.

Irish newspapers contain a wealth of genealogical information that varies depending on the type of features the newspaper published. The most useful include biographical notices, local civil authority meetings, court reports, and advertisements.

BIOGRAPHICAL NOTICES

Up to the mid-nineteenth century, birth, marriage, and death announcements tended to be reserved for social elites. Birth notices generally provided little detail beyond date, name of the father, and the gender of the child. Marriages and death notices were usually more informative. The former typically stated the names of the bride and groom and the name and residence of the bride's father (only rarely was the groom's father noted), while obituaries provided name, address, occupation, and date of death, sometimes adding praises of the deceased's character or a list of his achievements. In the second half of the century, the number of these announcements increased considerably and covered a much wider spectrum of society. Notices of deaths began to add funeral details, which can be a useful guide to finding headstones or cemetery records.

LOCAL CIVIL AUTHORITY ASSOCIATION MEETINGS

The minutes of the Board of Guardians or town commissioners were published in papers after every meeting and always listed those in attendance. Some of the later records even include verbatim reports of discussions. Summaries of the meetings held by local groups, such as sports and credit associations and the local port authority, were also regularly published along with the names of their officials.

COURT REPORTS

Rich with detail, reports from the Coroner's Court, the Petty Sessions Court, and the regular assizes (courts for more serious crimes) can add depth and color to a family history. Whether the subject of the court proceedings was a witness, defendant, or victim, the reports record a good range of personal information: name, residence, age, occupation, appearance, and relationships to others involved in the case.

ADVERTISEMENTS

Although most advertisements were designed to promote goods and services, some could better be described as announcements. They covered a range. Perhaps the most numerous were of a business nature, such as a change of address, a sale to a new owner, or the liquidation of stock following the death of the proprietor. Other notices reported personal or business bankruptcies, offered rewards for the return of lost or stolen property, or allowed husbands to publicly relinquish responsibility for the future debts of their wives.

B

The Dublin-based Irish Newspaper Archives offers more than sixty national, regional, and county titles spanning from 1738 to today. The database is available via subscription but is free to access at most libraries in Ireland.

Major online collections of historical Irish newspapers can be accessed at Irish Newspaper Archives <www.irishnewsarchive.com> (image **B**) and the British Newspaper Archive <www.britishnewspaperarchive.co.uk>. The latter database, which holds hundreds of British and Irish publications, is also available at Findmypast <www.findmypast.ie>. Ancestry.com has a browse-only collection of roughly thirty Irish newspapers spanning 1763 to 1890.

Ireland's "newspaper of record" is *The Irish Times*. It has the single most extensive online archive <www.irishtimes.com/archive> dating from the paper's launch in 1859; although a subscription is usually required, full and free access is available through any public library in the Republic of Ireland.

The NLI Newspaper Database <www.nli.ie/en/catalogues-and-databases-printed-newspapers.aspx> is the largest collection of newspapers on microfilm, but many county libraries and archives in Ireland also have significant holdings for their own region. The Public Record Office of Northern Ireland (PRONI) also has a sizeable microfilm collection <www.nidirect.gov.uk/sites/default/files/publications/newspapers-on-microfilm.pdf>.

Researchers with ancestral connections to northern counties should also check out *Eddies Extracts* <freepages.genealogy.rootsweb.ancestry.com/~econnolly>, a free-to-search database holding births, marriages, and death reports from the *Belfast Newsletter*, *Banner of Ulster*, *The Witness*, *Belfast Weekly News*, the *Northern Whig*, and many more regional titles. The collection also contains court and inquest reports, subscriptions lists, and other items of general historic and social interest. The earliest transcriptions date from 1825.

DIRECTORIES

The loss of almost all of Ireland's nineteenth-century censuses has created important subsets of printed Irish material that are more important than their publishers might ever have imagined.

RESEARCH TIP

Check the Date of Publication of Directories

Printed publications take time to make. As a result, every entry in a trades or street directory is at least six months out of date by the time of publication, so take that into account as you're researching your Irish ancestors in them.

Irish trade, postal, and local directories fall into this category. They performed a similar function to telephone directories before the Internet took over, providing point-in-time information about residents in a given area, and details of the goods and services available to them locally. The oldest directories that covered cities and larger towns may also have street-by-street listings of heads of households.

Directories (like *Slater's Directory*, image **C**) supply facts that are not always available or easy to find elsewhere. They are often the only source that states an ancestor's precise

C

The 1881 edition of *Slater's Directory* for Kanturk in the north of County Cork reveals the names and addresses of local nobility, corn merchants, school masters, grocers, bakers, and much more.

From the City to the Small Market Towns

Initially, trade directories focused only on the named city. The first was *Wilson's Dublin Directory*, which was published in 1751. *Pettigrew and Oulton's Dublin Almanac* (1834) was the next iteration, and it had street-by-street listings of heads of households that extended into the growing suburbs with each subsequent edition. Finally, the well-regarded *Thom's Directory*, which is still published, arrived on the capital's scene in 1844.

It wasn't until later that directories began to move significantly beyond city limits. The first provincial directory was John Ferrar's *Limerick Directory*, which was launched in 1769, and the second was Richard Lucas's *Cork Directory in 1787*. You can download it from **<www.limerickcity.ie/Library/LocalStudies/TradesStreetDirectories1769-1976>**.

But it was *Pigot's Commercial Directory of Ireland*, first published in 1820 and again four years later, that extended the coverage beyond the cities to include similar treatments of county towns and small rural towns, and included descriptions of these places for the first time. This formula was reprised by *Slater's Directory*, which ran through five editions from 1846 to 1894 and arranged its data by province and, alphabetically, by town. The nobility, gentry, and clergy are listed for every city and post/market town, along with separate lists of professionals and tradesmen, with their occupations listed.

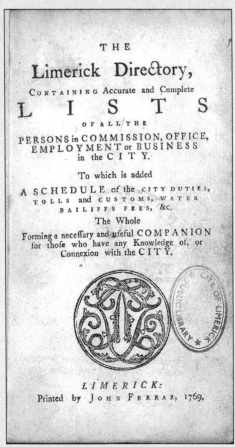

THE
Limerick Directory,

CONTAINING Accurate and Complete

L I S T S

OF ALL THE

PERSONS in COMMISSION, OFFICE, EMPLOYMENT or BUSINESS in the C I T Y.

To which is added

A SCHEDULE of the CITY DUTIES, TOLLS and CUSTOMS, WATER BAILIFFS FEES, &c.

The Whole

Forming a necessary and useful COMPANION for those who have any Knowledge of, or Connexion with the C I T Y.

L I M E R I C K:
Printed by JOHN FERRAR, 1769.

John Ferrar's published Ireland's first provincial directory in 1769. It is free to download at Limerick Library's Local Studies website.

occupation; someone loosely described in other documents as a merchant, for example, may be revealed through a directory to be a linen, wine, or timber merchant. Exact addresses are usually printed, too, making them very useful for family historians seeking residential details of ancestors in the pre-1901 census era. They also record the lives of people who were born and/or died before civil registration began.

Beyond the genealogical data they hold, directories deliver a lot of factual information regarding the day-to-day routines of an urban area at a certain period in time. Among the data typically printed in their pages:

- the post and coach arrival and departure timetables (and costs)
- the names and residences of local government and church officials
- dates of festivals, markets, and fairs
- the position of the planets and the time of tides

Here, you may be able to find out which school your ancestor attended—and even the name of the teacher. You could also learn the names and addresses of the local magistrates, bank managers, postmasters, clergymen, blacksmiths, boot menders, bakers, milliners, tallow chandlers, and egg dealers. Depending on how the directory is laid out, you may also be able to find out who lived on the same street.

On the downside, the poorest members of society—the landless laborers, small tenant farmers, factory workers, servants, and tenement dwellers—do not appear in directories. Nor do those who lived and worked outside urban areas.

Offline, the NLI <www.nli.ie/en/family-history-directories.aspx> and the Dublin City Library and Archive <www.dublincity.ie/dublin-city-library-archive> hold the best and most accessible collections of directories. County libraries and their local studies departments usually have strong local directory collections on their shelves, too. But for those unable to visit in person, many directories are now available online. An indispensable finding aid is the free Directories Database <swilson.info/dirdb.php>, which links to more than one thousand online copies of directories published between 1763 and 1986. Some are available for a fee; some are free.

For directories focused on Counties Antrim, Armagh, Down, Fermanagh, Londonderry, and Tyrone, PRONI has a strong but not quite complete collection covering the years 1819 to 1900. This has been digitized and is free to search online at PRONI's Street Directories database <nidirect.gov.uk/services/search-street-directories>. See the From the City to the Small Market Towns sidebar for more directories.

D

Numb 18,942   1073

The Dublin Gazette.

Published by Authority.

TUESDAY, SEPTEMBER 5, 1893.

The Dublin Gazette was issued from Dublin Castle from 1706 to 1921.

E

1076   THE DUBLIN GAZETTE, SEPTEMBER 5, 1893.

Post Office, Harold Edward Gibbings, Walter Blomfield Gregg, George Herbert Thornbury, Ernest Edwin Were, and Frederick George Williams.

Registrar-General's Office (Ireland), Robert Austin Cammack.

War Office, John Henry Owen.

Boy Clerks.

Charity Commission, Lionel John Budge.

Inland Revenue, Arthur Hall and Alfred Ernest Torbell (otherwise Lawrence).

National Education Office (Ireland), Henry Barrass Bell, Henry Patrick Boland, Richard Cronin, Andrew Taylor Emerson, William James Hadden, Nehemiah Stanley Harvey, George Huband, Patrick Hughes, Allan Gurwood McDonald, John Charles Mathews, Thomas Mellefont Steele, James Daniel Weir, and Francis Robert Alexander West.

Post Office, John Bernard Carroll (otherwise Hanlon), William Alfred Grant, Alfred Petrie Hunter, and Timothy Santry.

TRANSFERS, with the approval of the Lords Commissioners of Her Majesty's Treasury :—

Post Office, John Duncan, Clerk of the Second Division, from the Registrar-General's Office (Ireland).

War Office, Stanley Woodward, Clerk of the Second Division, from the Post Office.

Foreign Office, August 31, 1893.

The Earl of Rosebery, K.G., Her Majesty's Secretary of State for Foreign Affairs, has received a Despatch from Her Majesty's Representative at Belgrade, stating that the Servian Government have issued a Notice to the effect that, on and after the 15th of September next, all Travellers entering Servia from Austria-Hungary must produce their passports for the inspection of the Servian Authorities.

Fifteen-year-old Timothy Santry's appointment to the post office as a boy clerk was reported in both *The Dublin Gazette* and *The London Gazette*, as were his later promotions.

GAZETTES

Similar to newspapers, gazettes were originally published by the government's authority. *The London Gazette* was the first in Great Britain, and appeared in 1665. Many notices relating to Ireland were published in it, but in 1706, a distinct *Dublin Gazette* (image **D**) was established. This was issued from Dublin Castle published monthly until 1921.

While a state publication, *The Dublin Gazette* has earlier issues that are surprisingly full of genealogical information, with thousands of names recorded: its official announcements; news of appointments and promotions within the army, navy, and civil service; dissolved business partnerships, bankruptcies, and forced sales of land owned by debtors; reports

Hue and Cry:
The Police Gazette of the Royal Irish Constabulary

Better known as the *Hue and Cry*, Ireland's *Police Gazette* was published in Dublin on Tuesdays and Fridays by Alexander Thom & Co. from 1837. It was the official publication of the Royal Irish Constabulary (RIC) and was circulated to every police station across the island. It contains notices and reports of felonies committed and rewards for wanted felons from the thirty-two counties of Ireland, as well as the names and descriptions of army deserters, youngsters who had absconded from reformatories, wanted criminals, and habitual criminals newly released from prison under police supervision. In some cases, victims of the crimes are also referenced.

With so many names and descriptions, the *Hue and Cry* can be an invaluable source for the Irish genealogist. Identifying an ancestor in its pages can be illuminating, as the personal descriptions are fulsome and often include details of places associated with the individual. The following example, issued by the RIC in Killarney, County Kerry on 26 June 1863, shows this:

"Description of Daniel Philip Sullivan and Denis Sullivan, natives of Tiernaboul (Kerry), who stand charges with having, on the 13th day of June 1863, in the barony of Magunihy, parish of Killarney, violently assaulted Jeremiah Sullivan by striking him on the head with a spade: -

1. 20 years of age, 5 feet 5 inches high, slight make, fair complexion, thick face, blue eyes, long nose, fair hair; wore a dark cap, frieze coat, cord trowsers, blue vest. This man is still in the neighbourhood, but it is possible he may endeavour to start for America.

2. 52 years of age, 5 feet 6 inches high, slight make, pale complexion, thick face, blue eyes; wore a felt hat, frieze coat, knee breeches, blue vest."

A thirty-two-year span of issues (1863–1893) carrying some 150,000 indexed entries is available to search or browse at Ancestry.com. The NLI's holding of *Hue and Cry* runs from 1837 to 1917, with some gaps, and can be viewed by in-person appointment only.

from criminal and civil court cases; notices of rewards for felons and army deserters; and, in some eighteenth-century editions, even some notices of marriages, births, and deaths.

Unfortunately, *The Dublin Gazette* lost much of its local color after 1776, having been ordered by the government to concentrate on official announcements. It remains a useful source for genealogists, however. In my own family research, I was delighted to learn through the May 1893 edition that my then fifteen-year-old paternal grandfather—the son of an illiterate egg-dealer in Clonakilty, County Cork—had gained the second highest marks in that spring's civil service examination in Dublin. His subsequent first civil service appointment as a boy clerk in the post office was reported in both *The Dublin Gazette* (image **E**) and *The London Gazette* the following September, a reminder that items were often duplicated in these editions; if you cannot readily access the Dublin edition, you should certainly check out the free online London edition (see below).

After the partition of the island, the *Dublin Gazette* ceased publication and was replaced in 1922 by *Iris Oifigiúil* (Irish Official Journal), which is published free online <www.irisoifigiuil.ie>, while the *Belfast Gazette* was established in 1921 to serve the six counties of Northern Ireland. The Belfast, London and Edinburgh gazettes can be freely searched, via the All Notices tab, on one single website <www.thegazette.co.uk>.

A single complete online source for *The Dublin Gazette* does not exist. The largest free collection runs from 1750 to 1809 (inclusive) and can be downloaded from the Library of the Oireachtas (Irish Parliament) <opac.oireachtas.ie/liberty/libraryHome.do>. A word of warning: The searchable files are huge at 1–3GB each. The largest commercial collection can be searched at Newspaper Archive <newspaperarchive.com>, which holds forty-four editions from 1706 to 1908.

Offline, the NLI has a complete hardcopy run of *The Dublin Gazette* from 1708 to 1922, and microfilm copies from 1706 to 1780.

BOOKS, JOURNALS, AND ARTICLES

It used to be the case that only upper- and middle-class families were considered worthy of historical and genealogical study, and the shelves of many libraries are filled with books and journals recording their lives. *Burke's Peerage* <www.burkespeerage.com> and its sister titles should be a first port of call for sources on the aristocratic and gentry, while biographies of historical or cultural figures, regardless of their backgrounds, are generally easy to identify by a name search on Google <www.google.com> (or other search engines) and Wikipedia <www.wikipedia.org>.

For the lives of the less privileged and less exceptional families and individuals, genealogists have to dig a little deeper. For a lucky few, the effort will be well rewarded, perhaps with a fully documented pedigree or an account of the family or the ancestral

Create Your Own Library

Many books about the arrival of the Irish in North America can help you build up a good understanding of the Irish immigrants' experiences and provide context for your research. Some tell a history over several centuries, while others narrow down to a shorter time period or to certain groups of Irish immigrant (e.g., Protestants, women, or geographic areas of major settlement). Some examples include:

- *Emigrants and Exiles: Ireland and the Irish Exodus to North America* by Kerby A. Miller (Oxford University Press, 1988): Covers more than three hundred years of westward voyages from Ireland

- *Irish Immigrants in the Land of Canaan: Letters and Memoirs from Colonial and Revolutionary America, 1675-1815*, edited by Kerby A. Miller, Arnold Schrier, Bruce D. Boling and David N. Doyle (Oxford University Press, 2003): A specialized work on early Irish Protestant and Catholic migration to America

- *Mission of Our Lady of the Rosary for the Protection of Irish Immigrant Girls* by the New York Mission (Lauter and Lauterjung, 1900): Shares the history and successes of this New York Mission that cared for vulnerable young girl immigrants when they first arrived in the city.

- *The New York Irish*, edited by Ronald H. Bayor and Timothy J. Meagher (Johns Hopkins University Press, 1997): Collection of essays that tackles many aspects of life for the Irish in New York, from colonial times to the early 1990s

When narrowing down your ancestral research to specific US regions and cities, be sure to check out the thirty-plus Irish-themed books (many of them photographic histories) published by Arcadia Publishing **<www.arcadiapublishing.com>**. If you know the Irish city or county in which your ancestors lived, you'll also find the range of local history books and *Ireland in Old Photographs* series from The History Press **<thehistorypress.ie>**.

Researchers with connections to the north of Ireland might also seek out the *Ordnance Survey Memoirs of Ireland 1830-1840*, a forty-volume series published by the Institute of Irish Studies at Queen's University Belfast. These "memoirs" were intended to accompany the first detailed maps of Ireland, and here surveyors recorded not only the landscape but also buildings and antiquities, land-holdings and population, employment opportunities, traditions and superstitions, and all manner of characteristics and features of the villages and towns they visited. The project was discontinued before even half of the island had been surveyed, but the forty volumes (plus a modern index of people and place names) cover the seven counties of Ulster plus Counties Leitrim, Louth, and Sligo. Each volume covers a distinct area. The range is available from the Ulster Historical Foundation **<www.booksireland.org.uk/store/ordnance-survey-memoirs>**.

home at a particular period of time. Some of these may have been published as books or as articles for genealogical and local history journals.

Two excellent listings of such books and articles are *Bibliography of Irish Family History* by Edward MacLysaght (Irish Academic Press, 1982) and *Sources for Irish Family History* by James G. Ryan (Flyleaf Press, 1997).

Google Books **<books.google.com>**, the Internet Archive **<www.archive.org>**, and the NLI's *Sources* catalogue **<sources.nli.ie>** can help you identify unique publications, many of them out of print. Another useful source of free publications is Peter J. Clarke's Free Irish Genealogy eBooks site **<freeirishgenebooks.blogspot.co.uk>**, which has links to more than four thousand books and journals. The Family History Library also has many collections of Irish pedigrees and other genealogical material for Irish families and communities, as well as periodicals, books, and manuscripts. Explore the Catalog online **<www.familysearch.org/catalog/search >** by searching by place for Ireland (or a relevant place name), then looking under the Genealogy and Periodicals headings.

In addition to published histories or genealogies of specific families, a huge number of genealogical articles have been published by the many genealogical and historical societies in North America and Ireland. These features often include helpful advice for locating or using certain types of records, transcripts of passenger records and headstone inscriptions, and information about the services available in local archives. While some of these

RESEARCH TIP

Search More Broadly

When searching for published family histories or clues to your ancestors' lives, don't restrict your searches to your family surnames. Instead, look also for community, town, city, and ethnic histories in the areas they may once have called home. While your family may not be specifically named in such publications, you may learn a lot about their lives and the backgrounds of the people they lived among.

publications may be found in major genealogical libraries, most are only available from the society or organization itself.

The Periodical Source Index, known as PERSI, may be able to help you locate these publications. It holds more than 2.5 million entries from thousands of historical, genealogical, and ethnic publications, detailing articles, photos, and other material from the United States, Canada, Ireland, Britain, and Australia. The subject matter covers a wide range, from biography to naturalization records and from institutions to wills. An important function of such a large index is that it helps the researcher find material relating to locations distinct from the periodical in which they appear.

PERSI can be searched, free of charge, at Findmypast **<www.findmypast.com>**. As it is an index, it provides detail about the material—title and date, along with a description— but does not have the full article or image. However, Findmypast is working with the Federation of Genealogical Societies **<www.fgs.org>** to make the digital images available.

In the meantime, if the article you are interested in is not linked to the PERSI database, you can contact the publisher to find out how you might access the material (photocopies, digital issues, hard copies, etc.). Or you could search your local library's online catalog or WorldCat **<www.worldcat.org>**; the latter will generate a list of libraries that may hold the publication. Alternatively, you can order a copy of a PERSI periodical article via the Allen County Public Library's Genealogy Centre by completing an Article Request Form **<genealogycenter.org/docs/default-source/resources/articlerequest.pdf>**.

KEYS TO SUCCESS

Widen your search to newspapers published beyond the town or area where your ancestor settled. News stories—particularly obituaries—were often picked up by other titles when they had a connection to a former resident or employer.

Carefully record all your newspaper and printed sources searches. It's easy to lose track and find yourself covering over old ground.

Be flexible with name spellings when searching online indexes to printed sources. A woman may be referred to by the name of her husband (e.g., *Mrs. Patrick Ryan* for a married woman named Meghan Ryan) in obituaries or news stories, and people were often referred to by initials, abbreviations, and nicknames (e.g., *Jim, Jimmy,* or *Jas* rather than "James").

Persevere with large online catalogs of publications. They can be daunting at first, but once you become familiar with each one's idiosyncrasies, you'll find them highly efficient at hunting down the journals, books, and papers you want to locate.

12

Probate, Law & Order, Military, and Occupation Records

While earlier chapters of this guide have concentrated on single groups of records, this chapter is going to point you towards a wide range of material: probate, law and order, military, and occupational records. In each case, these collections may hold crucial genealogical information that can cast your research in a different light, or even simply add color to your family's story.

What they all have in common, however, is that they are not likely to be collections you can consult at an early stage of your research. In the majority of cases, you won't make much progress if you don't already have sufficient information to identify your ancestor from another person of the same name. But if you do have such detail *and* you find a candidate in these record sets, you may well stumble across a pot of gold.

PROBATE RECORDS

Testamentary records—whether a will or the administration of an estate—are most immediately useful for the details they can provide about an individual's immediate family: personal and business relationships, property specifications, and information about wealth. But these records can also provide information about extended family, such as the married names of sisters or daughters, or the addresses of relatives who had emigrated. They are also, apart from diaries, one of the few documents in which genealogists may learn about an ancestor's deepest feelings about his or her relatives and friends.

While discovering a will may well reward you with glorious detail, you'll face two unfortunate truths about pursuing testamentary records. Firstly, people who had no assets did not have to worry themselves about the ultimate disposal of their belongings, so most pre-twentieth-century probate records relate to landed families, made up of the professional classes and successful merchants. The second drawback is that the majority of Ireland's original testamentary records were destroyed in the 1922 fire at the Public Record Office (PRO) in Dublin.

From the fifteenth century to 1858, Irish probate records were under the jurisdiction of the Church of Ireland, specifically the church's Prerogative Court and the diocesan (or consistorial) courts. In most cases, the local diocesan court dealt with testamentary matters concerning its residents, granting probate of their wills or issuing letters of administration on the estates of those who died intestate (see The Probate Process sidebar). However, if the deceased's property had a value of more than five pounds in a second diocese, the will was sent to the Prerogative Court to be proved or to be assigned a grant of administration.

While this arrangement means that Prerogative wills are often those of the wealthiest individuals, it isn't exclusively so. It was also possible for the will of a small farmer with land on both sides of a diocesan border to require processing through the higher court, which was based in Dublin.

After 1858, responsibility for processing wills transferred to a new civil Court of Probate, which had a principal registry in Dublin and eleven district registries around the island. The wills previously filed with the diocesan courts were sent for safekeeping to the PRO in Dublin, where they were transcribed into Will Books. Indexes were then made to accompany these books, in alphabetical order of testator's name (image **A**).

The Probate Process

If an individual left a will setting out clear instructions for the disposal of their property and assets (their estate) to named beneficiaries, he or she is described as having died **testate**. In such circumstances, the court would confirm the process through legal documentation known as grants of probate.

When someone died without leaving a will, the deceased was described as having died **intestate**. An inventory of his or her property and assets would be prepared (usually by a relative) and put before the court, which would then decide on how the estate would be divided. In practice, the court would allow a relative to deal with the estate. The resulting legal documentation produced by the court would be known as "letters of administration."

From the will book for Cork District: An unusually short and simple will from Mary Flaherty dated February 27, 1890, in which she bequeaths to her brother Lawrence and sister Margaret "all the money or other property I possess for their use and benefit."

Access to Probate Records

As mentioned above, almost all of the original and register copies of will proved prior to 1900 were destroyed in the PRO Fire of 1922. Archives, historical societies, and the genealogical community have made huge efforts to unearth copies of the lost documents and either take them into safe custody or publish them for posterity. Estimates suggest about one-third of these wills have now been recovered, but this still leaves a gaping hole in the range of probate records available to family historians.

All the original manuscript calendars/indexes to the wills proved in the diocesan courts survived the 1922 fire, with only a few suffering damage. They are held at the National Archives of Ireland (NAI) and Public Record Office of Northern Ireland (PRONI), together with a few will and grant books and other manuscripts of the Prerogative Courts. Indeed, apart from those in private hands, nearly all probate records for the island of Ireland are held in just those two repositories. PRONI has a free online index to its surviving pre-1858 records <www.nidirect.gov.uk/services/search-name-search>, plus a database of wills calendar indexes and digitized will books (1858–1965) for grants of probate and letters of administration processed by the District Probate Registries of Armagh, Belfast, and Londonderry <www.nidirect.gov.uk/services/search-will-calendars> (image **B**). See the National Archives of Ireland Will Holdings sidebar for the collections NAI has made available online.

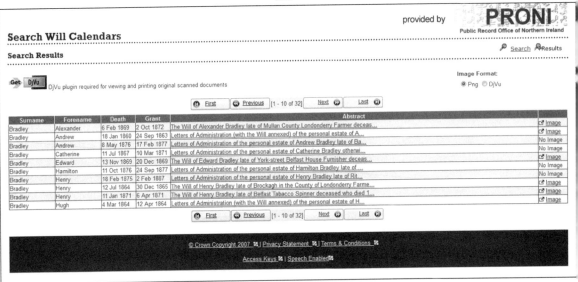

The Public Record Office of Northern Ireland (PRONI)'s wills calendar database includes index-only details from calendars as well as copies of will books processed by the district probate registries of Armagh, Belfast, and Londonderry.

Notably, Findmypast <www.findmypast.ie> has an Irish Wills Index that catalogs surviving documents held by the NAI (1484–1858): original wills, letters of administration or grants of probate, certified copies of original records, or transcripts or partial transcripts (e.g., an abstract) of records that genealogists transcribed before the wills were destroyed.

You can also search a small number of additional records for a fee on the (UK) National Archives' website <www.nationalarchives.gov.uk/help-with-your-research/research-guides/wills-1384-1858>; these relate to the wills of Irish people who died before 1858 and held property in England, which may have been proved in the Prerogative Court of Canterbury.

RESEARCH TIP

Choose the Superior Viewing Experience

Most, but not all, probate records for counties now in the Republic of Ireland are available free of charge on both the NAI's Genealogy site and on Findmypast. You need only to register with Findmypast to access the records without charge, and you'll find its view-and-maneuver options far superior to those offered by the NAI.

National Archives of Ireland Will Holdings

The NAI is one of the two major institutions to hold Irish will records. Check out these resources, some of which can also be found for a fee at Findmypast:

- **Diocesan and Prerogative Wills Indexes, 1595–1858:** These handwritten indexes and will books are arranged by diocese, and some are in a very poor and damaged state. Although the majority of records in this collection are indexes, will books compiled at the time the will was proved make up a small percentage of these records. A listing in these indexes does not mean the will has survived; you'll have to cross reference with the Irish Wills Index, available on Findmypast, to determine if the record still exists. Most of the surviving original records for the Republic are held by the NAI and digitized copies are online, free, at both NAI Genealogy site and Findmypast. (Note: The will books for Armagh, Belfast, and Londonderry are held by PRONI and are not online.)

- **Original Will Registers, 1858–1920:** The only will books lost in the 1922 fire were those for the principal registry based in Dublin and the Dublin district registry. All the other will books were held by the remaining district registries and survived, with only a few casualties. The books contain transcripts of each will, the wording of the grant, the date of transcription, and the date of the death of the testator.

- **Calendars of Wills and Administration, 1858–1920, 1922–1982:** This collection holds the calendars for all thirty-two historical counties of Ireland and, for 1918 to 1920, the calendars for the twenty-six counties of the Republic of Ireland. The more recent calendars (one per year from 1922) are incorporated into the main catalog of the NAI's main catalog (not the free Genealogy site) <**www.nationalarchives.ie/search-the-archives**>. Select the Simple Search option, type in *will calendars* with the year you want to search, then download the PDF. They are large files. The calendar entries for 1935 to 1949 are searchable via the main catalog and can be searched by name.

LAW AND ORDER RECORDS

Only a few years ago, court and crime records were beyond the search plan of most family historians, so they largely sat gathering dust in archives. Family historians rarely explored these vast record collections unless their research—often a newspaper report—had already unearthed a connection to a trial or court hearing. But digitization and indexing have recently released the store of genealogical and social information held within NAI collections, which cover only the twenty-six counties now in the Republic of Ireland. They come in two collections: the Irish Prison Registers, 1790–1920, and the Petty Sessions Court Registers, 1828–1912, which are described in the following sections. Other than these direct collections, the best place to find criminal trial, coroner inquests, and other court reports is from newspapers (see chapter 11).

Records for Counties Antrim, Armagh, Down, Fermanagh, Londonderry, and Tyrone can be accessed during an in-person visit to PRONI in Belfast, as they are not yet online.

Prison Registers

The NAI's entire collection of prison registers is online (for a fee) at Findmypast. While it isn't complete—some registers have not survived—this collection contains more than 3.5 million entries in forty-four registers and covers a range of detention facilities, from the local bridewell (typically attached to a police station) to county *gaol* (jail) and the "rehab" prisons for alcoholics known as Reformatories. The online collection includes registers from institutions in twenty of the twenty-six counties in modern-day Ireland. County Cork is well represented with fifteen custodial places included, and Dublin with six. The only counties (other than those in Northern Ireland) to not be included are Carlow, Cavan, Donegal, Monaghan, Roscommon, and Westmeath.

Individual entries can be quite detailed, including names, addresses, age, physical descriptions, places of birth, and information about next of kin, plus the specifics of the charges against the prisoner.

The level of crime reported in these records ranges dramatically from charges of high treason to leaving an employer without consent. Interestingly, drunkenness is the most common crime reported across the 130 years covered by the online collection, and it accounts for 25 percent of all incarcerations, followed by theft, assault, vagrancy, and rioting.

You'll notice a rise in the incarceration level beginning in 1849, when more than one hundred thousand people (many of whom were merely seeking refuge from the Famine) passed through the prison system. A week in the harsh prison institution at least meant reliable food and shelter, so parents would sometimes encourage children to commit a minor misdemeanor in order to get incarcerated and thus receive temporary nutrition.

Petty Session Court Order Books

The Petty Sessions Court was Ireland's lowest court, and it handled the vast bulk of both criminal and civil legal cases such as minor cases brought against individuals either by

---

RESEARCH TIP

Note the Prison's Location
In collections of prison registers, the "county" field relates to the *prison's* geographical location, not the permanent residence of the people named. Keep that in mind as you're searching for delinquent ancestors.

Research Tip: Find Your Black Sheep, Victims, and Witnesses
Records in the prison registers and petty sessions books extend beyond details of the accused and their crimes or misdemeanors. The complainants or alleged victims, witnesses, and arresting police officers appear in the Petty Session Books, while the next of kin was recorded in the prison registers. As a result, these collections are worth exploring even if your ancestors were as pure as the driven snow.

government officials, such as police constables, or other civilians. The presiding justice of the peace or local magistrate could impose a maximum punishment of one year's imprisonment; cases of a more serious nature were passed on to the Quarterly Sessions or Assizes Court. In practice, the majority of cases heard by the Petty Sessions Court resulted in the guilty party facing a fine, a few weeks in *gaol* (with or without hard labor), or a restriction to keep the peace for a specified period.

As with the prison registers collection, the most common charge brought before the Petty Sessions Court was drunkenness, representing about one in three cases. One in five charges related to revenue or tax discrepancies, typically shopkeepers or merchants using "light" weights and measures. Assault, poaching, failing to maintain boundary fences or obtain a dog license, and destruction of property also made regular appearances before the bench, as did local acts of nuisance (which often involved pigs, cattle, or sheep escaping from their pens and causing damage to crops and fences on public roads or a neighboring property).

Most of the surviving Irish Petty Sessions order books for the twenty-six counties of the Republic of Ireland date from 1858 to 1924, and the collection holds more than 22.5 million records. While the manuscript collection is accessible to personal visitors at NAI, your easiest access route to the records is via Findmypast. For a list of the courts included in the collection and their respective years of coverage, see <www.findmypast. co.uk/articles/irish-petty-sessions-order-books>. Alternatively, you can view the images on microfilm at FamilySearch Family History Centers. PRONI holds records for the six counties now in Northern Ireland, though they have not been digitized and can only be viewed by personal visitors to the Belfast office.

Many reports of cases before the Petty Sessions Courts made their way into local newspapers. If the story was sufficiently controversial, amusing, or salacious, parts of the report may even be verbatim, so you may learn the words spoken by your ancestor. More prosaic cases were not usually reported (except perhaps on a light news week), but your next research stop should be the local newspaper if you discover one of your ancestors recorded as a defendant, plaintiff, or witness in these order books.

MILITARY RECORDS

The main issue when researching Irish military ancestors is that, prior to the Partition of Ireland in 1922, Irishmen would have served in the British Army and British Navy. From the late 1700s until after World War I, large numbers of Irish men served, often as a way to escape the grinding poverty of life in Ireland or (in certain families) to uphold traditions.

Most of the surviving records are held in The National Archives (TNA) in Kew, London, and you'll find many useful guides on the TNA website. The "British Army Soldiers up to 1913" guide <www.nationalarchives.gov.uk/help-with-your-research/research-guides/british-army-soldiers-up-to-1913> is a good starting point and includes links to resources that you may want to explore, such as a collection of muster rolls and pay lists (c.1730–1898) and another of British army officers through 1913.

For researching soldiers who served before 1922, the most useful records are the pension/discharge collections, which can be accessed online via Findmypast and Ancestry.com. A military pension was due to any soldier after twelve years of service, and payments were administered by either the Royal Hospital Chelsea or the Kilmainham Hospital in Dublin. Upon discharge, a soldier had a choice, subject to any disabilities, of living at the hospital and being cared for within the institution, or living as an "out" pensioner (e.g., receiving regular pension payments from the hospital but living independently of it). The records of Irish soldiers can be found in both hospitals (whether they were "in" or "out" pensioners), and they contain brief biographical and service details including places of birth and enlistment.

Records for soldiers who fought in World War I can be surprisingly difficult to find, mainly because bombing during World War II destroyed a huge part of the collection. However, Ancestry.com, Findmypast, and FamilySearch.org have large collections of service records and pension records. In addition, medal index cards have survived for most soldiers, and these detail the campaign medals awarded to them. A useful guide to interpreting them can be found at 1914-1918.net <www.1914-1918.net/soldiers/interpret-mic.html>. In addition to medal rolls for World War I, rolls for the Boer War (1899–1902) can be viewed, unindexed, on the website of The National Archives, Kew, in series WO 100 (see WO 100/205 for Royal Irish Fusiliers and Connaught Rangers <discovery.nationalarchives.gov.uk/details/r/C3763969>). Findmypast has transcriptions of these within an indexed multi-source collection of Boer War records, and you can also view these records on Ancestry.com.

The NAI also holds a small collection of wills written by enlisted Irish men fighting with the British Army. Here, you can find records from the thirty-two historical counties, covering enlisted and non-commissioned soldiers who fought in the Boer War and in World War I. This collection is seriously incomplete; it includes only nine thousand wills, and thirty-five thousand Irishmen died in World War I alone. They can be searched and viewed free of charge on both the NAI and on Findmypast websites.

Records from TNA's Admiralty collection have survived more or less intact, and both Ancestry.com and Findmypast have good-sized collections dating back to the late 1700s. While Irishmen do feature in these collections, they are in relatively low numbers compared with those who joined the army.

Moving past records relating to WWI military action, Ireland has a significant collection of digitized material and indexes dating from the Revolutionary period in Ireland (1916 to 1921), held by the Irish Military Archives <www.militaryarchives.ie/en/home>. Among the available record sets are the Military Service Pensions Collection, which consists of applications for medals and pensions, the Bureau of Military History Witness

C

The Royal College of Physicians of Ireland's Roll of Licentiates in Medicine and Midwifery dates from 1866 to 1948 (Ref: RCPI/5/2/1/3). The RCPI has excellent archives and research facilities in Dublin, plus a free guide to using them.

Statements, and the 1922 Irish Army Census. The census registers record all soldiers in the National Army on November 12, 1922, and are particularly useful to researchers as they note the names of the soldier's next of kin.

OCCUPATIONAL RECORDS

Depending on your ancestor's line of work and the period you are researching, you may be able to find out more about your ancestor in records relating to his specific job or profession. This isn't possible for all types of work, but you may be surprised at what records are available. For example, good records survive for members of the military (see the previous section), the clergy, the Royal Irish Constabulary, and the medical (image **C**; see <www.rcpi.ie/heritage-centre>) and legal professions, while specialist archives and historical groups (often with no online presence) maintain records of certain trades and occupations. The Irish Railway Record Society in Dublin is an example of the latter; it has extensive but incomplete and unindexed records about railway employees, which are difficult to draw information from without a certain point of departure.

A first port of call for most trades and professions should be in local or national directories and almanacs. These were usually published annually, making it possible to track family names and locations, and maybe to conclude how the individuals were managing economically and in relation to their peers.

The best source of occupational collections is available at John Grenham's website <www.johngrenham.com/records/jobs_in.php#records>. From a menu of more than seventy occupations ranging from baker to coastguard and medical doctor to watchmaker, you can find all manner of resources including livery guilds, published directories of members, online training records, trade associations, and specialist libraries.

KEYS TO SUCCESS

Start your search of pre-1858 probate collections with the Irish Wills Index on Findmypast, as it will quickly highlight any surviving testamentary records for your ancestor.

If you have military ancestors, invest time to familiarize yourself with the workings of the dense website of The National Archives in Kew, London. Also, take advantage of its many free research guides.

Explore and enjoy the Petty Sessions Registers for your ancestor's home area. Even if you can't find any of your own ancestors, you'll learn a lot about the social environment in which they lived.

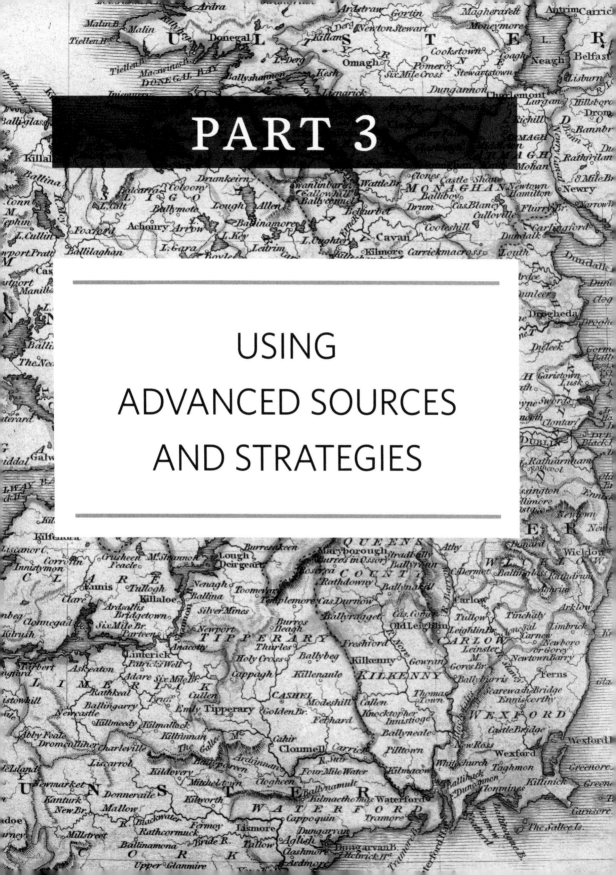

PART 3

USING
ADVANCED SOURCES
AND STRATEGIES

13

Putting It All Together

Throughout this book, you've learned about strategies and record types that will take your research from the United States to Ireland, then help you trace your family tree in the old country. Now, we'll look at two real-life examples of this book's research techniques in action.

AN ABUNDANCE OF FARRELLS: SEARCHING A COMMON NAME

Professional genealogist Nicola Morris of Timeline Research Ireland <www.timeline.ie> shares how she traced a family with a fairly common Irish name back through US records in order to identify the correct ancestral family.

♣ ♣ ♣

According to family lore, the Farrell family's grandfather, Jim, was Irish and had run away from home to board a ship bound for America. The relatively recent death of the family's own father (Jim's son), Donald, meant that the Farrells did not have anyone to ask for more specific family information, such as where Jim came from or the names of his parents. They wanted to visit the place in Ireland where Jim was born to find out more about the circumstances surrounding his departure and about their heritage, but they didn't

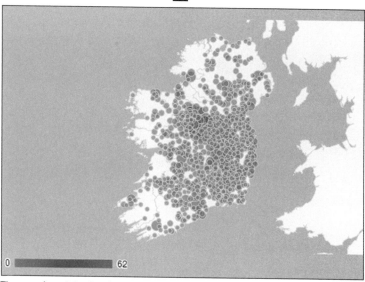

A

The map, from John Grenham's website, records the locations of all 3,548 Farrell households appearing in Griffith's Valuation (1848–1864). It's a common name, and one that is well spread across the island.

know where to go. They had tried searching for a Jim Farrell who was born in Ireland on various genealogy websites, but did not have enough information to identify their grandfather from the many records available (image **A**).

Unfortunately, the family's surname is common. *Farrell* traditionally means "man of valor" and is among the top-fifty most common Irish surnames, with the largest concentrations in Longford and other counties across the center of the island. Looking for a Jim Farrell without an approximate year or place of birth and without his parents' names would be a futile exercise.

With little information (and an unhelpfully common name to search), how should the Farrells start their research?

Before searching for anyone in Irish records, gather information from more recent US sources, such as the 1940 US federal census. We knew Jim's son, Donald Farrell, was born in the early 1930s in Waltham, Massachusetts, so we searched for a child under ten years of age who was residing with a father named Jim (or the more formal "James"). Sure enough, we were able to readily identify the family, living on Hagar Street in Waltham.

Here was Jim—James E. Farrell—a thirty-six-year-old machinist living with his wife, Alice C. Farrell, and their children James E. (aged 11), Donald F. (aged 8), and Richard H. (aged 6). But there was a surprise: *All* members of the Farrell family were recorded as having been born in Massachusetts. Either James E. Farrell (Donald's father) was not born in Ireland, or we had identified the wrong family.

To see if we could confirm this family as the correct one, we searched for Donald's recent death record. Unlike Irish death records, which have included parents' names only recently, US death records are a valuable resource for genealogical research and often record the names of the parents of the deceased. In this case, we learned that Donald Joseph Farrell was born in Waltham, Massachusetts on July 30, 1931, to parents James E. Farrell and Alice C. Sweeney, so we knew we were on the right track. We also now knew from the census record that Jim Farrell was actually born in Massachusetts in about 1904, and not in Ireland.

Earlier census returns told us more about him. In 1930, James E. and Alice C. Farrell had been married for two years, and they were living with their eldest son in Watertown, Massachusetts. The form also provided the vital confirmation: It was not James who had emigrated to the US, but instead his parents. Moving back in time again, the 1920 census revealed a sixteen-year-old James Farrell living in Waltham with his father, Patrick J. Farrell, a boilermaker in an iron foundry, and his mother, Mary E. Farrell. Young James worked as an errand boy in an office.

We searched the Massachusetts Town and Vital Records on FamilySearch.org and found the birth of a James Edward Farrell in Waltham. He was born on July 10, 1903, to Patrick Farrell, a boilermaker who was born in Ireland, and Mary A. Spellman.

But how could we be sure this birth record related to the same James E. Farrell who married Alice C. Sweeney in about 1928? We needed to find some evidence that corroborated our findings and would confirm the parents' names or James E. Farrell's date of birth. We looked for a marriage record for James and Alice C. Sweeney in the hopes that it would record James' parents names, but we couldn't find one.

Instead, we turned again to death records and found an entry for James E. Farrell in the US Social Security Death Index. The index's given date of birth (July 10, 1903) was consistent with the birth record, but his parents' names were not recorded. But we still had some luck: The index mentioned that in 1940, Patrick J. Farrell was living as a widower at Hagar Street, Waltham, in the house adjacent to his son, James.

Earlier census records confirmed that Patrick J. Farrell and his wife, Mary, were born in Ireland. Patrick emigrated in about 1892 and was naturalized; his wife emigrated about four years later, and they stated they had been married for nine years in 1910. This suggests they married in the United States after immigration, so we searched for their marriage record in Massachusetts—and this told us a great deal about them.

According to the marriage record, Patrick J. Farrell and Mary Spellman wed on April 24, 1901. Patrick was listed as a boilermaker, born in 1871 in County Louth, Ireland, and

Patrick Farrell's birth was registered by his mother, Catherine Hughes. She signed the register with an X, indicating she could not read or write.

the son of James Farrell and Catherine Hughes. Mary Spellman was born in 1875 in County Galway, Ireland, the daughter of Martin Spellman and Margaret Carthy.

Using census collections, marriage records, and different types of death records, we had connected the Farrell family in Massachusetts back to several surnames in Ireland. But we didn't want to stop there—we still don't know why Patrick came to the United States or where (specifically) he was from.

We began looking for more records in County Louth, where we believe Patrick J. Farrell was born in about 1871. Civil registration of births, marriages, and death became compulsory in Ireland in 1864, so this collection was a natural place to start the search. There are three registration districts in County Louth: Ardee, Dundalk, and Drogheda. A search of the civil birth index for all three districts between 1869 and 1873 found a number of newborns named Patrick Farrell, and it was impossible to identify which might be the correct entry. As a result, we had to look deeper.

A baby named Patrick was born to a James Farrell and Catherine Hughes on March 13, 1869, in Ardee, a small town on the banks of the River Dee. The certificate (image B) recorded that the father, James Farrell, was a weaver. This is a promising lead, and just might be our Patrick. We looked for a corresponding marriage record in the civil registration records, but failed to find one.

We turned to the Roman Catholic parish register for Ardee. The James Farrell and Catherine Hughes of Blackridge we found there married on October 25, 1863, just a few months before civil registration started. Unfortunately, the marriage witnesses, Pat McKenny and Anne Brannegan, were the only other names recorded on the marriage entry.

Having exhausted the parish register, we jumped back to civil registration records. These show Patrick was the fourth child of James and Catherine. His older siblings were Catherine (b. 1864), Edward (b. 1865), and Mary Anne (b. 1866), and he had a younger sister named Margaret (b. 1872). They were all baptized in the parish of Ardee.

This Patrick's father and brother appear on the 1901 census of Ireland, but Patrick is nowhere to be found. Our Patrick emigrated to the United States in the early 1890s, and that fact could explain his absence.

That same census describes James Farrell as a sixty-six-year-old widower (i.e., born about 1834). A farm laborer, he was living with his eldest son, Edward (whose name and relationship to James match with the Ardee parish register), and Edward's wife and children. Since James was a widower by 1901, we searched for a civil record of his wife's death in the Ardee registration district in the prior decades. We found only one Catherine Farrell who died between 1872 and 1901: a Catherine Farrell who died in the Ardee Work-house of "Phthisis" (tuberculosis) on March 16, 1873. In the record, she's listed as thirty-four years old and the wife of a laborer. Although her husband's name does not appear as the informant on her death certificate, she's likely the wife of our James Farrell; James did not have any children after 1872 (the year before this Catherine's death), and James' status as a widower in 1901 lines up.

So where does that leave the family story? We established that it was Patrick Farrell (not Jim) who emigrated, so that part of the myth has been busted. As for the rest, we might never know if he "ran away" to the United States. Based on the research we've gathered together, the Irish Farrell family (Patrick, his parents James and Catherine, and his siblings) do not appear to have occupied any land in their hometown of Ardee, and James Farrell worked as a weaver and laborer. There would not have been many employment opportunities for Patrick Farrell in Ardee in the 1880s and 1890s, and it may have been this limited future that prompted his emigration. Knowing more will require further research or another breakthrough, but we've come so far already.

KEEP CALM AND CARRIGAN ON: DOING COLLATERAL RESEARCH

Family Tree Books editor Andrew Koch of Ohio recently started researching his family tree. In this case study, he learns about his Carrigan ancestors, using records of both them and their extended family to place his ancestors in Ireland.

♣ ♣ ♣

I've always been enchanted by Irish culture: the lyrical names (Saoirse, Liam, Siobhan), the beauty of a well-played fiddle, the vibrance of St. Patrick's Day. Despite my decidedly German last name, I always hoped I had some Irish blood in me. Sure enough, tracing census returns back generations revealed my great-great-great-grandfather, James Carrigan. *Carrigan!* An Irish name if I've ever heard one. Kiss me, I'm one-thirty-second Irish!

	211	Hession Thomas	head		0	5000	R	no	M	W	43	S		no	yes
		Carrigan James	cousin					V	M	W	44	M	39	no	yes
		Lillian	cousin					V	F	W	53	M	43	no	yes

One of Andrew's biggest steps forward came while researching a distant relative: Thomas Hessian, his great-great-great-uncle's first cousin (Andrew's first cousin four times removed).

So what could I learn about the Carrigan line and where it came from? Minding my fundamentals, I started by researching James in US sources. From census records, online cemetery indexes, an Ohio death index, James' declaration of intention, a New York passenger list, and a Social Security death index entry for his daughter (my great-great-grandmother), I learned that Irish-born James (born about 1856) married and had his first son in England before immigrating to the United States, all in the same year: 1880. His English-born wife (Rose Flynn) and infant son (James Thomas) joined him in Cincinnati within the next couple years, and the couple had six more children (including my ancestor, Mayme) before Rose passed away in 1899 and James in 1914.

This was a great start, but I still had unanswered questions: Where in Ireland was James from, and what were his parents' names? A distant relative on Ancestry.com <www.ancestry.com> told me that James and his ancestors came from Dublin, but she didn't have concrete proof. She did, however, have James and Rose's marriage certificate and James Thomas' birth certificate. The documents revealed that James Thomas was born less than nine months after his parents' wedding (oops!), but the only other new information was the name of James' father: Patrick.

Likewise, my own research in Irish records was mostly fruitless. Civil registration didn't begin until a few years after James' birth, and I couldn't definitively find parish records with a potential hometown as broad as "Dublin." With some help from Claire Santry (this book's author), I had a lead—a clump of baptism records for "Corrigans" in St. Andrew's parish in Dublin. Each Corrigan had a Patrick and a Catherine as parents, and among the entries were a James, baptized in 1854 (relatively close to my James), and a Mary, baptized in 1853. But without more proof, I couldn't draw any conclusions.

Remembering the principle of collateral research, I knew it was time to search more broadly. With some reluctance, I started researching James and Rose's six children who weren't my direct-line ancestors: James Thomas (b. 1880), Patrick (b. 1882), William (b. 1886), Thomas (b. 1888), Rose Ann (b. 1889), and Catharine (b. 1892). For weeks, I searched WWI draft registration cards, federal census records, death certificates, Social Security claims, marriage records, and all the birth records I could find online. But none of them provided new information about my main line of Carrigans. I was losing hope, and came close to giving up.

But then came a breakthrough in the 1930 census. James Thomas and his wife, Lillian, lived in the household of a "cousin," a man named Thomas Hessian. *Hessian?* I'd never heard the name before, but I focused my research on the newcomer. Using his name and birth year, I found him with his brother and widowed mother (Irish-born Margaret Hessian) in the 1920 census. Skimming the record image, I was surprised to find James Thomas Carrigan and Lillian Carter listed on the same return page, then unmarried and living in separate homes; James Thomas, Lillian, and the Hessians were neighbors. But could the relationship run deeper? Could the Hessians be Carrigans? And if so, could they provide the connection to the old country that I've been looking for?

Determined, I searched high and low for records that might give me Margaret Hessian's maiden name. But her 1910 and 1920 census entries were inconsistent, giving different years for her immigration and birth. Without concrete dates, I couldn't find her in passenger lists, declarations of intention, or vital records. I didn't make significant progress until a Find A Grave <www.findagrave.com> entry for Thomas Hessian, who died in 1945 and was buried in St. Joseph's New Cemetery in Cincinnati.

And that's when I found my long-awaited pot of gold. Following a hunch, I found Thomas in the cemetery's online index of graves. His parents' names? Patrick Hessian and Margaret *Carrigan*. A match! But it gets even better: Margaret's burial entry revealed her parents' names as Patrick Carrigan and "X Haley."

With this in mind, I jumped back to Irish research and revisited the "Corrigan" lead. In 1880s-era Dublin, we have Catholic, Irish-born James (baptized in 1854) and Mary (baptized in 1853) who share Patrick Corrigan and Catherine (unknown maiden name) as parents; across the pond, we have Catholic, Irish-born James (born about 1856) and Margaret (born about 1854) who share a Patrick Carrigan and (unknown first name) Haley as parents.

So are my Carrigans the Corrigans from St. Andrew's in Dublin? My research so far suggests that is a possibility. The discrepancies in names and vital information aren't unusual. Mary and Margaret were similar (even interchangeable) names at the time, and birth years were less concrete in the 1800s than they are today.

But I shouldn't start calling myself a Dubliner yet. Only more research can prove or disprove my theory. Finding the maiden name of Patrick Corrigan's wife is a priority, as is searching Margaret's marriage, immigration, and naturalization records for any evidence of a hometown. But with a lack of other supporting evidence, this is my best find yet, and it wouldn't have happened if I hadn't researched my distant Hessian cousin.

14

What to Do When You Get Stuck

S ooner or later, all researchers run into a brick wall where the trail seems to have run
dry, no matter how hard they look. At some point, all paper trails inevitably come
to an end because the information they seek was never recorded. In Irish research,
this can sometimes happen frustratingly soon, especially in the areas hardest hit by poverty and famine, but the picture across the island is by no means uniform. Depending on
where they start, many researchers can and do move further backwards in time by one,
two, or more generations before the treasure chest of surviving records is emptied.

You may find more "natural" end points than brick walls. Brick walls are obstacles
that stop you from making headway in your research when you should reasonably expect
to make progress. Every researcher encounters them from time to time. They may occur
when you've followed a false lead, gathered facts that conflict with information you've
relied on, failed to distinguish between people with similar names and life dates, or found
a trail that simply goes cold.

These brick walls are the most frustrating features of family history research, but
they can often be overcome. Sometimes it might mean you need to backtrack and refresh
your memory. Were there snippets of information you didn't think were important? Do
you need to seek out new sources? Will collaborating with other genealogists deliver a

solution? This final chapter will highlight some alternative research methods to help you move out from the shadow of your research brick walls.

EXPLORE ALTERNATIVE DATABASES

When you've completed a lot of work but still haven't reached your goal, you probably don't want to me to advise you to do more research. But (unless you have magic research-solving dust to sprinkle over your work) you have to face the reality that still more work may be necessary.

Most researchers would probably admit to favoring one of the big sites over its rivals. Often, this favoritism is based more on familiarity than on objective facts, such as the range of record collections, superior search functions, or cost. However (despite some overlap in coverage), all the major databases contain distinctive selections of records, and you may find that going back over your research using a second or third database can open up fresh avenues. Just as important, they all have bespoke search engines so they often deliver different results when searching identical collections. Name-spelling treatments in particular differ between databases, so switching to a second or third site may unearth records for your ancestral family that slipped through the net in the first database you checked.

It may be hard to motivate yourself to start the rinse-and-repeat process, but you may make a breakthrough discovery once it's underway and you get used to the new database. In the process, of course, you'll also be casting a fresh eye over your earlier work, and that in itself could lead you to identify errors or conflicting information, revise your conclusions, or find new directions for your research.

REVISIT THE GENEALOGY BASICS

Even the most advanced researchers can sometimes benefit from taking their research back to the basics. In this section, I'll discuss two key techniques from earlier in this book that can help you conquer brick walls: whole-family genealogy and the FAN principle.

Chapter 2 introduced the concept of whole-family genealogy, in which researchers broaden their research to include both direct-line ancestors and all their siblings. While this obviously involves more work and takes more time, it helps you create the fullest and most accurate history of your family. Some researchers choose not to do it for practical reasons, while others might overlook it in their enthusiasm to jump back another generation.

For example, when your direct ancestors are not giving up their secrets or pointing a clear way back to Ireland, you can't ignore the whole-family genealogy approach. If your direct ancestor didn't leave the critical details of the family's townland of origin in an accessible record, perhaps a brother made sure to note it in his naturalization records. Maybe a sister made sure to add their mother's maiden name to a death announcement or family gravestone inscription, or someone in this extended family may have left the vital information you need to move your research further back in time. Similarly, researching the families of these siblings forward in time may help you identify living cousins who may have answers to your questions or share treasures such as photographs.

Another key tactic to consider is the FAN (Friends, Associates, Neighbors) principle discussed in chapter 3. Like most immigrants, Irish arrivals tended to cluster in communities made up of their own countrymen that they knew and understood, making the adjustment to their new home somewhat easier. As a result, seeking out the records of FANs who may not be related to your family might still turn up useful information.

You may need to extend your examination of FANs to anyone whose life intersected with that of your ancestor before or after death. Have you checked FANs' naturalization papers? If you made a list of all the FANs and looked at their naturalization papers, would any pattern emerge? Even if most don't provide a specific place of origin, some mention a county. What if you repeat the exercise for their witnesses? If you've already researched the FANs of your ancestor's life, widen this circle of FANs to include those who were named in his or her will or involved in probate proceedings.

LEARN MORE ABOUT THE COLLECTIONS

With the destruction of so many prime genealogical records—not least the nineteenth-century census returns and wills—Irish family historians have to rely on a number of records that were compiled for non-population reasons. For example, you probably understand why birth and death registrations were recorded, but can you explain the who, when, how, what, and why behind a set of Irish land records? If you think your ancestor ought to be appearing in a record set but you can't find him or her there, spend some time gathering background information about where and why the collection was taken: What was the original purpose of the records? How were they compiled? Who collected them, and who was recorded in them? This deeper level of understanding about a record set may explain why your ancestor is not recorded and help you find a work-around solution to extracting information from it.

COLLABORATE WITH OTHER RESEARCHERS

There really is a big wide genealogical world beyond the record databases, and it's worth venturing into. Sharing and learning from other family historians is one of the best ways to keep up-to-date with new resources and the ever-changing Irish genealogy scene.

"Give and take" would be an appropriate motto for the worldwide genealogical community. Family historians seem to have a strong streak of altruism in their veins, and they're a sociable group, too, as the number of US-based genealogy societies in appendix B demonstrates. I'd always recommend a beginner researcher join a society with a nearby Irish special interest group, because membership will provide immediate access to a whole range of knowledge, advice, and guidance from more-experienced researchers who can help keep you on the straight and narrow while you learn the ropes. Societies and interest groups also may offer lectures, access to their own specialized libraries, and cultural events that will help you learn more about your Irish heritage.

If you've identified a county or more localized place of origin in Ireland for your ancestor, you might consider joining a genealogical or historical society in Ireland. Localized historical groups are more numerous and can be found online; again, see appendix B for a list of some of the larger groups. By viewing their publications and (sometimes) their websites, you can learn a lot about the area where your ancestors lived and start to orient yourself around it without ever visiting the physical society headquarters. Whether focused on genealogy or history, such organizations on both sides of the pond publish newsletters, journals, and books that are crammed with valuable insights, and many work closely with their local and regional archives on transcription and indexing projects.

Another way to collaborate with experienced genealogists is through genealogy forums where you can respond to the questions of other researchers and (hopefully) get answers to your own queries. Ancestry.com has a busy forum like this: A huge international base of members makes for enlightening queries and responses and a likely place for discovering extended members of your family. You don't need an active subscription to use the Ancestry forum. Alternatively, if you're asking questions specifically about Irish research, you might like to try a forum based in Ireland such as Boards.ie <www.boards.ie/b/forum/1288> and RootsChat <www.rootschat.com/forum/ireland>, which both have some very knowledgeable and generous regulars happy to answer specific questions. Reading through some of the threads on these sites can be an education in itself!

Blogs are another way of extending your grasp of history, genealogical techniques, and a myriad Irish heritage and culture topics. You have a wide variety to choose from. Some are niche, while others have a wider focus. Some are professionally produced, while others are published by enthusiastic amateurs who may (or may not!) be true experts in their field. Most allow comments where you can pose questions or add your own views on the subjects under discussion.

And then there's Facebook, which plays a huge role in genealogy. On this social media behemoth, you can seek help, share advice or personal anecdotes, and connect with one another in a (usually) mutually supportive environment. Users have created hundreds of pages and groups specializing in family history.

Pages allow organizations, businesses, and individuals to post and share news and images. Researchers can follow and share the pages of their favorite archives, family history societies, database providers, and genealogy specialists, allowing them to keep up-to-date with the latest genealogical developments and releases, receive tips and hints on research techniques, and join in live Q&A sessions.

Groups have a narrower focus and provide a space for individuals to communicate about a common interest (e.g., Monaghan genealogy, Irish soldiers of the Great War, or Y-DNA surname groups). For example, you might need to know which cemetery or school would cover a particular part of Belfast, or whether any records of early eighteenth-century weavers survive for southwest Ireland. Facebook groups focused on this area may be able to provide the information.

DIG INTO DNA TESTING

It's sad to say that even after diligently completing all the steps and techniques outlined in this book, some researchers will be unable to unearth documentary proof of their family's place of origin in Ireland. A potential solution has emerged and become enormously popular: DNA testing. Millions of family historians have been tested in the hope of finding cousin matches, and there is no sign that the numbers have peaked.

Irish researchers, too, have embraced genetic genealogy research enthusiastically, curious to learn the stories of their extended families who left the island. Many of these researchers know the place of origin of their forbears, so finding DNA matches can open up many new avenues of research and even pinpoint where you could pick up the traditional trail.

There are several types of test, with Y-DNA and autosomal (atDNA) tests being the most popular and useful to genealogists. Because Y-DNA and (historically) surnames are passed from father to son down the generations, Y-DNA surname projects bring together disparate individuals who share the same surname. For example, if William O'Shea in Chicago joins the O'Shea Y-DNA project, his DNA test results will be added to the project's database and be scrutinized for any other O'Sheas who have similar DNA sequences. If William didn't know where in Ireland his family came from, for example, he may match with Dubliner Donal O'Shea, who has documentary proof that the family were living in Bandon, County Cork, in the late eighteenth century.

Autosomal testing has really grabbed the attention of family historians in the last few years. Unlike the Y-DNA test, atDNA inherited from both parents is analyzed, making it the better test for beginners. Your atDNA results will include a list of potential DNA

Go 'Off-Piste' With Ireland Genealogy Projects Archives

There is a whole world of online genealogical information beyond the mainstream commercial databases. Genealogy research seems to bring out the altruistic streak in people, with the result that Irish family historians have some excellent free, volunteer-led projects available for exploration.

With more than one hundred thousand photos and transcriptions of headstones and tens of thousands of transcriptions, the Ireland Genealogy Projects (IGP) Archives **<www.igp-web.com/IGPArchives>** has come a long way in the decade or so since it was launched. There you can find information from church registers; military, court, land, and will records; obituary columns; and other miscellaneous resources,. The Archives evolved as a natural supplement to IGP-web **<www.igp-web.com>**, a long-standing collection of "county" websites, each managed by a volunteer providing in-depth advice on researching family history at county level.

All the items on the IGP Archives' site have been donated by Irish family historians. Sometimes they donate transcriptions of documents—letters, deeds, leases, passenger tickets—that they've found among their own family's records or discovered serendipitously when exploring archive collections in major repositories. They donate their family's memorial or mass cards, old photographs of their ancestors, transcriptions of published town directories, and all manner of factual memorabilia that have the potential to solve other researchers' genealogical puzzles.

The huge number of headstone photographs is another example of the volunteers' generosity, and many volunteers spend their weekends and summer evenings snapping tombstones that others in the genealogical community may not themselves be able to visit. The site is updated weekly.

matches who have also tested with that company, plus an estimated degree of relationship for each of them (second cousins, third cousins, fourth cousins, etc). By comparing your research with a cousin match, you can try to determine which ancestors you share.

AncestryDNA **<www.ancestry.com/dna>**, the leading DNA-test provider, has made this easier by linking DNA tests to online family trees so you can quickly spot the surnames and locations you have in common. Other major testing companies are 23andMe **<www.23andme.com>**, Family Tree DNA **<www.familytreedna.com>**, and MyHeritage **<www.myheritage.com/dna>**. Note: You don't need to test with all four to find matches! A useful third-party tool such as GEDMatch **<www.gedmatch.com>** allows you to upload your raw DNA results to a central database.

A number of Irish DNA projects can also help you discover more relatives without having to test at multiple companies: the Ireland Y-DNA project

<www.familytreedna.com/groups/ireland-heritage/about>; the Ireland mtDNA project <www.familytreedna.com/groups/ireland-mt-dna>; and the Ulster Heritage DNA project <ulsterheritagedna.ulsterheritage.com/index.htm>. Also check out the Genetic Genealogy Ireland YouTube channel <www.youtube.com/channel/UCHnW2NAfPIA2KUipZ_PlUlw/videos>, which has free videos explaining how DNA tests can help you advance your family research.

KEEP UP-TO-DATE WITH RECORD RELEASES

With only a few exceptions, most of Ireland's major record collections have been digitized and are now available online. Even the majority of the exceptions are seeing some movement towards digitization, and many county archives have managed to earmark some funds for digitizing specialized collections in their care. Many of these are long-term projects being carried out without commercial involvement, and progress as funds and resources allow (To put it another: They're being completed slowly). As such, I would expect the records to be released in installments rather than as complete collections at some distant date.

Similarly, small groups of volunteers in Ireland and Northern Ireland continue to transcribe memorials in local graveyards, as well as documents, and other materials held by private individuals, parish authorities, museums, and local studies libraries. Finding out about these smaller scale releases across the pond means keeping your ear to the ground. My own blog <www.irishgenealogynews.com> aims to do that job for you, and there are many good international news-led Facebook pages worth following; download Katherine R. Wilson's regularly updated listing <socialmediagenealogy.com/genealogy-on-facebook-list> and tailor-make your own list, paying special attention to the pages that carry news stories about developments in the areas of Ireland and the United States that match the geography of your own research.

VISIT THE HOME LAND

Until fairly recently, Irish-Americans who discovered some clue to their immigrant ancestor's place of origin had to travel to Ireland to make any headway in their research, a hefty commitment in terms of both money (airfare, lodging, archive access fees, etc.) and labor (as research often required sifting through dusty archives or squinting at whirring microfilm images). Often their vacation would run out of time (or money) before they had a chance to visit the place their family had called home so many years before. They might return to the United States with little more than a glimpse of Ireland apart from the major repositories in Dublin and Belfast.

These days, heritage trips—no longer a research necessity—can be more relaxing, efficient, and fulfilling. Nearly all of Ireland's major genealogically useful record collections are now online (and most of them free, too), so most of the research can—and should—be done long before touching down on Irish soil. This way, you can spend your precious time in Ireland or Northern Ireland carrying out more advanced or specific research in the archives of the capital cities, enjoying sightseeing trips to the island's outstanding heritage attractions, and exploring the original home area. This more focused trip could give you time to receive expert guidance at the free genealogy services available at the National Library of Ireland (NLI) and the National Archives of Ireland (NAI), both of which run full-time Monday through Friday. They don't operate an appointment system; you just show up and wait your turn. (Incidentally, if you plan to research at the NLI, NAI, or the Public Record Office of Northern Ireland, be sure to check their respective requirements for reader or visitor cards on their websites, as you may need to show personal papers before a card will be issued.)

With the formal research accomplished, hopefully successfully, you'll then be free to head to your ancestral region, seek out the nearest heritage center or local studies library, visit the church where your ancestors once worshipped (and where, perhaps, more recent generations of family are buried), talk to locals, find the house or land that was once called home, and walk in their footsteps along the byways or village lanes that were once so familiar to your ancestors. Even if you can't locate the exact spot where they lived, "walking the ground" can be an emotional experience, and it shouldn't be rushed.

KEYS TO SUCCESS

- Don't give up at the first sign of a brick wall. We all encounter them from time to time, and they don't automatically spell the end of your quest.

- Learn about the records you are consulting. Understand the reasons they were gathered, who was targeted, and how they were compiled.

- Search alternative databases when you get stuck. Take advantage of free trials and free access periods when they are offered.

- Collaborate! Pick the brains of other Irish genealogists and historians by joining national and local societies, following specialist Facebook groups and social media accounts, and posting queries on online forums.

- Do your homework before making a research trip to Ireland. Most of the major Irish genealogical records are online, and many are free.

Latin in Irish Catholic Parish Registers

Many researchers with Irish Roman Catholic ancestors imagine they will have to face the seemingly impenetrable Irish language to understand their family's baptisms, marriages, and burials (although historical Roman Catholic burial records are rare). Fear not! Irish priests never used Irish in the registers of their church. Never. Instead, they used English or Latin. The latter occurs more frequently (but not exclusively) in the more rural parishes and along the western seaboard.

The good news for those family historians without a Classical background is that the standard of Latin among the Roman Catholic priesthood was, to be frank, pretty appalling. Rather than reveal their ignorance of how to correctly decline their nouns and verbs, the priests instead used abbreviations and recorded the essential details of the event in the same format, over and over again through the pages of the register. Breaking the "code" or "word pattern" used by an individual priest is rarely difficult, especially since the basic vocabulary of a baptism or marriage record is limited.

As a result, you'll need only a light Latin lesson to prime yourself for researching Latin church records. And since you'll be primarily looking out for the names of your ancestors, we'll start with names.

LATINIZED NAMES

Place names and surnames were not translated into Latin, but first names were. It is usually quite easy to translate these Latin names into English. Among women's names, you'll often find -*a* or -*am* has been added to a more familiar name: Ellena, Mariam, Caterina, and Brigitta are common examples. Men's names tend to get the "-*ius* treatment," as in Bartholomeus, Franciscus, Stephanus, and Jacobus.

Here are some of the less obvious Latin versions:

Males	
Carolus	Charles
Demetrius	Jeremiah, Jerome, Dermot, Darby
Dionysius	Denis
Eugenius	Owen, Eugene
Gulielmus	William
Ioannes	John
Jacobus	James
Joannes	John
Nigelus	Niall, Neil
Thaddeus	Timothy

Females	
Agna/Agneta	Agnes, Nancy
Hannah	Anne
Honoria	Hannah, Nora, Honora, Jane, Jean, Joan
Joanna	Jane, Joan

LATIN IN BAPTISM REGISTERS

A typical full-form Latin entry in an Irish Roman Catholic baptism register might read:

> *(Date +) Baptisavi Michaeli, filium legitimum Patricus Donovan et Anna Crowley de Courtmacsherry. Sponsoribus Johannes Sweeney, Marian Hayes.*

This might be abbreviated to:

> *(Date +) Bapt Michaeli, fl Patricus Donovan et Anna Crowley, Courtmshry. Sp John Sweeney, Marian Hayes.*

The translation is:

> "I baptized Michael, legitimate son of Patrick Donovan and Anne Crowley of Courtmacsherry. Godparents John Sweeney and Mary Hayes."

Baptism registers can also be kept in tabular form. Image **A** is a baptism register for Carolus (Charles) Kenny—name in the left column—that reads:

> *Rev'd Barthol' McEgan baptisavit Carolus film legm Joannis Kenny et Maria Godly cath loco Ballilaguane. Thoms Godly Ellena Keliher.*

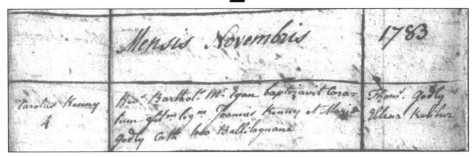

This baptism register is written in abbreviated Latin that is relatively easy to translate.

This can be translated as:

> "Reverend Bartholomew McEgan baptized Charles Kenny, legitimate son of John Kenny and Mary Godly from Ballilaguane."

The right column indicates that Thomas Godly and Ellen Keliher were the child's sponsors.

Here are some words you'll commonly find in baptism registers:

natus	birth
baptisatus	christened
nomen	first name
filia	daughter
filium/us	son
legitimum	legitimate
Pater	father
Mater	mother
parentes	parents
sponsores/sponsoribus	sponsors/godparents

LATIN IN MARRIAGE REGISTERS

A typical full-form Latin entry in an Irish Roman Catholic marriage register might read:

> *In matrimonium conjunxi sunt Thaddeus Buckley et Brigitta Lorigan, de Garranes. Testimonium: Cornelius White, Honoria Hayes*

The abbreviated version might read:

> *Mat con Thad Buckley, Brigitta Lorigan, Garranes. Con White, Honoria Hayes.*

The translation is:

"Timothy Crowley and Bridget Lorigan of Garranes were joined in matrimony. Witnesses Cornelius White and Nora Hayes."

The record in image **B** is another sample marriage register. This one reads:

Dionysium McCarthy et Mariam Bohane Disp[ensatio] rite obtenta in impedimento Consanguinitatis quod inter ipsis existebat in 4th et 4th gradibus Coram testibus Michaele McCarthyDuff et Anna McCarthy – Ego in Matrimonia – conjunxi Jeremias Molony

That can be translated as:

"Denis McCarthy and Mary Bohane duly obtained a dispensation from the impediment of consanguinity that existed between them in the 4th and 4th degrees. Before witnesses Michael McCarthyDuff and Anne McCarthy, I joined in marriage, Jeremiah Molony."

If you can decipher the handwriting, marriage registers like this one can be valuable resources.

Here are some words you'll commonly find in Latin marriage registers:

filia	daughter
filius/m	son
maritus, conjux	husband
uxor, marita, conjux	wife
matrimonium, copulatio, copulati, conjuncti	marriage
dispensatio	dispensation
banni, proclamentiones	marriage banns
consanguinati	blood-related
affinitatus	related by marriage between the two families, but not by blood
in tertio grado	second cousins
in secundus grado	first cousins
testimonium	witnesses

LATIN IN BURIAL REGISTERS

Historically, Irish Roman Catholic burial registers are rare, for reasons explained in chapter 8. Where they do exist, they tend to yield little genealogical information other than the name of the deceased and date of burial. In the sample register in image **C**, a priest in County Longford parish of Ardagh and Moydow followed the "burial-date/name-of-the-deceased-and-townland-of-residence" convention when writing up the burial record. He also added the women's maiden names and other details such as marital status (*inupta* for "unmarried"), age (*juvenis* for "young man," *senex* for "old man"), and relationship to other family members (*puella* for "daughter").

You might encounter some of the Latin terms used in burial registers or the general terms below. Otherwise, the only dedicated items of vocabulary you'll need are:

sepulti, sepultus	burial, buried
defuntorum liber/ordo	register of the deceased or requiem masses

Catholic burial registers are rare, and those that do exist (like this one) provided limited information.

GENERAL LATIN TERMS

In most parish registers, the Latin vocabulary used will be limited. Some common additional terms are below.

et	and
die	day
Mense/mensis	month
ano	year
domicililum	abode
loco	place
coram	in the presence of

You can find a more detailed list of Latin words and phrases found in genealogical records on FamilySearch.org <**www.familysearch.org/wiki/en/Latin_Genealogical_Word_List**>.

Irish Genealogy Research Societies

THE UNITED STATES

Northeast

BUFFALO IRISH GENEALOGICAL SOCIETY
Buffalo, NY
<www.facebook.com/
BuffaloIrishGenealogicalSociety>

CAPE COD GENEALOGICAL SOCIETY
Cape Cod, MA
<blog.capecodgensoc.org/p/special-interest-
groups.html>

**CONNECTICUT IRISH AMERICAN
HISTORICAL SOCIETY**
New Haven, CT
<www.ctiahs.com/genealog.htm>

FRIENDS OF IRISH RESEARCH
Brockton, MA
<www.friendsofirishresearch.org>

IRISH AMERICAN GENEALOGICAL SOCIETY
Philadelphia, PA
<www.facebook.com/pages/Irish-American-
Genealogy-Society/109616525814739>

IRISH AMERICAN HERITAGE MUSEUM
Albany, NY
<irish-us.org>

**THE IRISH ANCESTRAL
RESEARCH ASSOCIATION**
Newton, MA

IRISH/BRITISH GENEALOGY GROUP
New York City, NY
<www.meetup.com/
The-Irish-British-Genealogy-Group>

IRISH FAMILY HISTORY FORUM
Bethpage, NY
<ifhf.org>

MAINE IRISH HERITAGE CENTER
Portland, ME
<www.maineirish.com>

NEW YORK IRISH CENTER
Queens, NY
<www.newyorkirishcenter.org>

TROY IRISH GENEALOGY SOCIETY
Troy, NY
<www.rootsweb.ancestry.com/~nytigs>

**WESTCHESTER COUNTY
GENEALOGICAL SOCIETY**
Dobbs Ferry, NY
<www.rootsweb.ancestry.
com/~nywcgs/#Studygrp>

Mid-Atlantic and South

FAIRFAX COUNTY GENEALOGICAL SOCIETY
Church, VA
<fxgs.org/cpage.php?pt=18>

LEE COUNTY GENEALOGICAL SOCIETY
Fort Myers, FL
<lcgsfl.org/cpage.php?pt=12>

THE VILLAGES GENEALOGICAL SOCIETY
The Villages, FL
<vgsfl.org/cpage.php?pt=17>

WASHINGTON, DC FAMILY HISTORY CENTER
Kensington, MD
<www.wdcfhc.org/wordpress>

West

EASTSIDE GENEALOGICAL SOCIETY
Bellevue, WA
<www.rootsweb.ancestry.com/~wakcegs/
pages/irish_sig.html>

**MCCLELLAND IRISH LIBRARY
AND GENEALOGY RESEARCH CENTER**
Phoenix, AZ
<www.azirish.org/genealogy>

**SAN RAMON VALLEY
GENEALOGICAL SOCIETY**
Alamo, CA
<srvgensoc.org/sig.html#Irish>

SEATTLE GENEALOGICAL SOCIETY
Seattle, WA
<seattlegenealogicalsociety.org/content/
interest-groups>

**SOUTHERN CALIFORNIA
GENEALOGICAL SOCIETY**
Burbank, CA
<www.scgsgenealogy.com/interest-groups/
irish-group.html>

UNITED IRISH CULTURAL CENTER
San Francisco, CA

W.I.S.E. (WALES, IRELAND, SCOTLAND, ENGLAND) FAMILY HISTORY SOCIETY

Denver, CO

<www.wise-fhs.org>

INTERNATIONAL SOCIETY FOR BRITISH GENEALOGY & FAMILY HISTORY

Centennial, CO

<www.isbgfh.org>

Midwest

IOWA GENEALOGICAL SOCIETY

Des Moines, IA

<iowagenealogy.org/?page_id=196>

IRISH AMERICAN HERITAGE CENTER

Chicago, IL

<irish-american.org/tradition/genealogy>

IRISH GENEALOGICAL SOCIETY OF MICHIGAN

Detroit, MI

<miigsm.org>

IRISH GENEALOGICAL SOCIETY INTERNATIONAL

St. Paul, MN

<irishgenealogical.org>

IRISH GENEALOGICAL SOCIETY OF WISCONSIN

Milwaukee, WI

<www.igswonline.com>

IRISH HERITAGE CENTER OF GREATER CINCINNATI

Cincinnati, OH

<www.irishcenterofcincinnati.com>

KANSAS CITY IRISH CENTER

Kansas City, MO

<irishcenterkc.org/genealogy>

ST. LOUIS GENEALOGICAL SOCIETY

St. Louis, MO

<stlgs.org/about-us-2/
sigs-and-special-programs/
irish-special-interest-group>

IRELAND AND NORTHERN IRELAND

CLARE ROOTS SOCIETY

<www.clareroots.org>

CORK GENEALOGICAL SOCIETY

c/o Olive Coleman, 22 Elm Drive, Shamrock Lawn, Douglas, Co. Cork, Ireland

<www.corkgenealogicalsociety.com>

EAST CLARE HERITAGE GROUP

Ballyquin, Tuamgraney, Co. Clare, Ireland

<www.facebook.com/eastclareheritage>

FEDERATION OF LOCAL HISTORY SOCIETIES

(140+ groups)

<www.localhistory.ie/?page_id=403>

FEDERATION FOR ULSTER LOCAL STUDIES

(90+ groups)

<www.fuls.org.uk/fulsmembers.html>

GENEALOGICAL SOCIETY OF IRELAND

11 Desmond Avenue, Dún Laoghaire, Co. Dublin, Ireland

HUGUENOT SOCIETY OF GREAT BRITAIN & IRELAND: IRISH SECTION

<huguenotsinireland.com>

IRISH FAMILY HISTORY SOCIETY

13 St Assam's Drive, Raheny, Dublin 5, Ireland

<ifhs.ie>

NORTH OF IRELAND FAMILY HISTORY SOCIETY (11 branches)

Unit C4, Valley Business Centre, 67 Church Road, Newtownabbey, Co. Antrim, BT36 7LS, Northern Ireland

<www.nifhs.org>

RAHENY HERITAGE SOCIETY

68 Raheny Park, Raheny, Dublin 5, Ireland

<www.rahenyheritage.ie>

THE ULSTER GENEALOGICAL & HISTORICAL GUILD

Ulster Historical Foundation, The Corn Exchange, 31 Gordon Street, Belfast, BT1 2LG, Northern Ireland

<www.ancestryireland.com/membership>

WESTERN FAMILY HISTORY ASSOCIATION

<wfha.info>

WICKLOW COUNTY GENEALOGICAL SOCIETY

22 Wesley Lawns, Sandyford, Dublin 16, Ireland

<www.cigo.ie/wicklow-county-geneal-soc>

C

Irish Graveyard Research

Gravestone transcription projects used to be the staple social event for family history groups and the occasional local historian or graveyard enthusiast. Thanks to improved transcribing techniques, recent scientific survey innovations, and a keener interest in local history, Ireland's churchyards and cemeteries have become a focus of many commercial, educational, genealogical, and environmental groups, and family historians now have access to vast numbers of headstone transcriptions and photographs. Most of them are online, and the majority are free to access.

To find an ancestor's tombstone inscription, you need to know the place of burial. This isn't always straightforward because, historically, very few Roman Catholic churches kept burial registers, and the government has never required civil registration of deaths (introduced in 1864) to include a place of burial.

Researchers, therefore, have to rely on clues to discover where the deceased may have been buried. Church records, newspaper obituaries or funeral announcements, and probate records can offer some hints.

In practice, most of our ancestors were buried in a local churchyard, so you should be able to locate this place if you know the religious denomination of your forebears. You should bear in mind, however, that only the Church of Ireland had its own burial grounds until the early 1800s, and the majority of Irish families were too poor to identify their relatives resting place with anything other than an unmarked stone.

While gathering transcriptions from headstones is hugely welcomed, researchers lack a central database of records. Just like most of Ireland's genealogical records, these sources of family history details are scattered across a plethora of sites. The list in this section cannot claim to be comprehensive, as new projects are being launched all the time. However, it still covers the majority of online databases specializing in gravestone transcriptions and details of burial grounds.

BELFAST CITY BURIAL DATABASE

This database consists of burial records from 1869, though it does not include photos or inscriptions. The records are free to search, but acquiring an image of the register entry requires a small fee.
<www.belfastcity.gov.uk/community/burial-records/burialrecords.aspx>

BILLION GRAVES

Here, you'll find volunteer-donated photos and headstone inscriptions. The islandwide collection has low coverage at present but is expected to grow.
<www.billiongraves.com>

BRIAN CANTWELL'S MEMORIALS OF THE DEAD

Between 1970 and 1991, Brian Cantwell recorded headstone transcriptions from 24,400 memorials in 540 graveyards and churches, primarily from Counties Wicklow, Wexford, and (South) Dublin, but also some in Counties Clare, Cork, Galway, Kildare, and Sligo.
<www.findmypast.com>

DISCOVER EVER AFTER

Surveys of more than one hundred graveyards have resulted in a free searchable database of transcriptions and photographs of headstones, covering most (but not all) of Northern Ireland.
<www.discovereverafter.com>

ENFIELD & DISTRICT GRAVEYARDS

Local heritage groups have photographed, mapped, and transcribed headstones in burial grounds in the South Meath and North Kildare areas; find them for free here.
<www.enfieldgraveyards.com>

FIND A GRAVE

Volunteer-donated photos and headstone inscriptions. Its Ireland and Northern Ireland collections are tiny compared with those for the USA, but they are expected to grow in time.

FROM IRELAND

This website holds more than seventy thousand free gravestone inscriptions and headstone photos collected by genealogist Jane Lyons.
<www.from-ireland.net/ free-gravestone-records>

GALWAY BURIAL GROUND PLOT BOOKS

Here you can find free downloads of PDF files of Tuam Union burial plot registers dating from 1882 to 1920.
<www.galway.ie/digitalarchives>

GLASNEVIN

About 1.5 million Dubliners have been buried in this national necropolis since 1828. Burial registers can provide detailed information about the owner of graves and names of others in the same plot.
<www.glasnevintrust.ie/genealogy>

HISTORIC GRAVES

This website is the result of a community-based heritage project that digitally records and publishes historical graveyard surveys and stories. About two hundred burial sites have been surveyed and the results—transcriptions, photos, and local history stories—are free to access.
<www.historicgraves.com>

INTERMENT.NET

This large database of cemetery records includes those from Ireland, ranging from the 1600s to the 1900s.
<www.interment.net/ireland>

IRELAND GENEALOGY PROJECTS ARCHIVES

This volunteer-led archive holds more than one hundred thousand headstone photos and transcriptions, arranged by county and updated weekly.
<www.igp-web.com/IGPArchives/ headstones.htm>

IRISH GRAVEYARD SURVEYORS

Established in 2007, this firm surveys graveyards and cemeteries, creating maps of the plots and identifying tombstones by their inscriptions and local knowledge. The project, which has digitized photos and inscriptions, has worked in twenty-one counties across the island, with Counties Donegal and Mayo particularly well covered.
<www.irishgraveyards.ie>

IRISH WORLD

This site covers nine hundred cemeteries in Northern Ireland plus Counties Donegal, Monaghan, and Louth. You'll find only transcriptions here. While the index is free to search, full inscription and location details require payment.
<www.irish-world.com/gravestones/index. cfm>

KERRY BURIALS

This free database of seventy thousand records in 140 cemeteries is managed by local authorities in County Kerry.
<www.kerrylaburials.ie>

NORTHERN IRISH GRAVESTONE TRANSCRIPTIONS

Some 1,200 graveyards across the six counties of Northern Ireland are covered (not all comprehensively) in this collection from the Ulster Historical Foundation. Most transcriptions are pre-1900. Subscription or credits are required.
<www.ancestryireland.com/family-records/gravestone-inscriptions>

MOUNT ST. LAWRENCE, LIMERICK

Mount St. Lawrence was the city's main burial ground from 1849 until 1979 and contains the remains of seventy thousand people. All surviving headstones have been photographed and most of them have been transcribed; you can view them for free.
<mountsaintlawrence.limerick.ie>

WEST CORK GRAVEYARDS

Volunteers from Skibbereen Heritage Centre have surveyed sixteen West Cork burial grounds. The free database holds transcriptions of the headstones and links to photographs of the memorials.
<www.graveyards.skibbheritage.com/search.aspx>

D

Archives, Libraries, and Other Repositories in Ireland

National and Specialist Archives

DUBLIN CITY LIBRARY AND ARCHIVE
Pearse Street Library, 138–142 Pearse
Street, Dublin 2, Ireland
<www.dublincity.ie/main-menu-
services-recreation-culture/
dublin-city-public-libraries-and-archive>

GENERAL REGISTER OFFICE (GRO)
Werburgh Street, Dublin 2, Ireland
<www.welfare.ie/en/Pages/General-
Register-Office.aspx>

**GENERAL REGISTER OFFICE
OF NORTHERN IRELAND (GRONI)**
Oxford House, 49–55 Chichester St,
Belfast, BT1 4HL, Northern Ireland
<https://geni.nidirect.gov.uk>

LAND VALUATION OFFICE
Irish Life Centre, Abbey Street Lower,
Dublin 1, Ireland
<www.valoff.ie/en/
Archives_Genealogy_Public_Office>

NATIONAL ARCHIVES OF IRELAND (NAI)
Bishop Street, Dublin 8, Ireland
<www.nationalarchives.ie>
<www.genealogy.nationalarchives.ie>

NATIONAL LIBRARY OF IRELAND
Kildare Street, Dublin 3, Ireland
<www.nli.ie>
<http://registers.nli.ie>

**PRESBYTERIAN HISTORICAL
SOCIETY LIBRARY**
26 College Green, Belfast, BT7 1LN,
Northern Ireland
<www.presbyterianhistoryireland.com/
collections/library>

**PUBLIC RECORD OFFICE
OF NORTHERN IRELAND (PRONI)**
2 Titanic Boulevard, Belfast, BT3 9HQ,
Northern Ireland
<www.nidirect.gov.uk/proni>

REGISTRY OF DEEDS
Henrietta Street, Dublin 1, Ireland
<www.prai.ie/registry-of-deeds-services>

REPRESENTATIVE CHURCH BODY LIBRARY
Braemor Park, Rathgar, Dublin 14, Ireland
<www.ireland.anglican.org/about/
rcb-library>

SOCIETY OF FRIENDS LIBRARY
Swanbrook House, Morehampton Road,
Donnybrook, Dublin 4, Ireland
<www.quakers-in-ireland.org>

THE NATIONAL ARCHIVES (UK)
Kew, Richmond, Surrey, TW9 4DU, UK
<www.nationalarchives.gov.uk>

Regional Repositories

BELFAST CENTRAL LIBRARY
126 Royal Avenue, Belfast, Co. Antrim,
BT1 1EA, Northern Ireland
<www.librariesni.org.uk>

ARMAGH PUBLIC LIBRARY
43 Abbey Street, Armagh, Co. Armagh,
BT61 7DY, Northern Ireland
<armaghpubliclibrary.arm.ac.uk/wp>

CARLOW COUNTY LIBRARY
Local Studies Department, Tullow Street,
Carlow, Co. Carlow, Ireland
<www.carlowlibraries.ie/explore/
local-studies>

CAVAN COUNTY LIBRARY & ARCHIVES
Farnham Centre, Farnham Street,
Cavan, Co. Cavan, Ireland
<www.cavanlibrary.ie/Default.
aspx?StructureID_str=17>

CLARE COUNTY LIBRARY
The Manse, Harmony Row,
Ennis, Co. Clare, Ireland
<www.clarelibrary.ie/eolas/library/local-
studies/locstudi1.htm>
<www.clarelibrary.ie/eolas/coclare/
genealogy/genealog.htm>

CORK CITY & COUNTY ARCHIVES
33a Great William O'Brien Street,
Blackpool, Cork, Co. Cork, Ireland

CORK CITY COUNCIL

57 Grand Parade, Cork, Co. Cork, Ireland

<www.corkpastandpresent.ie>

CORK COUNTY LIBRARY

Reference and Local Studies,
Carrigrohane Road, Cork, Co. Cork,
Ireland

<www.corkcoco.ie/co/web/Cork%20
County%20Council/Departments/
Library%20%26%20Arts%20Service/
Find%20Your%20Local%20Library/
County%20Library>

DERRY CENTRAL LIBRARY

35 Foyle Street, Londonderry,
BT48 6AL, Northern Ireland

<www.librariesni.org.uk/Libraries/Pages/
Derry-Central-Library.aspx>

DONEGAL COUNTY LIBRARY

Rosemount, Letterkenny,
Co. Donegal, Ireland

<www.donegallibrary.ie>

DUBLIN CITY LIBRARY AND ARCHIVE

Pearse Street Library, 138–142 Pearse
Street, Dublin 2, Ireland

<www.dublincity.ie/main-menu-
services-recreation-culture/
dublin-city-public-libraries-and-archive>

DUBLIN SOUTH LIBRARY

Library Square, Tallaght,
Dublin 24, Ireland

<www.southdublinlibraries.ie>

DÚN LAOGHAIRE-RATHDOWN

dlr Lexicon, Haigh Terrace, Moran Park,
Dún Laoghaire, Co. Dublin, Ireland

<http://libraries.dlrcoco.ie>

FINGAL LOCAL STUDIES & ARCHIVES

Clonmel House, Forster Way,
Swords, Co. Dublin, Ireland

<www.fingalcoco.ie/community-and-leisure/
libraries/archives-and-local-studies>

ENNISKILLEN LIBRARY

Halls Lane, Enniskillen, BT74 7DR,
Northern Ireland

<www.librariesni.org.uk/Libraries/Pages/
Enniskillen-Library.aspx>

GALWAY LIBRARY HEADQUARTERS

Local History Collection, Island House,
Cathedral Square, Galway, Ireland

Archive <www.galway.ie/en/services/more/
archives/#d.en.24425>

Library <www.galway.ie/en/services/
library/galwaylocalhistory>

KERRY LIBRARY

Local History & Archives Department,
Moyderwell, Tralee, Co. Kerry, Ireland

<www.kerrylibrary.ie/local-history-amp-
archives.html>

KILDARE LIBRARY & ARCHIVES

Riverbank Arts Centre, Main Street,
Newbridge, Co. Kildare, Ireland

<www.kildare.ie/Library/
KildareCollectionsandResearchServices/
Archives>

KILKENNY COUNTY LIBRARY

Local Studies, John's Green House, John's Green, Kilkenny, Co. Kilkenny, Ireland
<www.kilkennylibrary.ie/eng/Our_Services/Local_Studies>

LAOIS COUNTY LIBRARY

Aras an Chontae, J F L Avenue, Portlaoise, Co. Laois, Ireland
<www.laois.ie/departments/libraries/services/local-research>

LEITRIM COUNTY LIBRARY

Áras An Chontae, Carrick on Shannon, Co. Leitrim, Ireland
<www.leitrimcoco.ie/eng/Services_A-Z/Library/Archives>

LIMERICK COUNTY ARCHIVES & LOCAL STUDIES

Merchant's Quay, Limerick, Ireland
<www.limerick.ie/archives>

LIMERICK CITY LIBRARY & LOCAL STUDIES

The Granary, Michael St, Limerick, Ireland
<www.limerickcity.ie/Library/LocalStudies>

LONGFORD COUNTY LIBRARY

Local Studies & Archives, Deanscurragh, Longford, Co. Longford, Ireland
<www.longfordlibrary.ie>

LOUTH COUNTY ARCHIVES

Old Gaol, Ardee Road, Dundalk, Co. Louth, Ireland
<www.louthcoco.ie/en/Services/Archives>

MAYO COUNTY LIBRARY & LOCAL STUDIES

John Moore Rd, Gorteendrunagh, Castlebar, Co. Mayo, Ireland
<www.mayolibrary.ie/en/LocalStudies>

MEATH COUNTY LIBRARY & LOCAL STUDIES

Railway Street, Navan, Co. Meath, Ireland
<www.meath.ie/Community/Libraries/LocalStudies>

MONAGHAN COUNTY LIBRARY & LOCAL STUDIES

98 Avenue, Clones, Co. Monaghan
<www.monaghan.ie/en/services/library/localhistory>

OFFALY COUNTY LIBRARY LOCAL STUDIES & ARCHIVES

Tullamore Central Library, O'Connor Square, Tullamore, Co. Offaly, Ireland
<www.offaly.ie/eng/Services/Libraries/Local-Studies-Archives-Collection>

ROSCOMMON COUNTY LIBRARY

Abbey Street, Roscommon, Co. Roscommon, Ireland
<www.roscommoncoco.ie/en/Services/Library/Local_Studies_and_Archives>

SLIGO COUNTY LIBRARY REFERENCE AND LOCAL STUDIES

Westward Town Centre, Bridge Street, Sligo, Co. Sligo, Ireland
<www.sligolibrary.ie/sligolibrarynew/LocalStudies>

TIPPERARY LOCAL STUDIES & ARCHIVES

The Source, Cathedral Street, Thurles, Co. Tipperary, Ireland
<www.tipperarylibraries.ie/tipperary-studies>

TYRONE COUNTY LIBRARY

1 Spillars Place, Irishtown Road, Omagh, BT78 1HL, Northern Ireland
<www.librariesni.org.uk/Libraries/Pages/Omagh-Library.aspx>

WATERFORD COUNTY & CITY ARCHIVES

High Street, Waterford,
Co. Waterford, Ireland
<www.waterfordcouncil.ie/departments/culture-heritage/archives/index.htm>

WESTMEATH COUNTY ARCHIVES SERVICE

County Library Headquarters, County Buildings, Mount St., Mullingar, Co. Westmeath, Ireland
<www.westmeathcoco.ie/en/ourservices/library/explorewestmeath/localstudies/archives>

WEXFORD COUNTY ARCHIVE

6A Ardcavan Business Park, Ardcavan, Co. Wexford, Ireland
<http://wexfordcountyarchive.com>

WICKLOW GENEALOGY & ARCHIVE SERVICE COUNTY BUILDINGS

Whitegates, Wicklow Town,
Co. Wicklow, Ireland
<www.wicklow.ie/archives-genealogy-service>

Other Useful Addresses

CENTRE FOR MIGRATION STUDIES

Ulster American Folk Park, Mellon Road, Castletown, Omagh, Co. Tyrone, BT78 5QY, Northern Ireland
<www.qub.ac.uk/cms>

COUNCIL OF IRISH GENEALOGICAL ORGANISATIONS (CIGO)

31a All Saints Road, Raheny, Dublin 5, Ireland
<www.cigo.ie>

GLASNEVIN CEMETERY – GENEALOGY RESEARCH CENTRE

Finglas Road, Dublin 11, Ireland
<www.glasnevintrust.ie/genealogy>

GUINNESS ARCHIVE

Guinness Storehouse, St. James's Gate, Dublin 8, Ireland
<www.guinness-storehouse.com/en/archives>

NATIONAL FOLKLORE COLLECTION

John Henry Newman Building, Newman Building, Stillorgan Road, Belfield, Dublin 4, Ireland
<www.ucd.ie/folklore/en>

County and Heritage Genealogy Centers

The Irish Family History Foundation (IFHF), a not-for-profit organization based in New-bridge, County Kildare, has coordinated a network of heritage and genealogy centers across Ireland for more than thirty years. In addition to preserving and sharing Irish heritage, these centers have created Ireland's largest online database of baptism, marriage, and burial registers from a number of denominations, including Roman Catholic, Church of Ireland, Presbyterian, Methodist, Baptist, and Quaker records **<www.rootsireland.ie>**.

You can also find collections of civil records (birth, marriage, and death), plus a good number of gravestone inscriptions, for more than half the island's historical counties. Consult the Online Sources menu **<ifhf.rootsireland.ie/generic.php?filename=centres/ifhf/sources.tpl>** to view the detailed lists of records held in each county database.

In addition to transcribing records and maintaining their online database via the RootsIreland website, all IFHF heritage and genealogy centers offer paid research services to clients. Some—but by no means all—also have visitor facilities and provide exhibition or lecture space, books for sale, and tourism information. Some operate within local libraries.

If you've hit a research roadblock—or you'd like to learn more about a particular center's holdings—contact the appropriate center for assistance.

ANTRIM

Ulster Historical Foundation
The Corn Exchange
31 Gordon Street, Belfast
BT1 2LG, Northern Ireland, UK
Tel: +44 028 90 661988
E-mail: enquiry@uhf.org.uk

ARMAGH

Armagh Ancestry
The Navan Centre
81 Killylea Road, Armagh
BT60 4LD, Northern Ireland, UK
Tel: +44 28 3752 1800
E-mail: researcher@
armaghbanbridgecraigavon.gov.uk

CARLOW

Carlow Library Genealogy Service
Tullow Street, Carlow Town
Co. Carlow, Ireland
E-mail: genealogy@carlowcoco.ie

CAVAN

Cavan Genealogy
1st Floor, Johnston Central Library, Farnham St, Cavan
Co. Cavan, Ireland
Tel: +353 (0) 49 4361094
E-mail: cavangenealogy@eircom.net

CLARE

Clare Heritage and Genealogical Centre,
Church Street, Corofin
Co. Clare, Ireland.
Tel: +353 (0) 65 6837955
E-mail: clareheritage@eircom.net

CORK (NORTH AND EAST)

Mallow Heritage Centre
27/28 Bank Place, Mallow
Co. Cork, Ireland.
Tel: +353 (22) 50302
E-mail: mallowheritagecentre@gmail.com

DERRY

Derry Genealogy
Derry City and Strabane District Council
Tower Museum, Union Hall Place,
Derry-Londonderry
BT48 6LU, Northern Ireland, UK
Tel: (028) 71372411
E-mail:genealogy@derrystrabane.com

DONEGAL

Donegal Ancestry
Old Meetinghouse, Black Lane, Ramelton
Co. Donegal, Ireland
Tel: +353 74 9158285
E-mail: info@donegalancestry.com

DOWN

Ulster Historical Foundation
The Corn Exchange
31 Gordon Street, Belfast
BT1 2LG, Northern Ireland, UK
Tel: +44 028 90 661988
E-mail: enquiry@uhf.org.uk

DUBLIN (NORTH)

Swords Historical Society
Carnegie Library, North Street, Swords
Co. Dublin, Ireland
Tel: +353 (1) 8400080
E-mail: swordsheritage@eircom.net

DUBLIN (SOUTH)

Dun Laoghaire Heritage & Genealogy
Craft Courtyard, Marlay Park,
Rathfarnham
Dublin 16, Ireland
Tel: +353 (0) 1 4954485
E-mail: cmalone@dlrcoco.ie

FERMANAGH

Irish World Heritage Centre
51 Dungannon Road, Coalisland,
Co. Tyrone, B71 4HP, Northern Ireland, UK
Tel: +44 028 8774 6065
E-mail: info@irish-world.com

GALWAY (EAST)

East Galway Family History Society
Woodford Heritage Centre, Woodford,
Loughrea, Co. Galway, Ireland
Tel: +353 (0) 90 9749309
E-mail: galwayroots@eircom.net

GALWAY (WEST)

Galway Family History Society West
St. Joseph's Community Centre, Shantalla
Co. Galway, Ireland
Tel: +353 (0) 91 860464
E-mail: galwayfshwest@eircom.net

KILDARE

Kildare Genealogy
Newbridge Library, Main Street
Newbridge, Co. Kildare, Ireland
+353 (0)45 448350
E-mail: kildaregenealogy@iol.ie

KILKENNY

Rothe House Trust Ltd
Rothe House, Parliament Street
Kilkenny, Ireland
Tel: +353 (0) 56 7722893
E-mail: kilkennyfamilyhistory@
rothehouse.com

LAOIS

Irish Midlands Ancestry
Bury Quay, Tullamore
Co. Offaly, Ireland
Tel: +353 (0) 5793 21421
E-mail: info@offalyhistory.com

LEITRIM

Leitrim Genealogy Centre
Ballinamore
Co. Leitrim, Ireland
Tel: +353 71 9644012
E-mail: leitrimgenealogy@eircom.net

LIMERICK

Limerick Genealogy, Lissanalta House
Dooradoyle, Co. Limerick, Ireland
Phone: +353 61 496542
E-mail: research@limerickgenealogy.com

LONGFORD

Longford Genealogy
17 Dublin Street
Longford, Co. Longford, Ireland
Tel: +353 (0) 43 41235
E-mail: longroot@iol.ie

LOUTH

Louth County Library
Roden Place, Dundalk
Co. Louth, Ireland
Tel: +353 (0) 42 9353190
E-mail: referencelibrary@louthcoco.ie

MAYO (NORTH)

Mayo North Heritage Centre
Enniscoe, Castlehill
Ballina, Co. Mayo, Ireland
Tel: +353 (0) 96 31809
E-mail: northmayo@gmail.com

MAYO (SOUTH)

South Mayo Family Research Centre
Main Street, Ballinrobe
Co. Mayo, Ireland
Tel: +353 (0) 949 541214
E-mail: soumayo@iol.ie

MEATH

Meath Heritage Centre
Town Hall, Castle St
Trim, Co. Meath, Ireland
Tel: +353 46 9436633
E-mail: meathhc@gmail.com

MONAGHAN

Monaghan Genealogy
6 Tully, Monaghan Town
Co. Monaghan, Ireland
E-mail: theomcmahon@eircom.net

OFFALY

Irish Midlands Ancestry
Bury Quay, Tullamore
Co. Offaly, Ireland
Tel: +353 (0) 5793 21421
E-mail: info@offalyhistory.com

ROSCOMMON

Roscommon Heritage & Genealogy
Company
Church Street, Strokestown
Co. Roscommon, Ireland
Tel: + 353 71 9633380
E-mail: info@roscommonroots.com

SLIGO

Co Sligo Heritage and Genealogy Society
Aras Reddan, Temple St, Sligo Town
Co. Sligo, Ireland
Tel: +353 71 9143728
E-mail: heritagesligo@eircom.net

TIPPERARY (NORTH)

North Tipperary Genealogy Centre
The Governor's House, Kickham Street
Nenagh, Co. Tipperary, Ireland
Tel: +353 (0) 67 33850
E-mail: tipperarynorthgenealogy@
eircom.net

TIPPERARY (SOUTH)

Bru Boru Cultural Centre
Rock of Cashel, Cashel
Co. Tipperary, Ireland
Tel: +353 (0) 62 61122
E-mail: eolas@bruboru.ie

TYRONE

Irish World Heritage Centre
51 Dungannon Road, Coalisland
Co. Tyrone, B71 4HP, Northern Ireland, UK
Tel: +44 028 8774 6065
E-mail: info@irish-world.com

WATERFORD

Waterford Heritage
Genealogy Centre, Jenkins Lane,
Waterford City
Co. Waterford, Ireland
E-mail: mnoc@iol.ie

WESTMEATH

Dún na Sí Heritage Centre,
Knockdomney, Moate
Co. Westmeath, Ireland
Tel: +353 (0) 90 6481183
E-mail: dunnasimoate@eircom.net

WEXFORD

Co. Wexford Heritage and Genealogy
Society
Riverbank, Main St, Newbridge
Co. Kildare, Ireland
Tel: +353 (0)45 448350
E-mail: enquiries@rootsireland.ie

WICKLOW

Wicklow Family History Centre
County Archives, County Buildings, Station Road, Wicklow Town
Co. Wicklow, Ireland
Tel: +353 404 20126
E-mail: wfh@eircom.net

Two further heritage centers in County Cork complete the IFHF network but do not maintain their record databases on RootsIreland.ie:

CORK CITY ANCESTRAL PROJECT

Cork County Library, Carrigrohane Road, Cork City,
Co. Cork, Ireland
Tel: +353 (0)21 4285648
E-mail: corkancestry@corkcoco.ie

SKIBBEREEN HERITAGE CENTRE

The Old Gasworks Building, Upper Bridge Street, Skibbereen
Co. Cork, Ireland
Tel: +353 (0)21 40900
E-mail: info@skibbheritage.com

F

Publications and Websites

PUBLICATIONS

Books

GENEALOGY

Finding your Irish Ancestors in New York City, by Joseph Buggy. Genealogical Publishing Co., Inc.

Irish Methodists—Where do I start?, by Steven C Smyrl. CIGO.

Tracing Your Irish Ancestors (4th ed.), by John Grenham. Gill & Macmillan.

A New Genealogical Atlas of Ireland (2nd ed.), by Brian Mitchell. Genealogical Publishing Co., Inc.

The Surnames of Ireland (6th ed.), by Dr. Edward MacLysaght. Irish Academic Press.

Tracing Derry-Londonderry Roots, by Brian Mitchell. Genealogical Publishing Co., Inc.

IRISH HISTORY

Atlas of Irish History, edited by Séan Duffy (2nd ed.). Gill & Macmillan.

Colonial Ulster: The Settlement of East Ulster, 1600–1641, by Raymond Gillespie. Cork University Press.

The Great Hunger—Ireland 1845–9, by Cecil Woodham Smith. Hamish Hamilton.

This Great Calamity, The Irish Famine, 1845–52, by Christine Kinealy. Gill & Macmillan.

A History of Ireland in 250 Episodes, by Jonathan Bardon. Gill & Macmillan.

Modern Ireland, 1600–1972, edited by R. F. Foster. Oxford University Press/Penguin.

Tudor Ireland: Crown, Community and the Conflict of Cultures, 1470–1603, by Steven G. Ellis. Longman.

IRISH-AMERICAN HISTORY

The Forgotten Irish: Irish Emigrant Experiences in America, by Damian Shiels. The History Press Ireland.

Immigration of the Irish Quakers into Pennsylvania 1682–1750, by Albert Cook Myers. Genealogical Publishing Co., Inc.

The Irish Americans: A History, by Jay P. Dolan. Bloomsbury.

The Irish at Home and Abroad, a quarterly journal (1993–1999) by Dwight A. Radford and Kyle J. Betit.

The Irish Bridget: Irish Immigrant Women in Domestic Service in America, 1840–1930, by Margaret Lynch-Brennan. Syracuse University.

The Irish Catholic Diaspora in America, by Lawrence J. McCaffrey. Catholic University of America Press.

The Irish in the American Civil War, by Damian Shiels. The History Press Ireland.

The Irish Way: Becoming American in the Multiethnic City, by James R. Barrett. Penguin.

The Pre-Revolutionary Irish in Massachusetts, 1620–1775, by George F. Donovan, Saint Louis University.

The Scotch-Irish in America, by Henry Jones Ford. Genealogical Publishing Co., Inc.

Magazines

IRISH ROOTS MAGAZINE
Quarterly, print and digital
<www.irishrootsmedia.com>

FAMILY TREE MAGAZINE
Bi-monthly, print and digital
<www.familytreemagazine.com>

WEBSITES

Blogs

BRITISH GENES
British and Irish genealogy news

FREE IRISH E BOOKS

Free online books on Irish history and genealogy

<www.freeirishebooks.blogspot.ie>

IRISH GENEALOGY NEWS

Daily news of record releases, database plans, archive and library developments, genealogy and history events, product discounts, book launches, etc.

<www.irishgenealogynews.com>

JOHN GRENHAM

Comment and observation on Irish genealogy developments

<www.johngrenham.com/blog>

TOWNLAND OF ORIGIN

Irish genealogical research in North America

<www.townlandoforigin.com>

IRISH IN THE AMERICAN CIVIL WAR

Irish emigration and Irish involvement in the American Civil War

<www.irishamericancivilwar.com>

DNA

IRELAND Y-DNA

<www.familytreedna.com/groups/ireland-heritage>

IRELAND DNA RESEARCH PROJECT

<www.livingdna.com/en-gb/irish-dna-research-project>

IRISH DNA FACEBOOK GROUP

<www.facebook.com/groups/329021130499449>

GENETIC GENEALOGY IRELAND

<www.ggi2013.blogspot.ie>

<www.facebook.com/groups/300082013464522>

<www.youtube.com/channel/UCHnW2NAfPIA2KUipZ_PlUlw/videos>

Forums

BOARDS

<www.boards.ie/b/forum/1288>

ROOTSCHAT

<www.rootschat.com/forum/ireland>

History

CENTURY IRELAND

Multi-media history of Ireland, 1913–1923

<www.rte.ie/centuryireland>

DUCHAS

A digitized version of the National Folklore Collection of Ireland, including free access to Schools' Collection

<www.duchas.ie>

HISTORY IRELAND

Magazine telling the history of Ireland from earliest times to contemporary (Bi-monthly; print and digital)

IRISH HISTORY PODCAST
Articles, videos, and podcasts on Irish historical themes and events
<www.irishhistorypodcast.ie>

Records

ANCESTRY
Essential for US-based research, with extensive US records and a sizeable Irish collection
<www.ancestry.com>

ASK ABOUT IRELAND
Free access to Griffith's Valuation collection including maps
<askaboutireland.ie/griffith-valuation>

BRITISH NEWSPAPER ARCHIVE
Large collection of local and national Irish newspapers; included in FindMyPast's Ireland and World collections
<www.britishnewspaperarchive.co.uk>

CATHOLIC PARISH REGISTERS
National Library of Ireland's free collection of unindexed digitized Roman Catholic registers (images only) to 1880/81
<registers.nli.ie>

COMMONWEALTH WAR GRAVES COMMISSION
Details of Irish dead who fought with British and Commonwealth forces during WWI and WWII; includes photos and locations of graves and memorials
<www.cwgc.org>

FAMILYSEARCH
Free access to sizeable collection of Irish record sets and indexes (Check the Catalog section for digitized records accessible only via Family History Centers.)
<www.familysearch.org/search/collection/list#page=1&countryId=1927084>

FINDMYPAST.IE
Largest single collection of Irish records, also featuring British, US, and Canadian collections. Many of the Irish record sets (including all those available on the National Archives of Ireland's Genealogy website but with a more flexible search engine) are free to access with only a registered account.
<www.findmypast.ie>

GENERAL REGISTER OFFICE (GRO) IRELAND
Application forms to request civil birth, marriage, and death certificates, and "research copies," plus online ordering facility for some years
<www.welfare.ie/en/pages/apply-for-certificates.aspx>

GENERAL REGISTER OFFICE OF NORTHERN IRELAND (GRONI)
Database of civil birth, marriage, and death records including images of certificates
<https://geni.nidirect.gov.uk>

IRISHGENEALOGY

Official Irish government research database for civil registration (all-Ireland), plus church records for Carlow, Cork, Dublin City, and Kerry
<www.irishgenealogy.ie>

IRISH GENEALOGICAL RESEARCH SOCIETY

Several unique databases, some free, some only accessible by members
<www.irishancestors.ie>

IRELAND GENEALOGY PROJECTS & ARCHIVES (IGP-WEB)

Free transcribed records and photos donated by researchers around the world
<www.igp-web.com>

IRISH NEWSPAPERS ARCHIVES

Local and national newspapers, Ireland and Northern Ireland
<www.irishnewsarchive.com>

MILITARYARCHIVES

Free databases include collections focused on the Revolutionary and Civil Wars, plus an Army census from 1922
<www.militaryarchives.ie>

NATIONAL ARCHIVES (UK)

Since Ireland was part of Britain for much of its history, many collections—especially military records—are held in this UK repository.
<www.nationalarchives.gov.uk>

NATIONAL ARCHIVES OF IRELAND

Free access to most of the major national collections including census, wills, land records, and more
<www.genealogy.nationalarchives.ie>

NATIONAL LIBRARY OF IRELAND

Several catalogs of its own holdings plus those of archives around the country and articles published in local journals
<www.nli.ie/en/intro/catalogues-and-databases-introduction.aspx>

PUBLIC RECORD OFFICE OF NORTHERN IRELAND (PRONI)

Northern Ireland's major repository with free access to Revision Books, Wills, Street Directories, and Historical Maps
<www.nidirect.gov.uk/information-and-services/public-record-office-northern-ireland-proni/search-archives-online>

REPRESENTATIVE CHURCH BODY LIBRARY

The RCB Library is repository for the archives of the Church of Ireland. It is digitizing and transcribing baptism, marriage, and burial registers and other church papers as resources permit through its free Archive of the Month series. See List of Registers for up-to-date advice on location of surviving records.
<www.ireland.anglican.org/about/rcb-library/list-of-parish-registers>

ROOTSIRELAND

Largest single database of transcribed church registers of many denominations, civil birth, marriage and death records for some counties, plus other records

<www.rootsireland.ie>

List of online sources for each county

<www.rootsireland.ie/ifhf/generic.php?filename=sources.tpl&selectedMenu=sources>

ULSTER HISTORICAL FOUNDATION

Free collections, most from Ulster and Northern Ireland

<www.ancestryireland.com>

Miscellaneous

CLAIMING CITIZENSHIP

Information for those claiming citizenship through an Ireland-born grandparent

<www.citizensinformation.ie/en/moving_country/irish_citizenship/irish_citizenship_through_birth_or_descent.html>

GENEALOGY ON FACEBOOK

Regularly updated list of Facebook pages and groups for genealogy around the world

<www.socialmediagenealogy.com/genealogy-on-facebook-list>

IRISH ANCESTORS

Mostly free reference source for records with maps, county-by-county listings, and useful surname-mapping tools

<www.johngrenham.com>

IRISH GENEALOGY TOOLKIT

Free online beginner guide to Irish genealogical research

<www.irish-genealogy-toolkit.com>

LOCAL BOOKS

Online bookstore specializing in books by local authors and Irish emigrants, many of which are not available elsewhere online

<www.localbooks.ie>

MAPS OF IRELAND

Free repository of historical and contemporary maps of Ireland, which users can view together

<maps.osi.ie/publicviewer/#V2,578432,756724,0,10> (Republic of Ireland)

<www.nidirect.gov.uk/services/search-proni-historical-maps-viewer> (Northern Ireland)

NATIONAL ARCHIVES OF IRELAND FLICKR

Photostream of vintage photos

<www.flickr.com/photos/nlireland>.

PLACENAMES DATABASE OF IRELAND

Free maps and topographical resources, plus a glossary of Irish words used in placenames

<www.logainm.ie>

SHANE WILSON

Miscellaneous free tools for maps, land divisions, place names searches, a directories database, and a townland database

INDEX

PHOTO CREDITS

COVER

Top left (cross): Obtained via Getty Images: Danita Delimont/Gallo Images/ Getty Images

Bottom left (woman): Courtesy the New York Public Library

Right (men): Courtesy the New York Public Library

CHAPTER 2

Image A: Courtesy of Paul Gorry, MAGI

Image B: Image reproduced courtesy of the National Library of Ireland

CHAPTER 3

Image A: Courtesy of FamilySearch.org

Destination: New York sidebar: Courtesy of CastleGarden.org

Image B: Courtesy of Ancestry.com

CHAPTER 4

Image A: By Marshall Henrie (Own work) [CC BY-SA 3.0 (**<http://creativecommons. org/licenses/by-sa/3.0>**)], via Wikimedia Commons

CHAPTER 5

Image C: Based on a map in *A New Genea- logical Atlas of Ireland, 2nd Edition*, by Brian Mitchell. Courtesy of Genealogical Publishing Company, Baltimore, MD **<www.genealogical.com>**

Image D: Based on a map courtesy the National Library of Ireland.

Exploring the Index of Townlands sidebar: Image reproduced with permission of Shane Wilson

Image E: Based on image courtesy of **<JohnGrenham.com>**

CHAPTER 6

Image A: Courtesy of General Register Office of Ireland

Image C: Courtesy of **<JohnGrenham.com>**

CHAPTER 7

Image A: Image reproduced with permission of Shane Wilson

Image B: Courtesy of IrishGenealogy.ie

Image C: Image reproduced courtesy of the National Library of Ireland

Images D and E and the Searching the Indexes sidebar: Courtesy of IrishGenealogy.ie

CHAPTER 8

Images A and B: Images reproduced courtesy of the National Library of Ireland

Images C, D, and E: © RCB Library

Image F: Image used with permission from the Presbyterian Historical Society

CHAPTER 9

Images A, B, and C and the Exploring the NAI Census Database and Records Alternatives: Census Search Forms sidebars: Reproduced with thanks to the Director of National Archives (of Ireland) for permission to publish

CHAPTER 10

Image B and Griffith's Valuation Online sidebar: Courtesy of **<AskAboutIreland .com>**

Land Act Purchases sidebar: Courtesy of Deputy Keeper of the Records, Public Record Office of Northern Ireland. Reference number: VAL/12B/19/13D

CHAPTER 11

Missing Friends/Information Wanted Advertisements sidebar: Image used by permission of the New England Historic Genealogical Society

Image C: Image courtesy of Cork City Libraries

From the City to the Small Market Towns sidebar: Image courtesy of Limerick City & County Libraries

Images D and E: Images reproduced courtesy of the National Library of Ireland

CHAPTER 12

Image A: Image reproduced with thanks to the Director of the National Archives (of Ireland) for permission to publish

Image B: Courtesy of the Deputy Keeper of the Records, Public Record Office of Northern Ireland

Image C: Reproduced by kind permission of the Royal College of Physicians of Ireland

CHAPTER 13

Image A: Courtesy of **<JohnGrenham.com>**

Image B: Courtesy of **<irishgenealogy.ie>**

Image C: Courtesy of **<www.ancestry.com>**

APPENDIX A

Images A, B, and C: Image reproduced courtesy of the National Library of Ireland

*All images not noted are in the public domain, have no copyright restrictions, or were created by the author.

ACKNOWLEDGEMENTS

The pages of a book are rarely written in isolation, and this *Irish Genealogy Guide* is no exception. Many kind genealogists, both professional and hobbyist, as well as archivists, librarians, friends, and even a husband have contributed advice, suggestions, and image research, and have allowed me to dip into their huge stores of knowledge and experience to help bring this guide together. I greatly appreciate their time and generosity: Kyle Betit, Eric Bignell, Claire Bradley, Joe Buggy, Eddie Connolly, Maris Cotter, Paul Gorry MAGI, John Grenham MAGI, Dr Susan Hood of the RCB Library, Ciara Kerrigan of the National Library of Ireland, Brian Mitchell MAGI, Nicola Morris MAGI, Meadhbh Murphy of the RCPI, Sean J. Murphy, Tom Quinlan of the National Archives of Ireland, Stephen Scarth of the Public Record Office of Northern Ireland, Stephen Smyrl MAGI, and Shane Wilson.

I would also like to thank my editor, Andrew Koch, for his motivation and patient guidance during the editing process.

ABOUT THE AUTHOR

A full-time freelance journalist for more than thirty years, Claire Santry has three specialities: Irish genealogy, architecture, and travel. She has written for many Irish, UK, and US newspapers and magazines, including *The Guardian*, *Belfast News Letter*, the *Washington Post*, *Visitor Ireland*, *Britain*, *Family Tree* (UK), and *Family Tree Magazine* (US), and publishes both the well-established Irish Genealogy News blog <www.irishgenealogynews.com> and its stablemate website Irish Genealogy Toolkit <www.irish-genealogy-toolkit.com>. She is a Fellow of the Irish Genealogical Research Society and editor of its monthly members bulletin, which carries news of record releases and other developments in Irish family history.

Claire's work has taken her to many far flung corners of the globe, and she lived and worked in Paris, France, for a spell, but she now divides her time between England and Ireland. When she finally packs away her suitcase, she and her husband plan to settle near her childhood home in County Carlow.

DEDICATION

To my much loved parents, who had the good sense to be Irish.

ISBN: 978-1-4403-4880-8

Other Family Tree Books are available from your local bookstore and online suppliers. For more genealogy resources, visit **<shopfamilytree.com>**.

21 20 19 18 17   5 4 3 2 1

DISTRIBUTED IN CANADA BY FRASER DIRECT

100 Armstrong Avenue

Georgetown, Ontario, Canada L7G 5S4

Tel: (905) 877-4411

DISTRIBUTED IN THE U.K. AND EUROPE BY

F&W Media International, LTD

Brunel House, Forde Close,

Newton Abbot, TQ12 4PU, UK

Tel: (+44) 1626 323200,

Fax (+44) 1626 323319

E-mail: enquiries@fwmedia.com

fw

a content + ecommerce company

PUBLISHER AND COMMUNITY LEADER: Allison Dolan

EDITOR: Andrew Koch

DESIGNER: Julie Barnett

PRODUCTION COORDINATOR: Debbie Thomas

4 FREE

FAMILY TREE templates

- decorative family tree posters

- five-generation ancestor chart

- family group sheet

- bonus relationship chart

- type and save, or print and fill out

Download at <ftu.familytreemagazine.com/free-family-tree-templates>

MORE GREAT GENEALOGY RESOURCES

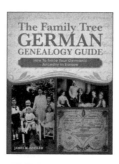
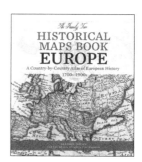